T0401956

Interfacing Science, Literature, and the Humanities / ACUME 2

Volume 15

Edited by

Vita Fortunati, Università di Bologna

Elena Agazzi, Università di Bergamo

Massimo Salgaro

Stylistics, Stylometry and Sentiment Analysis in German Studies

The Operationalization of Literary Values

With 32 figures

V&R unipress

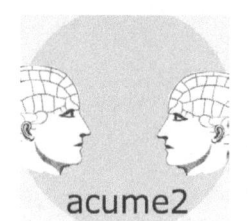 

MIX
Papier aus verantwortungsvollen Quellen
FSC® C083411

Bibliographic information published by the Deutsche Nationalbibliothek
The Deutsche Nationalbibliothek lists this publication in the Deutsche Nationalbibliografie;
detailed bibliographic data are available online: https://dnb.de.

Volume published with the contribution of the University of Verona – Department of Foreign
Languages and Literatures.

This project has received funding from the European Union's Horizon 2020 research and innovation
programme under the Marie Skłodowska-Curie grant agreement No 860516.
ELIT – H2020-MSCA-ITN-2019

© 2023 by Brill | V&R unipress, Robert-Bosch-Breite 10, 37079 Göttingen, Germany,
an imprint of the Brill-Group
(Koninklijke Brill NV, Leiden, The Netherlands; Brill USA Inc., Boston MA, USA; Brill Asia Pte Ltd,
Singapore; Brill Deutschland GmbH, Paderborn, Germany; Brill Österreich GmbH, Vienna, Austria)
Koninklijke Brill NV incorporates the imprints Brill, Brill Nijhoff, Brill Hotei, Brill Schöningh,
Brill Fink, Brill mentis, Vandenhoeck & Ruprecht, Böhlau, V&R unipress and Wageningen Academic.
Unless otherwise stated, this publication is licensed under the Creative Commons License
Attribution-Non Commercial-No Derivatives 4.0 (see https://creativecommons.org/licenses/
by-nc-nd/4.0/) and can be accessed under DOI 10.14220/9783737015707. Any use in cases other
than those permitted by this license requires the prior written permission from the publisher.

Cover image: Fingerprint
Printed and bound by CPI books GmbH, Birkstraße 10, 25917 Leck, Germany
Printed in the EU.

Vandenhoeck & Ruprecht Verlage | www.vandenhoeck-ruprecht-verlage.com

ISSN 2197-1390
ISBN 978-3-8471-1570-0

Contents

1.   The Common Roots of Stylistics and Stylometry

In 2018, at the archaeological site of Pompeii, archaeologists discovered a villa that had been under renovation when Mount Vesuvius erupted and destroyed the town. An inscription found at the site indicated a date: 17 October 79. This finding was extremely relevant because it allowed the moment of the eruption, which, according to the writings of Pliny the Younger, took place on August 24, 79 CE, to be post-dated. Although Pliny's dating had always been considered reliable, other findings, such as pomegranates found in fire pits or the presence of plants that produce berries in autumn, seemed to corroborate revision of the date of the eruption.

In a site such as Pompeii, interdisciplinary teams of archaeologists, art historians, historians, and bioarchaeologists work together to reconstruct and study the social and cultural reality of a Roman town, preserved for centuries. A multidisciplinary approach provides richness because it allows convergence and complementarity in methodology. Different disciplines fill in gaps in a variety of ways, and dialogue among them increases the reliability of their findings.

In 2016, only a few years before this discovery, I began to collaborate with Simone Rebora, whose background is in engineering and Digital Humanities. His background was very different from mine, namely German Studies and cognitive and empirical approaches to literature. When we first began to work together, our partnership, as is often the case in Italy, was grounded in mutual friendship, and we had neither a specific research field nor a specific method in mind. Rather, our "method" was more a product of our different personalities and approaches to the study of literature. To quote Spitzer, it was more a "habitual procedure of the mind" than a "program regulating beforehand a series of operations [...] in view of reaching a well-defined result" (Spitzer 1988: 36). But this initial perspective was somehow wrong. Looking back at our joint publications over recent years, what emerges is that our apparently spontaneous collaboration had developed into an intentional methodology. In retrospect, I see at least four features that have characterized our shared work:

1. We always started from a theoretical question in literary theory or literary history and tried to address it through quantitative analysis.
2. We consistently benefited from the interplay among such different disciplines as literary theory, stylometry, stylistics, empirical aesthetics, and archival research.
3. We maintained an open dialogue among these disciplines to avoid hierarchies.
4. Our focus was predominantly on German literature from the nineteenth to the twenty-first centuries.

Our starting point in questions of literary theory or history required a scientific procedure known as operationalisation (see Chapter 2), the process whereby concepts are transformed into a series of operations and in which "a bridge [is built] from concept to measurement" (Moretti 2013: 3). I had used this method over at least the last decade to provide answers to research questions. The collaborative studies in which I was involved with psychologists, psycholinguists, and literary scholars had focused on such diverse topics as literariness (Salgaro 2015; 2018b), empathy (Salgaro & Tourhout 2018; Salgaro *et al.* 2021), and literary prestige (Salgaro *et al.* 2018; 2020). In my interdisciplinary research with Simone Rebora I applied this approach to very different authors, ranging from Goethe's, Kafka's and Musil's late style (Rebora & Salgaro 2018) to contemporary writers such as Florian Meimberg (1975-) (Salgaro 2022) and Daniel Glattauer (1960-) (Salgaro 2021a). We focused largely on the period from the beginning of the twentieth century through such authors as Felix Salten (1869–1945) (Rebora & Salgaro 2022), B. Traven (1882–1969) (Salgaro 2022a), and Robert Musil (1880–1942) (Dimino *et al.* 2021; Rebora *et al.* 2018; Salgaro 2019). Part of this research has been deepened or thoroughly revised for this publication.

I would label this approach the "operationalisation of literary values," the subtitle of this book. Explicitly or implicitly, we constantly rate literary texts—for example, when we write a review, when we buy a book, or when colleagues and friends ask us for reading recommendations. "Literary value," then, simply means the attribution of value to a literary text, but in the sense used here, it also refers to a peculiarity of literary reading or of topics or features that are appreciated in the field of literary theory. Literary value is itself a research topic in the field of literary studies (Chapter 7).

A writer's characteristic style is surely such a literary value inasmuch as the most important authors can be recognized by their writing styles. The most well-known adjective defining a literary style is "Kafkaesque," which can also be used to denote unexplained and mysterious events in everyday life (Salgaro 2008). When attributing value, literary scholars tend to isolate the identifiable features in the style of the authors they study so as to distinguish these authors from others. Specialists can thus recognize a Shakespearean or Dantesque style.

The word "style" has sometimes been applied to the way language is used in a particular historic period, genre, or literary movement—for instance, epistolary, Romantic, or Victorian style. The phrase "late style" is also attributed to a phase of an author's production that results in a way of writing that differs from earlier phases or from the work of peers. Johann Wolfgang Goethe was described as "Olympian" for his balance in his maturity, a characteristic for which he was both exalted and censured. But literary value is not attributed solely to writing. Empathy, one of the main features of literary reading, is also considered a value in the field (see Chapter 8) because it is a cognitive ability that can be improved by literary reading.

The operationalisation of literary values implies an approach that requires a combination of disciplines and paradigms. In my everyday life, this scientific approach has taken the form of a dialogue with students and colleagues of different disciplines such as Simone Rebora, Pasqualina Sorrentino, Gerhard Lauer, Winfried Menninghaus, Paul Sopčák, Arthur Jacobs, Jean-Yves Tano and many others. Without this dialogue I would never have been able to broaden my scientific horizons and create bridges between different disciplines, and for that I am grateful.

1.1. The Ineffability of Literary Style

Many of the research tools used in the studies showcased in this book are typical of the Digital Humanities and empirical aesthetics. Most of them also belong to the subfield of stylometry, which is the application of statistics to the study of authorial style. Stylometry has benefited from enormous development thanks to the digitization of texts and computer-based analyses. The theoretical and methodological roots of stylometry are much older than the Internet and its scientific paradigms are not unprecedented in the humanities. Stylistics, for example, can be considered an ancient predecessor. To highlight the common epistemological roots of stylistics and stylometry, I will reconstruct the birth and evolution of stylistics in the last century.

Carlo Ginzburg indirectly showed the common epistemological roots of stylistics and stylometry in his 1979 essay, "Clues: Roots of an Evidential Paradigm" (Ginzburg 2013). This ground-breaking paper began by exposing the "Morellian method"—i.e., the examination of minute details in a painting (fingernails or the shape of fingers, toes, and earlobes, for example) to identify its creator. Morelli wanted to trace every museum piece to its maker, but his method was heavily criticized for being mechanical and positivistic. Assuming that "the art connoisseur resembles the detective who discovers the perpetrator of a crime (or the artist behind a painting) on the basis of evidence that is imperceptible to most people" (Ginzburg 2013: 97–98). Ginzburg was able not only to draw a line between the Morellian method and Arthur Conan Doyle's detective strategies, but also to draw connections to Freud's essay, "The Moses of Michelangelo," published in 1914, in which Freud refers to Morelli's method as a neighbour of psychoanalysis. Freud found in Morelli a method based on marginal elements, even "rubbish," that he considered highly significant. These elements escaped the control of the artist and thus expressed individuality.

According to Ginzburg, a common feature connected Morelli, Doyle, and Freud. All three were medical doctors who delivered diagnoses based on the observation of superficial symptoms (Ginzburg 2013: 102). Around the decade 1870–1880, this "presumptive paradigm" based on "medical semiotics" started to assert itself in the humanities. For Ginzburg, however, the history of the paradigm could be traced to primeval times during which humankind lived from hunting and was forced to examine, collect, and reconstruct the infinitesimal traces (tracks, spoor, etc.) of their prey. What characterized this hunting practice was "the ability to construct from apparently insignificant experimental data a complex reality that could not be experienced directly" (Ginzburg 2013: 103).

Such a presumptive paradigm necessarily implies the impossibility of grasping a reality. Hunters do not "know" or "experience" their prey, but, in collecting the traces an animal has left behind, they can reconstruct the story of the animal. Similarly, the doctor who collects and observes symptoms understands the history of the individual disease though, "the disease in itself is out of reach" (Ginzburg 2013: 105). In various fields, the paradigm demands similar intellectual operations: analysis, comparison, classification.

The semiotic paradigm Ginzburg reconstructed is typical for qualitative research in fields such as medicine, philology, or history. Unlike quantitative research, which follows a Galilean paradigm and is unconcerned with individuality, qualitative approaches focus on "individual cases, situations, and documents, precisely *because they are individual*" (Ginzburg 2013: 106). For qualitative research the impossibility of quantifying is the result of the unavoidable presence of the individual element. Following Ginzburg, "the more that individual traits were considered pertinent, the more the possibility of attaining exact scientific knowledge failed" (Ginzburg 2013: 111). In order to avoid sacrificing knowledge of the individual element, the humanities had to develop a different paradigm "founded on scientific knowledge of the individual" (Ginzburg 2013: 112).

In his essay, Ginzburg followed this semiotic, divinatory, and conjectural paradigm, whose main goal is to capture individuality. This perspective is not new, however. For example, Francis Galton proposed in 1888 that individuals could be distinguished through fingerprints. Whether or not this form of knowledge can be labelled "scientific" is of no consequence. What is relevant is that it is present each time the uniqueness of an observed phenomenon is a decisive element in a scholar's research. This kind of knowledge can be used for both natural phenomena and for cultural artefacts, as Ginzburg affirmed:

> Morelli set out to identify, within a culturally conditioned system of signs such as the pictorial, those which appeared to be involuntary, as in the case with symptoms (and the majority of clues). And in these involuntary signs, in the "material trifles"—a calligrapher might call them "flourishes"—comparable to "favorite words and phrases" which "most people introduce into their speaking and writing unintentionally, often without realizing it," Morelli recognized the surest clue to an artist's identity. (Ginzburg 2013: 118)

In quoting Morelli, Ginzburg not only reconstructed the semiotic paradigm previously defined but, indirectly and unintentionally, also provided an efficient definition of "stylometry"—the study of style through quantitative methods. Like the Morellian method in art history, stylometry in literary studies focuses on negligible features of literary texts to find an author's stylistic fingerprint. Its analyses are based on word frequency, of which the most frequent are usually the most trivial (function words such as "and," "in," "I," etc.). Surprisingly, the relative frequency of these apparently unimportant elements makes it possible to recognize an individual style and sometimes even to attribute it to a specific author. The individual style, like the disease in the individual, is "out of reach." What we can quantify or observe are the "symptoms" of this style—that is, the linguistic features that give rise to style.

An author's style is an individual and unmistakable trait. It is what psychologist called, at the end of the nineteenth century, a "Gestalt." In his 1890 essay, "Über Gestaltqualitäten," Christian von Ehrenfels introduced the concept for the first time (von Ehrenfels 1890). For him the Gestalt was the sum of diverse elements, though this perceptual whole was different from the sum of individual parts. "By Gestalt qualities we understand such positive imaginative contents," von Ehrenfels noted, "which are bound to the presence of imaginative complexes in consciousness, which in their turn consist of elements separable from each other" (von Ehrenfels 1890: 285). Von Ehrenfels suggested melody as an example of a Gestalt: though it consists of individual tones, a melody is much more than the sum of tones. Gestalt psychologists observed that human beings tend to perceive patterns or configurations rather than individual components, a view that is sometimes summarized in the maxim, "the whole is more than the sum of its parts." Among various Gestalt qualities, patterns and similarities can be recognized just as similarities between melodies by two different composers can be identified without the need to specify the nature of the (un)likeness. In this context, von Ehrenfels introduces the concept of style:

> Like the similarities of the phylogenetic products of nature, the similarities of human
> products, when viewed from the point of view of stylistic affinity, are largely based on
> Gestalt qualities. What is called a sense of style in an artistic field should consist of
> nothing other than the ability to perceive and compare the Gestalt qualities of the
> category in question (von Ehrenfels 1890: 279).[1]

As early as the 1920s, the first generation of Gestalt psychologist found that works
of art were also a Gestalt: the whole produced by chromatic, acoustic, and linguistic relations—that is, Gestalten that acquired a unique expressive value.

Scholars such as Johannes von Allesch reflected on the relation between works
of art and their critics or connoisseurs. The meaning of a work of art always
contains "irrational" or "ineffable" elements that are born from the unique
encounter between the work of art and the viewer. In von Allesch's words, "The
artwork is not the painting or the color, it is created in our idea of it" (von Allesch
1921: 35), meaning that the nature of a Gestalt of a work of art depends upon the
whole in which it is embedded. A "degree of fulfilment" can exist between the
ideas that occur to an observer or reader of a work of art and the work's actual
content or features—as Allesch pointed out: "The content of a work of art is its
well-understood form" (von Allesch 1921: 110), while the reception a work of art
receives changes from person to person and depends on personal experience,
individual circumstances, tradition, and cultural niche (von Allesch 1921: 54). In
that sense, the reader's concept is highly individual. Literary style may also be
considered a Gestalt because it is the outcome of various elements that readers
must perceive as a whole.

Another important concept of literary theory, "foregrounding," stems from
the psychology of Gestalt (Gregoriu 2018). This concept refers to the human
capacity to perceive shapes, separating them from the "ground." Literary foregrounding can also be linked to style because it typically involves a deviation or a
stylistic distortion of some sort through an aspect of a text that deviates from the
linguistic norm (Burke & Evers 2018), though fictional characters are also foregrounded as they emerge from grounded settings.

The beginning of the twentieth century was very productive for the concept of
literary style to which Leo Spitzer, an outstanding philologist considered one of
the founding fathers of stylistics, made an important contribution. Not coincidentally, Ginzburg quoted Spitzer's study of neologisms in Rabelais in which
Spitzer used scant clues as indicators of the author's worldview (Ginzburg 2013:
124). The affinity between Spitzer and Ginzburg is shown in the following quotation in which Carlo Ginzburg used exactly Spitzer's adage to describe the
linkage between quantitative studies and individuality:

---

1 All quotations extracted from non-English texts (German, Italian, French) have been translated by the author of the book.

I was forearmed by the adage *individuum est ineffabile* [the individual (thing) cannot be grasped]. Could it be that any attempt to define the individual writer by his style is doomed to failure? An individual stylistic deviation from the general norm must represent a historical step taken by the writer, I argued: it must reveal a shift in the soul of the epoch, a shift of which the writer has become conscious and which he would translate into a necessarily new linguistic form. (Spitzer 1988: 13)

That one of the founding fathers of stylistics questioned whether "any attempt to define the individual writer by his style [was] doomed to failure" may seem astonishing. Individuality cannot be grasped by the literary critic, who can only observe the shift, or the stylistic deviation, in the style of the writer with regard to the "soul of the epoch." The observation and description of this shift was Spitzer's lifelong task.

1.2. The Birth of Stylistics

Along with Leo Spitzer (1887–1960), Charles Bally (1865–1947), whose roots lay in classical rhetoric and poetics, is considered one of the founding fathers of stylistics (Burke 2018a). Both published their works on literary stylistics in the first part of the twentieth century, a productive and fertile period for literary theory and stylistics. Bally's *Précis de Stylistique* (1905) is commonly used to mark the beginning of literary stylistics—that is, the linguistic analysis of a literary writer's stylistic possibilities. He is widely recognized as one of the co-editors, alongside Albert Sechehaye, of Saussure's *Cours de Linguistique Générale* (1916). Because Saussure did not begin teaching his course in general linguistics until 1907, there is no reason to see Bally as having simply applied Saussure; rather, he employed his knowledge of German linguistics in what he called "stylistique." In *Traité de Stylistique Française*, Bally (1970: 12) set out to study the "expressive resources of a whole language," noting that stylistics could be "general, collective, or individual" and were not focused solely on writers' individual "style." For Bally, language expressed the emotions and thoughts of the speaker. Thus, he emphasized the affective uses of language, its musical and rhythmic qualities, and the varieties of possible expression such as homonyms (Bally 1970: 44–46). The affective valence that "denotes" linguistic expression is out of reach for the linguist who cannot grasp the "intellectual or affective dominants" of a linguistic utterance (Bally 1970: 152).

As a consequence, interdisciplinarity was required. In Bally's view, stylistics lay between linguistics and psychology as a research field, and the object of research in stylistics was properly the "verbal expression" and not "the thought" (Bally 1970: 13). Abstract meaning could be expressed in various ways depending upon the emotional state of the speaker or writer. Thus, Bally found no purpose in studying grammatical rules but was interested instead in all the possibilities of a language's "expressive resources" in varying contexts. Bally wanted to look at entire linguistic systems, especially of the French language, and his definition of stylistics differed from approaches that studied the language of a single author. To Bally, the object of stylistics was not literary style because any individual writer's means of combining linguistic elements lay outside his research. He was interested in systems, not the case, and literary and scientific language were simply "specialized languages" (Bally 1970: 244).

What is interesting is Bally's differentiation of the quantitative and qualitative elements of language. Concerning the "future scientific study of styles," he was convinced that "certain features of literary expression that are striking are often negligible, while others that are unnoticed are veritable distinctive signs" (Bally 1970: 244). He considered the quantitative elements of word frequency by comparing words with a similar meaning but used with varying frequencies (e.g., *mer* and *océan*, *presqu'île* and *peninsula*; Bally 1970: 171). If two words were synonyms, the less frequent was used when the "affective dominant" was bigger. Bally considered the "statistics of usage" (Bally 1970: 205) as stylometry would do some decades later. Certain rare words seemed to belong to foreign languages either because they denoted an uncommon element or were not frequent, and he considered that the appropriateness of a word depended highly upon the context in which it was used, on its "milieu" (Bally 1970: 217). That, in turn, depended upon the social roots, education, and professional background of the individual.

Resonances of Hippolyte Taine's theory can be perceived in this concept of milieu. An individual's vocabulary tends to be adapted to his or her milieu. Bally distinguished three possible social definitions of a linguistic expression: collo-quial language or an expression of a lower or a higher "milieu" (Bally 1970: 217; 224). In this context, the definition of "*écart*," a deviation or rupture, becomes central. A linguistic element can produce a "rupture" when it is experienced as too popular or too vulgar (Bally 1970: 225) or it can be judged as "written" language, which is different from literary. Literary language produces a rupture with regard to spoken and common language. The "literary expression is only beautiful as a contrast," Bally wrote (1970: 249), and common language had to be at the core of education in contrast to the "sublime deformations" of language introduced by geniuses like Racine, Corneille, or Victor Hugo (Bally 1970: 249). "Qualitative features" also determined the value of a word—for example, when pejorative suffixes were used (Bally 1970: 177).

In terms of stylistics, Jean Starobinski highlighted the differences between Charles Bally and Spitzer in this way: while Bally was interested in *langue*, Spitzer focused on *parole*. Spitzer himself translated this difference into his own words, noting that, while Bally studied *Sprachstile*, he himself was devoted to *Stil-sprachen* (Starobinski 1970: 8–9).

Spitzer shared with Bally a double scientific background in linguistics and literary studies. He conceived of stylistics as a bridge between linguistics and literary history because he saw, in the literary style of an author, a revelation of the intellectual context of an age. Spitzer himself was, in some ways, a "mythic" intellectual figure, one considered "omniscient," and was able to read and write in five languages (Paccagnella & Gregori 2010: x). Critics have always highlighted the link between Spitzer's work and his life in Austria, where he was born, and later in Germany, Turkey, and the USA.

In *Linguistics and Literary History* (1948) Spitzer conceived literary stylistics as the historical and comparative study of style (Spitzer 1988: 13). His goal for literary stylistics, then, was to relate the thesis that style reflected cultural knowledge to the methods of linguistics, which offered a validated descriptive model. In pursuing that goal, he offered a new definition of the relationships between style, language, and knowledge in which literary style was a form of cultural activity and, therefore, neither an independent aesthetic value nor a function of characteristic linguistic features. For him stylistics helped to extract the ideology and cultural framework that were a part of an author's production because the production of literature and language were always influenced by historical context.

Style has always been defined by neighbouring disciplines such as rhetoric, structuralism, philology, poetics, and criticism. In contrast, Spitzer claimed, "I had in mind the more rigorously scientific definition of an individual style, a linguist's definition that would replace the casual, impressionistic remarks of literary critics" (Spitzer 1967: 11). Spitzer defined literary style as the highest form of discourse and believed that the overall goal of stylistics was to uncover the characteristic elements that could be used to interpret both the focal point of the expressivity of a literary text and its place in a cultural tradition. The core of his method was to find a "common denominator" in the deviations of literary texts from the general usage of language. Spitzer wrote:

> In my reading of modern French novels, I had acquired the habit of underlining expressions which struck me as aberrations with respect to general usage, and it often happened that the underlined passages, taken together, seemed to offer a certain consistency. I wondered whether it would be possible to establish a common denominator for all or most of these deviations. Could not the common spiritual etymon, the psychological root, of several individual "traits of style" in a writer be discovered, just as we have discovered an etymon common to various fanciful word formations? (Spitzer 1967: 11)

In his 1930 essay "Zur sprachlichen Interpretation von Wortkunstwerken/On the Linguistic Interpretation of Literature," Spitzer sought to display practical examples of his method, which he based on the premise "that any psychic or spiritual excitement which deviates from our normal mental habits finds utterance in a corresponding verbal deviation from normal usage so that, inversely, we may infer an emotional centre of the psyche from any deviation from the linguistic norm, and a verbal peculiarity must mirror a psychic peculiarity" (Catano 1988: 86). This feature of stylistics may be phonological, semantic, or syntactic but would always reveal itself against the background that philology showed to be current for the cultural context in question.

Many theoreticians have speculated on the existence or "supposed existence" of the Spitzerian method (Paccagnella & Gregori 2010: x–xi; 262–64). According to Spitzer, the creative process induces a "solidification of the psyche in the language." A literary work is foremost a mirror of a "unique and unrepeatable experience" (Spitzer 1988: 447). This process was not enclosed in creative individuality as were neologisms. Rather, "they are the passage from parole into langue, to use Saussure's terms." Accordingly, the birth of neologisms was, for Spitzer, the best example of how the author deviated from everyday language. Neologisms were the consequence of an emotional experience that needed a specific means of expression. This phenomenon can be observed both in such writers as Rabelais and Christian Morgenstern and in advertising texts and in the nicknames Spitzer's wife invented for their son. In his words:

> [I]n my study "Puxi" (1927), I treated the semantic radiation of a less pathological but no less passionate feeling, that of mother love—showing how, in one individual case, this passion succeeded in attracting a world into the orbit of the pet name given a child by its mother. Can we, then, imagine that religious and philosophical currents, which have spread over vast areas of civilization and have completely transformed the lives of their followers (as have Pythagoreonism or Christianity), should not also have been highly powerful forces for linguistic transformation [and that they were], although less varied in whimsical and arbitrary ways, even more firmly established and enduringly effective because of the momentum given by the unanimity and extent of religious passion? (Spitzer 1967: 6)

Spitzer's linguistic interests surely covered a wide spectrum. The subjects of his studies ranged from high-brow and traditional writers of all epochs to everyday linguistic use such as the speech of Italian soldiers captured during the First World War (Spitzer 1920) or a mother's nicknaming of her son (Spitzer 2016). Spitzer saw language as an "outward crystallization of the 'inward form' [...] the lifeblood of poetic creation" (Spitzer 1988: 21). But artistic creativity was not limited to a canonical aesthetic dimension alone. A mother or a soldier could become linguistically creative if their emotional states urged them to find new or unconventional forms. Even advertising texts could share features with literary texts (Spitzer 1988: 331). In such cases of an "aesthetics from below," as Gustav Theodor Fechner would have called it, originality derived from the rupture with reference to a specific linguistic habit or context. The "balanced notion" of Spitzer's style follows Starobinski: "neither particular, nor universal, but a detail in the moment of universalization [that] implicates a rebellion of one individual and his reconciliation through his *work*" (Starobinski 1970: 23).

In his early works, Spitzer employed Freud's psychological model, which placed a writer's individual linguistic wordplay at centre stage. Freud's importance to Spitzer lay in his analysis of the logic of the unconscious and, thus, justified the individuality of literary style. In this perspective, historical changes in language were legitimated by the psyche of the author (Spitzer 1988: 21–22). The goal of stylistics was not limited to a description of parallels between the writer's emotional experiences and word choices, however, but consisted of rooting these parallelisms in the writer's psyche. The use of psychoanalysis in his early works gained Spitzer criticism, for example by David Lodge (Lodge 1966: 54). In his later works Spitzer would increasingly read literary texts as aesthetic artefacts without references to the mind that produced them.

In many of his essays, Spitzer affirmed his commitment to the German tradition of hermeneutics, and the "hermeneutic circle" introduced by Schleiermacher was a source of inspiration for Spitzer's interpretative method. Schleiermacher claimed that every interpretation implied a pre-understanding, yet any understanding of a literary work was changed in the act of reading. The act of interpretation implied the paradox that each part can be known only in terms of the whole and the whole only through its single elements. These cultural elements can be of varying natures—for example, "one must try to see the manifold cross-relationships between the detail (the advertisement) and the whole (our civilization)" (Spitzer 1988: 330). In his "circle of understanding" (Spitzer 1988: 24), Spitzer adapted this perspective to locate the minute particularities of ordinary linguistic features or in a literary text to larger cultural entities in which they were embedded. By embracing the paradigm of hermeneutics, he distinguished between "science, which dealt with things that could be measured and weighed" and hermeneutics, which dealt with "knowledge irreducible to 'scientific treatment'" (Spitzer 1988: 33).

The psychic portrait that the stylistician pursues is a construct of investigation, though stylistics is uninterested in biographical facts. In his analysis of *Bubu de Montparnasse* (1905) by Charles-Louis Philippe, Spitzer (Spitzer 1988: 41–83) noted a massive use of causal cues, such as "because of." He defines these marks as "spies," in Italian "*spie*," using the same term Ginzburg had used in his essay (Spitzer 1988: 43). Such linguistic markers were "individual formulations" that signaled writers' "originality in conspicuous deviations" (Spitzer 1988, 44). In Spitzer's view, these uncommon uses expressed a writer's *Weltanschauung*. The "pseudo-objective motivation" expressed in Philippe's style highlighted a fatalistic worldview and a humorous sympathy with the underprivileged fictional characters in the novel. Because fictional characters must be realistic for readers,

Philippe described their actions "against the background of general norms" (Spitzer 1988: 55).

But Spitzer's method, which sought to preserve the uniqueness of a writer's style, did not reject quantitative approaches. The causal cues observed in Philippe's novel seemed quite prosaic. As Spitzer observed, "the less this common prepositional phrase is linked with other words from everyday life, the more poetic it appears to be. Conversely, the more common the phrase used to achieve the new effect, the more successful the stylistic innovation" (Spitzer 1988: 48). In other contexts, he recognized the "principle of repetition" (Spitzer 1988: 336; 433). The differential value determined the deviation effect of a literary feature as well as its success. Spitzer found an example of this comparative approach in Wöfflin's *Principles of Art History* in which, "through a series of parallelisms in which he described, by contrasting them with another, classical and baroque art, he succeeded in defining these two styles" (Spitzer 1988: 126). As we have just seen, the two artistic movements illuminate themselves reciprocally and their definition emerges *ex negativo* in relation to one another.

Spitzer studied neologisms in Rabelais and searched for their descendants, finding them in such celebrated writers as Gautier, Balzac, and Céline (Spitzer 1988: 29–31). By comparing the style of these authors, he emphasized that he was not able to capture the individuality of their style but only the differences between them. In his words, "Victor Hugo is not Rabelais, although there may be Hugo-esque traits in Rabelais [and] Rabelaisian traits in Hugo" (Spitzer 1988: 30). What appeared to be central in Rabelais could be unimportant in Hugo and vice versa. Spitzer warned that stylistics was able only to draw lines connecting the ideas of these authors but could not determine their individuality. Characteristically, he again used the Latin adjective "*ineffabile*," which had appeared in the quotation regarding the impossibility that quantitative studies could express individuality. Literary works of art were, for him, unique in themselves, undefinable and in-effable, like a solar system, a product of a constellation of different historical lines and a particular social climate (Spitzer 1988: 30). It was precisely the freedom of the writer that sought deviation, and the writer filled this gap by writing the text and entering into communication with language and society. As Spitzer defined it, the writer established originality through deviations that could be quantified and observed in experiments. Not unexpectedly, in one of his early essays, he envisaged the possibility of carrying out experiments in linguistics:

> In linguistics, the ability to carry out experiments has always been lacking. The natural sciences can vary the starting conditions in a systematic way (that is, through an experiment) and observe the results of changes to discover causal nexuses, while linguistic research must always register its results and hypothesize variations in a more-or-less speculative way. War has given rise to "experiments" in various sectors…. It is nature itself that carried out a wide sociological experiment. (Spitzer 1920: 1)

Spitzer's wish would be fulfilled only years later in the field of "empirical studies of literature" (Salgaro 2021b). Some critics have considered his method to be "empirical" (Paccagnella & Gregori 2010: xi). At the time he wrote, however, he could not know that experiments in linguistics would be possible, and he certainly could not have prophesized the coming of the computer which permitted an immensely powerful increase in analysis, comparison, and classification. In 1949, Padre Busa collaborated with IBM to digitalize the *Index Thomisticus*. From that moment on, it became clear for linguistics and stylistics that the computer made it possible to recognize patterns and traces that the human eye either could not grasp or could perceive only with great effort. Thanks to computers, the reading and rereading Spitzer envisaged could be exchanged for a more efficient "distant reading."

1.3. The Development of Stylistics As a Science between 1945 and 2000

Wolfgang Kayser's *The Linguistic Artwork/Das sprachliche Kunstwerk*, first published in 1948, is, on the one hand, an introduction to literary analysis and, on the other, a handbook that provides evidence of the guiding concepts of literary theory in Europe after the Second World War (Paccagnella & Gregori 2010: 6). Kayser absorbed Bally's and Spitzer's theories on style and proposed stylistics as the core of his the "science of lyrics" (Kayser 1948: 272–73). He defined the old stylistics as normative—that is, a kind of manual that prescribed a "correct" use of language. He divided the new stylistics into three branches. The first one, he argued, is inspired by Ferdinand de Saussure, who distinguished between *langue*—that is a linguistic system—and *parole*—that is, the individual use of language. Charles Bally followed his mentor by studying the emotional and affective function of linguistic expression. As part of the Geneva school, he tried to grasp language as a whole without focusing on individual expressions such as literary texts.

Scholars like as Karl Vossler and Leo Spitzer, who considered fantasy and creativity to be the real engines of the evolution of language, formed the second branch that Kayser identified (Kayser 1948: 275). In this branch of studies, style was linked to a writer's personality and originality.

The third kind of stylistics was related to the fine arts in which the features of a certain painter or of an epoch were named. Here, style meant the "harmonization of external forms" and the "expression of the individual's inner world" (Kayser 1948: 277). These words bring strongly to mind the concept of style as Gestalt.

Despite these differences, Kayser concluded that the three branches agreed in considering style the "unitary expression of something individual" (Kayser 1948:

281). In this sense, it could be defined as an expression of an inner world, of the personality of its creator. A landscape or a tree could not be "stylish." For Kayser, the problem was that authors could use different styles in their works and that some writers, for example during the Baroque period, suppressed their uniquely individual features in an effort to abide by the prescriptions of that time. He added that the "presumptive paradigm" of Ginzburg was also valid—that is, that the individuality of a personal style could not be grasped in a unique text which could only serve as a "source of evidence" when placed in relation to other texts.

Consequently, Kayser proposed his own definition: "style is, viewed from outside, the unity and individuality of creation; viewed from the inside, the unity and individuality of perception" (Kayser 1948: 292). According to him, the broad concept could be identified in particular works as well as in specific writers or epochs. Although Kayser attempted to link his concepts to the observation of textual and formal features, his definition was not empirically observable and remained essentially fuzzy ("the ineffable-identical"). Kayser also criticized psychoanalytic approaches, such as those of Spitzer's early work. He preferred to identify differences between linguistics and stylistics from a quantitative perspective:

> Linguistics is interested in the unusual linguistic forms of a text. If a phenomenon appears only one time, it will attract attention. Stylistics, however, is interested in linguistic expressions that are, on the basis of their frequency, characteristic for the composition of a certain work as a whole. "Continuity creates style," Flaubert once said. These common forms are stylistic traits. The more expressive and efficient they are, the easier stylistic traits are to recognize, the more they constitute phenomena that differ from "common" language. (Kayser 1948: 100–101)

As an example of such deviations, Kayser quoted a poem in which articles were missing. He considered this an example of an easily recognizable and expressive stylistic trait. As stylistic analysis cannot dismiss historical contextualization, Kayser held that the individual style of a work was easier to recognize in the context of what is "common and normal in the language and in comparison with homologous contemporary works" (Kayser 1948: 101) and that rhetorical figures did not play a significant role in the "new stylistics." In Kayser's view, syntax, rhythm, construction, and position of words were more important, as was, obviously, the content. He thus proposed different examples of his stylistic analyses in his examination of Novalis' *Heinrich von Ofterdingen* and Mallarmé's *Apparition*.

After WWII, stylistics seemed to offer a way to bring literary criticism closer to the natural sciences. In his 1959 article, "Criteria for Style Analysis," Michael Riffaterre observed that subjective impressionism and normative rhetoric had long interfered with "the development of stylistics as a science" (Riffaterre 1959: 154). In his view, linguistic analysis should facilitate an exact and objective use of literary language, and he organized his essay into short, numbered paragraphs in an effort to reflect scientific praxis. He also used abbreviations such as SD (stylistic device) and AR (average reader) and employed concepts such as informants, uncommon in the vocabulary of literary criticism.

Riffaterre held that elements of stylistics could be be distinguished from "neutral" ones because they conveyed an expressive, affective, or aesthetic emphasis without altering the content, and he conceived of the writer as the "encoder," who encrypted his message in such a way that the reader could "decode" it easily (Riffaterre 1959: 156–57). In the process of decoding, stylistic features limited freedom of perception. The nature of the relationship between this fixed encoding and readers' variable decoding, however, remained unclear. The linguist saw literary texts as a "mine of data" to reconstruct a past phase of the language, an expression that recalls the "data mining" of contemporary Digital Humanities. The stylistician's job was to consider the effect a text has at the time of its publication and to collect the reactions of average readers to determine stylistic devices "objectively." Riffaterre's method thus differed from Spitzer's, whose method Riffaterre considered "impressionistic" because it relied on the stylistician's own observations and interpretations of linguistic clues (Riffaterre 1971: 163–64).

For Riffaterre "the linguistic norm is virtually unobtainable" (Riffaterre 1971: 168) and the "deviation" from the linguistic norm is not assessed abstractly but through experimentation of the readers' embodied norms. Thus, Riffaterre relied on stylistic context—that is, a linguistic pattern broken by an unpredictable element. He assembled a catalogue of stylistic devices on the semantic and phonetic level in a given text, though he admitted that the average reader could also misinterpret neutral elements as stylistic devices. Alternately, some stylistic devices (metaphors, e. g.) could become clichés and thus would not be perceived as ruptures of linguistic patterns. Despite the unreliability of textual decoding, Riffaterre believed stylistics could become a science if it renounced the "subjective apprehension of the elements of style" (Riffaterre 1971: 174).

Ironically, and for the same reasons, David Lodge believed that stylistics could not be scientific (Lodge 1966: 60). In his view, the deviation from linguistic usage determined by French and German stylisticians was by no means enough to determine the literary identity of a given text. In the French tradition, the definition of style as "*écart*"—that is, deviation—has been very common. Bruneau (1951) defined literary style as authors' voluntary deviations from the grammatical norms of ordinary language. In his words, "Stylistics is the science of deviations" (Bruneau 1951: 6), while Lodge noted that common linguistic elements could also be constituents of literary structures (Lodge 1966: 55). He argued that similarities and differences existed between stylisticians and critics: the similarities relied upon the concept of the linguistic element, which was determined by context. From the perspective of stylisticians, context was language considered as a whole; for critics, it was the individual text in which the linguistic feature was embedded. Lodge held that stylistics could not replace literary criticism because it aimed for scientific status while criticism dealt with values. Nevertheless, literary criticism could benefit from the accurate terminology employed in linguistic analysis.

In fact, Lodge saw modern stylistics as largely a European phenomenon, arguing that North Americans "have no Spitzer or Auerbach" (Lodge 1966: 52). In Lodge's view, American critics mistrusted formal analysis and description and remained unconvinced by stylisticians' tendency to explain and interpret artists in psychological terms. In the 1950s, he felt, the academic tradition of close reading had forgotten Spitzer's lesson (Lodge 1966: 55–56).

The gap between North American and European criticism was confirmed by Catano (1988) in establishing his theories on style within the North American tradition. For European stylisticians, the core of literary stylistics was the study of linguistic efficiency through fine-grained descriptive procedures, whereas the close reading advocated by North American New Criticism drifted toward objective analysis of literary texts. In Catano's words, "Spitzer's ongoing struggle to match an acceptable descriptive methodology with a post-Romantic epistemology of style remains the central problem to be solved by modern stylistics" (Catano 1988: 3). Romantic and Post-Romantic theories have qualified literature and literary style as acontextual, floating above social context. Conversely, Catano sought a re-evaluation of stylistics in North America that tied epistemology and literary style together by describing the social motivations behind the use of language (Catano 1988: 14).

After 1950, the North American tradition of stylistics headed toward more scientific and formal approaches. Amid this shift, a critical problem linked to interpretation arose. The drive for objectivity in the new stylistics involved the blatant separation of linguistic methodology from critical interpretation, and interpretation itself became an issue. At this stage, Stanley Fish challenged the separation between description and interpretation in many of his essays, especially in those devoted to stylistics (Fish 1980: 68–97; 246–268). In his essay, "What is Stylistics and Why are They Saying Such Terrible Things about It?" he sarcastically conducted "a saturation bombing of stylistics" (Fish 2000: 247).

The first object of Fish's attack was Michael Riffaterre. In *Literature in the Reader: Affective Stylistics* (1970), Fish challenged the distinction between standard and poetic languages (Fish 2000: 60). For him, "stylistic devices" that compelled readers' attention were traits typical of literary language and did not alter the meaning of the text; rather, they placed emphasis on some of its parts. Fish criticized the radical separation of style and meaning and their placement into hierarchies. In Riffaterre's understanding, style was important whereas content could be overlooked. Presenting himself as an "advocate of the rights of the readers" (Fish 2000: 15), Fish did not deny the relevance of cataloguing formal features; he merely insisted that the value of these features could only be determined by their function in the experience of the reader. He therefore appreciated Riffaterre's shift of focus from the text to the reader.

From Fish's perspective, "everything is a stylistic fact" (Fish 2000: 65) and no distinction between linguistic and stylistic facts could therefore be made. Consequently, he proposed the rejection of the concept of style. Stylistics appeared to Fish to be a reaction to the subjectivity of literary criticism and "an attempt to put criticism on a scientific basis" (Fish 2000: 70). In his view, this attempt was a reaction to the fear of interpretation and was doomed to fail; it reflected, as he put it, "the desire to be relieved of the burden of interpretation by handing it over to an algorithm" (Fish 2000: 86). Fish disapproved of what he considered stylisticians' attempts to determine context-free elements or primes and to build the determination of meaning upon them. To Fish, stylisticians aimed to establish an inventory of fixed relationships between observable data and meanings, and he condemned what he considered their positivistic attempt to replace the subjectivity of literary studies with objective techniques of description and interpretation.

In *How Ordinary is Ordinary Language?* (1973), Fish confronted the presumed distinction between ordinary and poetic language, arguing that literature was defined by specific linguistic and formal features. For him, literature was not a specific category of text but was rather a product of a way of reading (Fish 2000: 97) and he refused every essentialist concept of literature. Riffaterre, whose concept that literary language was a "deviation" of standard language characterized by different stylistic features, again served Fish as a case in point. He argued against this "positivist assumption" as follows:

> The same assumption underlies the attempt (often undertaken by the same people) to isolate style, which is usually defined either as a distinctive way of employing the rules of ordinary language (style as choice) or as a departure from those same rules (style as deviation). Since the choice (between alternative expressions) does not affect the content of the utterance but merely puts a personal stamp—an emphasis—on it, and since the deviation is from the same content (even to the extent sometimes of obscuring and overwhelming it), the two notions depend on and leave intact the norm of ordinary language and are thus more or less parallel to the two definitions of literature (message-plus and message-minus) dictated by the same norm. The search for style, like the search for an essentialist definition of literature, proceeds in the context of an assumption that predetermines its shape. (Fish 2000: 110)

Some lines later, Fish provocatively proposed the eradication of the concept of style which, in his view, was not a feature of writing but the reflection of an ideology.

In the second part of *What is Stylistics?* Fish took his criticism even farther by arguing that objectively defined linguistic features could only be blended into stylistic analysis through the subjective analysis of the critic (Fish 2000: 246–68). Thus, the analysis of formal linguistic features could not overcome the inherently interpretative nature of linguistics and stylistics. In Fish's critical view, the representatives of stylistics were not aware of what they were doing because they were blinded by methodological and ideological premises. Their formal descriptions, in other words, seemed to be interpretations from the start (Fish 2000: 257).

In academic contexts, both the notion of historical distance and the climate of critical debates have changed over the last forty years, and reconstructing Fish's arguments against stylistics may seem anachronistic. What continues to make Fish relevant is that he placed meaning not in the text but in the act of reading. He did not ask his students what texts meant but what they *did*. In stylistics, as in other critical approaches, he argued against subjugating readers to the critical theses of stylistics and other critical schools (Fish 2000: 15).

1.4. The Encounter between Stylistics and Stylometry after 2000

Starobinski had already identified the "recognition of the stylistic deviation (*écart*) with regard to the common use" (Starobinski 1970: 19) as the starting point of Spitzer's stylistics. The literary work exposed its uniqueness against the background of a social fact: common use, everyday language. The keywords of stylistics are, according to a contemporary critic, "deviation" and "highlighting".

Intended as divergence from a norm (Gregoriu 2018: 90–94), deviation can be internal or external. If the expression detaches itself from the norms of its language, genre, or cultural or contextual use, it is considered external. It is internal when it occurs on the phonological, lexical, or syntactical level (Montini 2020: 128). A good example of a semantic deviation might be a rhetorical figure such as the metaphor in which a word is endowed with a new, figurative meaning. All these forms induce a phenomenon called "foregrounding" (Montini 2020: 130), the literary theory of which is linked to literariness (Salgaro 2015). Another excellent example of semantic deviation is Dylan Thomas' poem "A Grief Ago" (Jeffries & McIntyre 2010: 31–32), in which the poet employed a grammatical transgression that pushed readers to find the deeper meaning of the expression in the poem's title.

In a Western academic context, stylistics has always occupied an uncomfortable position between such disciplines as linguistics and literary studies and has had the tendency to articulate itself in a variety of subdisciplines: corpus stylistics, stylistic pragmatics, historical stylistics, and cognitive stylistics. Since its appearance, stylistics had much in common with linguistics, and Starobinski called Spitzer's method a "fecund coming and going" between stylistics and linguistics (Starobinski 1970: 12)—for example, in the use of empirical linguistic data to confirm the theories of stylistics. Leech defined stylistics as a "bridge discipline" (2008: 2) whose hybrid status demonstrates its aim to explain the relation between language and artistic function (Leech & Short 2007: 13).

Leech and Short (2007: 42) also reflected on "the problem of 'measuring' style," which, in their view, should consider not only the occurrences of words but also co-occurrences and placement. Consequently, the ideal of a completely objective description of style is a myth, because literary scholars can only attempt to observe what is frequent or infrequent in a text (Leech & Short 2007: 51). Based on this assumption, Leech and Short consider deviance to be "the difference between the normal frequency of a feature, and its frequency in the text or corpus"; that is, a statistical notion (Leech & Short 2007: 48).

In stylistics, no agreement exists regarding the features required for an adequate account of style and no infallible technique is known for selecting what is significant because all texts have their individual qualities. Nonetheless, Leech and Short point out, four categories are likely to yield stylistically relevant information: "lexical categories, grammatical categories, figures of speech, cohesion and context" (Leech & Short 2007: 75). For literary texts, "foregrounding" is a typical stylistic effect that "foregrounds" an element against the background of more common expressions in everyday language. With their study, Leech and Short provided not only a foundation for what they called the "new stylistics" but many tools that can be used to describe the style of literary texts.

The beginning of the twenty-first century has proven to be a golden moment for the "new stylistics" as the publication of a series of handbooks shows (Burke 2018b; Stockwell & Whiteley 2015; Sotirova 2016). A more recent trend in stylistics seems to be "cognitive stylistics," which offers a range of tools and theories for researching interactions between texts and readers' mental representations and cognitive processes (Bell *et al.* 2021; Harding 2018). Other contemporary studies understand style as an umbrella term in philosophical and cultural debates focusing on authors like Pynchon was a "master of stylistic disguise" (Herrmann *et al.* 2020: 357). All recent research on style seems to agree that "much rests on the intuition and personal judgement of the reader" (Leech & Short 2007: 4). Suggesting that style does not remove the individual element, Jeffries and McIntyre (2010) wrote that:

> We cannot expunge our personal response from our analysis and would never want to. Like the natural and social scientists, we are human analysts, not machines. But like them [...] we do think that it is incumbent upon us a) to produce proper evidence and argumentation for our views, and to take counter-evidence into account when making our interpretative claims, b) to make claims which are falsifiable and c) to be explicit and open about our claims and the evidence for them. This does not constitute a claim to be

natural scientists, but merely to be systematic, open, honest and rational. (Jeffries & McIntyre 2010: 171)

This position is in line with David Lodge's argument (1966) that

> every writer displays his own unique "signature" in the way he uses language, something which all his works, however diverse, have in common, and which distinguishes them from the work of any other writer [...]. Modern linguists have applied the concept universally, and ascribe to every individual speaker an "idiolect" or way of using language which is unique. (Lodge 1966: 50)

Stylometry, of course, shares the methodological questions raised by stylistics. According to Kestemont (2014), what happened to the concept of style is that "scholars' subjective intuitions (*Gelehrtenintuition*, connoisseurship) [...] in style-based authorship-studies firmly contrast with today's prevailing criteria for scientific research, such as replicability or transparency (Kestemont 2014: 59–60). In his words, a rupture or turning point exists in the passage from stylistics to stylometry, though many continuities exist as well.

Stylometry is a subfield of computational literary studies, which is itself a subfield of the wider research area of Digital Humanities (Rebora 2020b) and shares common ground with corpus stylistics (Burke & Mahlberg 2018: 380). More specifically, computational literary studies use computers to analyse literary texts. Through statistical analysis of linguistic uses, stylometry attempts to "measure" the style of authors, thus discerning their latent "authorial footprints."

Much debate has taken place regarding the beginnings of stylometry. My aim is not to retrace the historiography of stylometry but rather to highlight the paradigms it shares with stylistics. The first attempts to study authorial style on the basis of an analysis of the statistical frequency of words were carried out by de Morgan and Mendenhall in the nineteenth century. They assumed that an author could be distinguished by the average length of the words she or he used. As Holmes wrote:

> The origins of stylometry date back to 1851 when the English logician Augustus de Morgan suggested in a letter to a friend that questions of authorship might be settled by determining if one text does not deal in longer words' than another [...] His hypothesis was investigated by Thomas Mendenhall, an American physicist, in the 1880s who subsequently published the results of his labours in measuring the lengths of several hundred thousand words from the works of Bacon, Marlowe, and Shakespeare [...] His legacy was to show that word length is not an effective authorial discriminator but he did find similarities between Shakespeare and Marlowe which, to this day, are still being investigated albeit with vastly more sophisticated techniques! (Holmes 1998: 112)

These methods yielded only partial results. The first successful results in stylometry were obtained by Frederick Mosteller and David L. Wallace (Mosteller &

Wallace 2007), who determined the authorship of the Federalist Papers (published in 1787–1788).

As these examples show, the methods of stylometry were elaborated before the introduction of computers (Stalder 2016: 21); it has been also the case for computational literary studies (Rebora 2020b). In 1964, German literary scholar Roy Wisbey founded the first Literary and Linguistic Computing Centre at the University of Cambridge, and, in 1970, together with Michael Farringdon, he organised the first international symposium "The Computer in Literary and Linguistic Research" (Pichler & Reiter 2020: 3). In 1973, the first professional association, the Association for Literary and Linguistic Computing, was founded at King's College, London.

The term stylometry is even older, though it remains unclear who was the first to use it. In Russian literary studies, N. A. Morozov (1854–1946) introduced the term stylometry in 1915 with the aim of investigating stylometric laws along the lines of other disciplines that found regularities in nature and social life (Kelih 2008: 48).

In 1921, the Russian Academy for the Arts was born in Moscow with the intention of providing an interdisciplinary and unifying perspective on the study of the arts (Plotnikov 2014: 8–9). The institute consisted of a philosophical, a sociological, and a physical-psychological section. In the institute's initial stage, the well-known painter, Wassily Kandinsky, was its head. The most prominent Russian psychologists of that time, Alexander Luria and Lev Vygotsky, worked for the institute to study reactions to artistic artefacts (Plotnikov 2014: 311).

In addition to empirical aesthetics, the precursor of another empirical method of literature was also developed at the Russian Academy for the Arts—computational literary studies, the quantitative assessment of literary style that is widespread in the digital humanities today. As regards empirical methods of literature, it was Boris Jarcho (1889–1942) who introduced the quantitative and statistical investigation of the stylistic, rhetorical, and content-based features of literary texts (Hansen-Löve *et al.* 2013: 411–426; 442–452).

Since its very first appearence stylometry was linked to the field of authorship attribution research. Starting at the beginning of the twenty-first century, this methodology has been further refined with the use of computers. In 2002, in attempts to determine authorship attribution in a collection of English poets, John Burrows proposed the so-called Delta, which he defined as the distance between one text and a group of texts. He fine-tuned his methods on a collection of English poets.

The calculation of Delta is based on complex mathematical insights (Evert *et al.* 2017: 5–7), though the procedure is extremely simple: (1) a list is generated containing the most frequent words in a collection of digitized texts; (2) for each text, the frequency of use of the words that make up the list is measured; (3) the "distance" between the texts is calculated by comparing the different frequency lists using a formula. The reasons for Delta's effectiveness are not entirely clear, though it may be that this measure is able to grasp the unconscious selection of function words—that is, articles or adverbs, for example—by an author (Kestemont 2014: 60). The approach is very similar to Morelli's method for determining the authorship of a painting (Kestemont 2014: 61).

The range of potential methodologies adopted by stylometry varies enormously and may focus on such aspects as punctuation marks, parts of speech, sentence structure, and even character sequences. The aim of this method can be authorship attribution but also the placement of a text or a group of texts into a genre. It has been used successfully to attribute literary texts in German, English, and Italian. More detailed analyses follow in Chapters 3–4.

Another kind of "keyness analysis" is the so-called "Zeta analysis," which attempts to grasp the linguistic features of texts. Zeta analysis follows an even simpler logic than Delta: given two groups of documents, (1) each text is divided into a number of segments of equal length; (2) for each word contained in the two groups, the proportion of the segments in which it appears is then calculated; and (3) the Zeta value of a word is then obtained by subtracting the two values (Rebora 2020b: 24). When Zeta analysis was applied to texts written by Shakespeare, it was able to show his distinctive use of the word "gentle."

With the digitization of millions of texts, the concept and the study of style are changing. Other important side-products of stylometric analysis are trees and diagrams that provide insight into a specific whole corpus at one glance. This visualization, which is a typical phenomenon of scientific work in the digital age, has strong explanatory power. As Eder shows, these diagrams enable conclusions about literature to be drawn from a distant-reading perspective—that is, through a visual interpretation of groupings and separations of several samples (Eder 2017: 51).

Herrmann, von Dalen-Oskam, and Schöch (2015) reviewed the ways in which style has been defined since 1945 in Dutch, German, and English literary studies to find the missing link between stylistics and stylometry. In their reconstruction, style is a thorny concept expressed in up to six different definitions, for example: "as higher-order artistic value (assessed through aesthetic experience)"; "as the holistic gestalt of single texts"; as "an expression of individuality, subjectivity, and/or emotional attitude of an author or speaker"; as "an artefact that presupposes (hypothetical or intentional) selection from among a set of alternatives"; and "as a deviation from some type of norm, involving (quantitative or cognitive) contrast" (Herrmann *et al.* 2015: 30).

Most of the theoreticians of literary style mentioned earlier can be classified within this list. The fifth definition, in particular—style as deviation—would include many of the most important stylisticians such as Spitzer and Bally. The second definition, style as a Gestalt, would place theoreticians like Ginzburg or Kayser together because of their belief that style is ineffable.

Even for contemporary stylisticians, the concept of style is fuzzy and enigmatic. Michael Maar began his more than 600-page-long 2021 monograph on style in German literature with the question "What is style?" His answer was as complicated as the question. There is no good nor bad style, he observed. "Each style is unique, that is its definition" (Maar 2021: 12). The sensitivity for style was not predetermined but was rather a feeling for something that cannot be measured but is nevertheless real. For Maar, style was an individual phenomenon that could not be separated from the personality of the author. It was a Gestalt that merged thought and sound, rhythm and concept (Maar 2021: 18). Interestingly, Maar did not consider every important author as a stylist: literary authors such as Balzac, Henry James, Stefan Zweig, and Heinrich Böll were read despite their style. While some authors have a personal style, others impress for their "non-style" or lack of a style. Paradoxically, style can also be expressed by what is not written, and Maar cites examples of great literature in which the dash or other punctuation expresses what cannot or should not be told (Maar 2021: 478–79; 505–06).

Following the elucidation of his very personal criteria, Maar presented an impressive and comprehensive history of German literature in which he introduced the biography of each author briefly and then moved on with a succinct description of that writer's style. One example of this style of criticism is his comparison of two of the main writers in the German canon, Franz Kafka and Thomas Mann:

> One grew up in Prague in a middle-class Jewish general store, the other in Lübeck in a senator's villa. One died of tuberculosis, unmarried and childless, at the age of forty; the other lived twice as long, celebrated his golden wedding anniversary, and fathered six offspring. One published two and a half books during his lifetime; the other was awarded the Nobel Prize once and nominated twice, leaving a thirteen-volume edition of his works […] One is the purest author in the German language; the other perhaps the richest. Thomas Mann, so completely different from Kafka, is not overestimated but underestimated as a stylist. (Maar 2021: 347–48)

One of the six definitions Herrmann, von Dalen-Oskam and Schöch proposed for the concept of style was that "any linguistic feature that can be formally defined and its frequency measured computationally implies a quantitative analysis of literature" (Herrmann *et al.* 2015: 30). This concept is at the core of their essay, which attempted to find both the overlap in and the boundaries between "mainstream" and "computational" (or "empirical") literary stylistics. This branch of studies is stylometry, a computational approach to style, and its methods have been applied for authorship attribution but also to questions of literary history and to the description of author, genre, and period style (e. g., Jannidis & Lauer 2014). Herrmann and her co-authors stressed that, in general, "statistical approaches to style adhered to the maxims of the scientific method, with three levels of empirical adequacy: of observation, of description, and of explication" (Herrmann *et al.* 2015: 35). Following these authors, "style" in the Digital Humanities is anything that can be measured in the linguistic form of a text, including sentence length, word length, or punctuation.

At the end of their paper, Herrmann and her co-authors defined style as "constituted by the combination of many possible features and should be seen as a complex system, with features situated at different linguistic levels" and "not limited to deviations from grammaticality or some supposedly neutral norm" (44). Their definition was designed to provide common ground for research in a new paradigm of style studies that was emerging as much from literary studies as from stylistics and computational linguistics.

By proposing their own theory, Herrmann and co-authors distinguished their approach from traditional stylistics. One of the main differences is in the concept of style which "is not something unique to literary works; rather, every text has a certain kind of style" (Herrmann *et al.* 2015: 46). Another difference relied upon rejection of the "deviation paradigm." The definition adopted by Hermann and her co-authors departed from the need for contrast developed by most earlier scholars of stylistics. They regarded style as something that could be observed in a single text or text sample without explicit comparison or contrast with other units. Furthermore, stylistic features could be seen as objective qualities of texts that offered a firm basis for hermeneutic acts of sense-making—that is, textual interpretation.

Although the Herrmann group made a relevant contribution to the contemporary concept of style, it was primarily concerned with the differences between stylometry and traditional stylistics. In contrast, the reconstruction of its evolution in the previous paragraphs shows that three elements guarantee the common ground between the two disciplines:

a)   Literary Style as Ineffable

Studies that follow the research paradigm studied by Carlo Ginzburg hold that the individuality of a style cannot be fully grasped by stylistic analysis. They argue that individuality can only emerge through comparison. The pioneers in stylistics considered style to be "ineffable," and, although style emerged from data as a result of the frequency of linguistic patterns, the "core" of individuality could not be expressed. Every stylistician has sought to quantify linguistic features that characterize an epoch, a genre, or a writer. Bally, for example, considered the "statistics of usage" of certain stylistic traits (Bally 1970: 205), Kayser their frequency (Kayser 1948: 100–101), and Spitzer their "principle of repetition" (Spitzer 1988: 336, 433). But the "scientific knowledge of the individual" (Ginzburg 2013: 112), as studied in stylistics, demands the analysis and categorization of all the symptoms of this quality that come to the surface. In Ginzburg's words, it is "the ability to construct from apparently insignificant experimental data a complex reality that could not be experienced directly" (Ginzburg 2013: 103).

To put it simply, the individuality of a writer, which is to say the core of style, remains ineffable.

Because stylometry is a form of "distant reading," it can capture linguistic elements and a great deal of information that a reader's cognitive system does not allow. But the individuality of writing style grasped by software in stylometry also remains something of a "black box"—that is, stylometry can produce specific results, though how it does so is not clear. In line with this reasoning, Kestemont (2014) expressed the hope that stylometry could move from "black magic" to theory. The fact that Delta algorithms consistently perform differently in different languages and that these differences can be explained only partially is an enigma for stylometry. Other researchers in stylometry observe that virtually no other algorithm exists that has been used as much as Delta though "there is still no theoretical framework to explain its success" (Evert *et al.* 2017: 8).

The operation of the Delta measure seems to clash with the interpretation of the concept of style. This practice shares some common ground with what is called "modelling" in the Digital Humanities (McCarty 2007). In practice, Delta "models" authorial style as a pattern of usage frequencies of a few hundred relatively frequent words (on which the calculation of the stylometric distance is based), inevitably trivializing the complexity of writing style in literature (such as the structuring of the discourse, the ordering of sentences, and the Jakobsonian selection of words). Yet Delta works precisely because, in flattening everything into a mere spectrum of frequencies, it manages to grasp, at least indirectly, the majority of these aspects and make them measurable (Rebora 2020: 30). In this sense, both stylistics and stylometry try to quantify the linguistic markers of style without being able to grasp the uniqueness of style per se.

b)   The Deviation Paradigm

As shown in the previous paragraphs, stylistics and stylometry both affirm deviations within the styles of two or more authors, including those related to common language, to the norms of the epoch, or to a literary genre. Deviation has been a core notion for stylistics starting from Bally to Montini (Montini 2020). Rebora (2020b: 25) has noted the common ground between the Zeta analysis of stylometry and the structuralist interpretation of style as a deviation from the norm (see Spitzer 1966; Riffaterre 1971), highlighting the close link between stylometry and the corpus linguistics. In fact, corpus stylistics uses statistical methods to classify texts into categories on the basis of the co-occurrence of distinctive linguistic phenomena, one of which is "keyword in context." Once a word, whose use is statistically different from the norm, has been identified, the passages in which it appears are extracted and analysed, creating a practice that Mueller (2012) has called "scalable reading." The Delta measurement is also considered a deviation, as Evert et al. comment: "Burrows thinks about style here in a way known from stylistics: style is the deviation from a norm" (Evert *et al.* 2017: 5). Consequently, the style of an author can only be assessed in relation to a reference corpus or the style of other authors.

c)   The Scientific Status of the Disciplines

Since Bally and Spitzer, stylisticians have quantified stylistic features and carried out experiments (Spitzer 1920: 1). The attempt to corroborate observations through quantitative analysis is shared by stylometry, which bases its methods on statistics. Since their beginnings, both stylistics and stylometry have sought to create an interdisciplinary research field combining linguistics and literary studies. Important representatives of stylistics, such as Bally and, later, Riffaterre, advocated a scientific status for their discipline (Riffaterre 1959: 154). This, too, unites stylistics and stylometry.

Contemporary stylometry follows in the footsteps of stylistics through the continued use of a range of methods to answer the questions it poses. Both follow a much older "presumptive paradigm" that Ginzburg observed in our ancestors —for example, in hunters. In the chapters that follow, I will follow this paradigm: Like a detective, I will collect the hints; like a hunter I will observe the traces the prey left in the forest. The goal of the "investigation" or "hunt" will be to collect the markers of the style of a genre, an epoch, or of an author whose individuality emerges through comparison with other markers or features. Depending on the research questions, stylistic analysis of literary texts will be integrated with stylometric analysis, sentiment analysis, archival research or empirical studies of readers' reactions. Here, the paradigm described by Carlo Ginzburg will take the form of interdisciplinary research.

2. Operationalisation in Literary Studies

Gregory Crane's 2006 article, *What Do You Do with a Million Books?*, seems *a posteriori* prophetic. The crucial question in his title is both rhetorical and fascinating, and the "million books" he mentions refer to the number of books that had already been digitized when he wrote:

> We are beginning to see the rise of vast libraries of digital books. The Million Book Project at Carnegie Mellon had as of November 2005 already scanned more than 600,000 books. Even more ambitiously, Google has created a consortium of libraries to build a massive digital collection: one of the partners alone—the Harvard University Library system—contains more than 15,000.000 items. Recent research by OCLC has counted the total number of unique books that will be digitized by the Google Print project at over 10.5 million. The Open Content Alliance is offering a more transparent framework for mass digitization, and such industry forces as Yahoo and Microsoft are beginning to develop digital collections with millions of books. (Crane 2006)

No library that preserves printed books can match these numbers, and Crane recognized that the quantitative effects of the digital revolution would, at some point, also become qualitative: "The change in scale alone is staggering, with quantitative change so great that qualitative effects are likely to follow" (Crane 2006). The main issue has been to find tools for the extraction of useful information from stored records. OCR technology, for example, makes it possible to digitize texts and can analyse page layouts and parse out footnotes, headers, tables of contents, and indices. Machine translation is another tool, even for historical languages. The most important tools seem to be linked to "data extraction", which allow humanists to draw succinct information and generate higher-level inferences from a huge body of data.

Digitization offers literary theory the big data of digitized archives, but, at the same time, raises the problem of creating corpora from which data can be extracted. For corpora that include contemporary publications and some online texts, the problems of copyright or data protection exist. Because it is common to carry out contrastive analyses in stylometry, more than one corpus must be created. In some cases, data from a "content corpus" are analysed against data from a "reference corpus." For example, in order to identify the features of Goethe's late style, the content corpus of his mature writings must be contrasted with the reference corpus of his early works. As we will see further on, digitization has profoundly changed the production, distribution, and consumption of literature in the digital age and created a new ecosystem that Simone Murray has baptized the "digital literary sphere" (Murray 2018). The Internet has offered new spaces for writing and publishing, beginning with self-publishing. In general, the whole system of communications among publishing houses, writers, and readers has been revolutionized, becoming more direct and informal thanks to social media. The "rating culture" that characterizes today's digital lives, which pushes us to review and evaluate hotels, restaurants, and drivers, also affects the evaluation of books, where tension continues to grow between reviews as forms of high cultural criticism and the amateur reviews fostered by Amazon or websites like Goodreads (Chapter 7). The architecture of the Internet itself plays a role in the distribution and democratization of critical authority.

As Adriaan van der Weel (2011) has noted, the digital revolution has also been a third reading revolution. Digitization is challenging the "Order of the Book" that has formed the basis of Western culture and other cultural traditions. In a digital environment, a literary text always runs the risk of "digital obsolescence" (van der Weel 2011: 181)—that is, the deterioration of physical materials. All digital texts lack the typical paratextual features of printed books—typography, cover art, size, colour, etc.—and look identical regardless of provenance or quality. It has been shown that the loss of materiality affects perceptions during literary reading. The most interesting effect has been in the measure of so-called "medium awkwardness": subjects reading on an iPad reported that holding and manipulating the medium was awkward (Mangen & Kuiken 2014). On digital devices, readers tend to "skim" and "shallow read" rather than engage in the deep reading that is more typical for printed books (Maryanne Wolf & Stoodley 2018; Salgaro 2022a).

Reading inferiority on digital devices has been observed in several studies and has led to attitudes that have seemed critical of technological innovations (Delgado *et al.* 2018). Others have extolled the potential of these new technologies to open literature to new, hitherto unknown users and applications (Lauer 2020). Consider that literature can now be enjoyed on computers, tablets, e-readers, or smartphones.

In 2013, in his book *Distant Reading*, Franco Moretti offered a groundbreaking statement regarding the impact of digitization on literary studies:

> In the last few years, literary studies have experienced what we could call the rise of quantitative evidence. This had happened before of course, without producing lasting effects, but this time it is probably going to be different, because this time we have digital

databases and automated data retrieval [...] When it comes to phenomena of language and style, we can do things [with them] that previous generations could only dream of. (Moretti 2013a: 212)

This mass of data demands that "close reading" be complemented by "distant reading," allowing "patterns among billions of sentences" of digitized texts to be identified (Moretti 2013a: 164). The main drawback of close reading is that it considers only a small group of canonical texts and neglects the thousands beyond the canon. Moretti was aware that the goal of the distant-reading approach was to capture large systems like the "Western European Novel" (Moretti 2013a: 49) on a theoretical level.

The exploitation of big data requires a methodological revolution by literary scholars who generally "listen" to literary texts to interpret them. According to Moretti, digitized archives "are not messages that were meant to address us, and so they say absolutely nothing until one asks the right question." This "encounter of the formal and the quantitative" (Moretti 2013a: 164–65), which characterizes the studies described in the following pages, fascinated him.

2.1. Quantitative and Qualitative Research in the Social Sciences

To understand the interaction between quantitative and qualitative research, an examination of the methodology employed by the social sciences, which have been dealing with this issue for some time, may be of service. When sociology was born in the middle of the nineteenth century, its founders shared a naive belief in the natural sciences. The foundations of sociology, therefore, appeared in the context of positivism. In Germany, the controversy between quantitative and qualitative research, the so-called *Methodenstreit* or, literally, "methodology dispute," began in the early twentieth century (Weitin 2021: 115ff). Post-positivist thinking in the second part of twentieth century replaced a concept of science that was based on a mechanistic model of reality, the certainty of scientific laws, and faith in the progress of humankind.

At that point in the history and evolution of the scientific paradigm, probability and uncertainty entered the equation. Although the social sciences lost their certainties as a result, they didn't abandon empiricism (Corbetta 2014: 28). Toward the end of the nineteenth century, the German sociologist Max Weber took an interpretative approach to social phenomena and rejected the parallelism between sociology and the natural sciences. For him, the core of sociological understanding was *Verstehen*—that is, the attempt to capture the uniqueness and non-replicability of social phenomena. Carlo Ginzburg called this the "presumptive paradigm" (see Chapter 1). Following in these two traditions, varying in the methods of social-science research become clear: the quantitative and the qualitative (Corbetta 2014: 39ff), the differences between which were summarized by Corbetta (2014: 51) in a table partially reconstructed here (Table 1) with a focus on concepts relevant to literary criticism:

	QUANTITATIVE RESEARCH	QUALITATIVE RESEARCH
Relation theory research	Structured, logically following phases, deduction (theory precedes observation)	Open, interactive
Concepts	Operational	Orientated, open, in progress
Psychological interaction between researcher and observed phenomenon	Scientific observation, detached, neutral	Empathic identification in the perspective of the studied object
Representativeness	Statistical representative sample	Single cases, not statistically significant
Mathematical and statistical techniques	Intense use	No use
Implications of the results	Generalizable	Specific

Table 1: Quantitative Research and Qualitative Research

Moving to another area of science, ethnographic fieldwork can provide a good example of qualitative research. Ethnographers engaged in "participant observation" adopt an ecological approach, involving themselves with the objects of study in their natural environment (Ronzon 2008: 15). The ethnographer in the role of participant-observer doesn't manipulate the context, as happens with experimental work in the lab. Rather, ethnographers observe the research object, which may be an event, a person, or a phenomenon, in the "real world," capturing its uniqueness and originality. Guided by Francesco Ronzon, ethnographic observation does not exclude observers' subjectivities; instead, it recognizes the individuality of the researcher, who belongs to a particular culture, society, and group with specific beliefs, motivations, and interests. In this view, the interpretation of observed data assumes high relevance, and the endeavour to find the correct method for each case leads to a certain "methodological pluralism" in ethnographic research (Ronzon 2008: 20).

In recent years, a third paradigm has emerged that attempts to combine qualitative and quantitative approaches; it rejects methodological orthodoxy in favour of methodological appropriateness (Patton 1990; Bryman 2003). For scholars of this mode of study, the legitimization of quantitative or qualitative analyses depends upon the research object (Corbetta 2014: 70).

The concept of *operationalisation* serves as a bridge in the dialogue between quantitative and qualitative research and was first introduced by P. W. Bridgman in 1927 in his *Logic of Modern Physics*. In explaining "the operational point of view," he wrote:

> To find the length of an object we have to perform certain physical operations. The concept of length is therefore fixed when the operations by which length is fixed are fixed: that is, the concept of length involves as much and nothing more than the set of operations by which length is determined. In general, we mean by any concept nothing more than a set of operations; *the concept is synonymous with the corresponding set of operations…* [T]he proper definition of a concept is not in terms of its properties but in terms of actual operations. (Bridgman 1927: 5–6)

Although the concept of operationalisation originated in physics, it has sparked heated debates in such other subjects as philosophy and psychology (Chang 2021). As described in the *Dictionary of Social Research Methods*, it is "the mapping of a research question onto a dataset or study design" (Elliot *et al.* 2016). Matthew DeCarlo offered a more contemporary definition of operationalisation as "the process by which researchers conducting quantitative research spell out precisely how a concept will be measured" (DeCarlo 2018). Operationalisation works by identifying specific indicators used to represent the studied concepts. For example, the concept of "well-being" can be framed as physical health, emotional health, work environment, life evaluation, healthy behaviours, and access to basic necessities. Empirical work in a specific area can provide very specific examples of how important concepts have been measured in the past and what sorts of indicators have been used.

Taking DeCarlo as a guide, an operational definition consists of: (1) the variable being measured, (2) the measure that will be used, and (3) the way in which the results of that measure will be interpreted. It is not always easy to find the right measure for a variable. To measure a variable such as age, the best option would be simply to ask, "How old are you?" Most social variables are not that simple, however, but scales have been developed in many areas and validated by research. Concepts in quantitative and qualitative research are different because the concepts in a qualitative study are defined by researchers' interpretations, but operationalisation in quantitative research, in DeCarlo's view, requires a more open-ended approach.

For Corbetta (2014: 89), similarly, operationalisation meant "translation from theoretical language to empirical language" or, in other words, the transformation of a concept into empirically observable properties. The operationalised property of a research object thus constitutes a variable. He mentions two examples. First, the concept of "cultural level" (89) can be operationalised as "level of education," which can be measured as "non-graduate, high school diploma, PhD, etc." Second, the concept of "weight" can correspondingly be expressed in the property "weight of a book" and operationalised with the measure of a specific weight (Corbetta 2014: 93). As these examples show, such properties allow the quantification, measurement, and classification of a phenomenon.

Even a concept like empathy, one of the most common reactions to fictional characters, can be operationalised. One of the main problems with the concept of empathy is that its concept, as it has developed over the last hundred years in such areas as aesthetics, psychology, the neurosciences, and literary theory, lacks clarity and precision. Not surprisingly, a 2019 paper identified up to forty-three distinct definitions of empathy in academic publications (Pinotti & Salgaro 2019).

In an environment of such conceptual fuzziness, "operationalisation can provide a new perspective for transparent theory-building and development regarding empathy and its sub-constructs" (Surma-aho & Hölttä-Otto 2022: 12). Surma-aho and Hölttä-Otto, for example, described five core concepts of empathy (empathic understanding, empathic design research, empathic design action, empathic orientation, and empathic mental processes) as well as six potential operationalisations.

2.2. The Introduction of Operationalisation into Literary Studies

Operationalisation is not limited to the social sciences. Recently, it has been applied to the field of literary theory as well. Here is Franco Moretti's pithy definition:

> [Operationalisation] describes the process whereby concepts are transformed into a series of operations—which, in turn, allow all manner of phenomena to be measured. Operationalising means building a bridge from concept to measurement, and then to the world. In our case, [the bridge] is from the concepts of literary theory to some form of quantification and then to literary texts. (Moretti 2013b: 3)

After describing the concept of operationalisation, Moretti moved on to the operationalisation of narrative space as it was allocated to a particular character, using the procedure to analyse a character's "space" within a narrative structure. In plays, the space devoted to each character is easy to determine because words are distributed among the various speakers. Moretti took Racine's *Phèdre* as an example. In that tragedy, Phèdre utters 29% of the words; Hyppolite, 21%; Thésée, 14%; and so on (Moretti 2013b: 3).

After calculating these frequencies, Moretti reflected on the importance of numbers which, alone, could not create new theories or generalizations. For him, measurements in literary theory made some concepts "real" by proving that something corresponded to them in the world of fiction (Moretti 2013b: 6). In his view, the number of words given to a particular character revealed the meaning that the character brought to the play, but such a correlation was not precise across all plays. In some, the protagonist occupied the most space (*Macbeth*, for example); in others, such as *Antigone*, the protagonist had fewer lines than other characters. In Moretti's view, the measurement of "character space" indicated that the protagonist was "only a special instance of the more general category of centrality" (Moretti 2013b: 10). Numbers could show that the protagonist was a tool captured by readers' sense of individual character while "character-space" was the realization of a theory that wanted to understand something "that does not fall under the domain of our senses—that is, the *relations* among characters" (Moretti 2013b: 11). As he stated:

> That is why, in the end, operationalisation produced more than the refinement of already-existing knowledge: not the protagonist, improved, but an altogether new set of categories. Measurement as a challenge to literary theory, one could say, echoing a famous essay by Hans Robert Jauss. This is not what I expected from the encounter between computation and criticism. I assumed, like so many others, that the new approach would change the history, rather than the theory of literature and, ultimately, that may still be the case. But as the logic of research has brought us face to face with conceptual issues, they should become the task of the day, countering pervasive clichés regarding the simple-minded positivism of digital humanities. Computation has theoretical consequences—possibly, more than in any other field of literary study. The time has come to make them explicit. (Moretti 2013b: 11)

A few lines later, Moretti correctly recognized that most literary concepts were not designed to be quantified. To show this, he tried to link Hegel's conception of tragic conflict with empirical data from *Antigone*. In considering examples, Moretti questioned the connection posited by Hegel between face-to-face confrontations and face-to-face encounters in tragedies. In both parts of his essay, Moretti showed that operationalisation favoured the leap from measurement to reconceptualization. Operationalisation struck him as the key to answering the question "What Do You Do with a Million Books?":

> Digital humanities may not yet have changed the territory of the literary historian, or the reading of individual texts, but operationalizing has certainly changed and radicalized our relationship to concepts: it has raised our expectations, by turning concepts into magic spells that can call into being a whole world of empirical data; and it has sharpened our scepticism, because, if data revolt against their creator, then the concept is in real trouble. A theory-driven, data-rich research program has become imaginable, bent on testing, and, when needed, falsifying the received knowledge of literary study. Of this enterprise, operationalisation, will be the central ingredient. (Moretti 2013b: 15)

Recently, operationalisation seems to be gaining ground in literary theory and has inspired a "reflective text analysis" (Pichler & Reiter 2020: 57).[2] Pichler and

---

2 "What we mean by reflective text analysis is not a theory but a practice characterised by three aspects: (i) the division of a question into sub-questions must always account for the oper-

Reiter (2021) tried to operationalise the terminology of traditional literary studies so that it could be used in computational literary studies. By operationalisation, they meant the development of a method for tracing a (theoretical) term back to text-surface, that is to a linguistic phenomenon. The aim of such operationalisation was not the interpretation of a text but the development of procedures for the manual or automatic recognition of text passages, which is common in the Digital Humanities (Pichler & Reiter 2021: 4).

They used a concrete example to test this procedure by applying it to Norbert Altenhofer's "model interpretation" (*Modellinterpretation*) of Heinrich von Kleist's *The Earthquake in Chile*. This confrontation with Altenhofer's hermeneutic theory falsifies the notion that "the digital humanities have escaped confrontation with the great aesthetic and scientific culture of the 20th century" (Moretti 2022).[3] This Altenhofer work was chosen because it revealed many of the author's own background assumptions regarding literary theory. At the centre of Altenhofer's hermeneutic theory is the thesis that the meaning of literary works is not given but is constructed from the dialectic of the general and the individual in a work's language and form. Thus, the meaning of texts is always in abeyance and never static (Pichler & Reiter 2021: 8), which contributes to a sense that Kleist's texts are enigmatic. Pichler and Reiter encountered many difficulties in trying to operationalise Altenhofer's approach because many concepts, such as "mysteriousness" (*Rätselhaftigkeit*) were vague. These scholars raised questions regarding whether the terminology of literary studies could be traced in this way to text-surface phenomena, and they proposed various ways by which such definitions could be converted into manual or automatic recognition. Because they employed tools from computational linguistics that can only partially be transferred to computational literary studies, researchers are left to decide which kind of operationalisation is the most adequate. As the authors noted, "in principle, however, it should be noted that the algorithmic approach requires a high degree

---

ationalisation of the concepts relevant to it; this results in a mutual conditional relationship between the division into sub-questions and the operationalisation of concepts. (ii) In the empirically based validation of the operationalisation(s) and the interpretation of findings, explicit and implicit as well as theoretical and practical presumptions must be considered. (iii) All work steps must be carried out in the context of disciplinary knowledge, which must also be reflected upon critically with regard to the practice and results of analysis" (Pichler & Reiter 2020: 57–58).

3 In *Falso Movimento/Wrong Movement* Franco Moretti (2022) reflected on the reasons why the Digital Humanities have not changed our knowledge of literature. According to him, what is missing most is a reference theory: "Perhaps it is that we were all completely unprepared for the advent of new research technologies. Unprepared deep down, and not because we did not know anything about statistics." Moretti seems not to consider fully the young age of the discipline given that time is needed to build a proper methodological framework.

of explicitness and clarity of the terms, as this is the only way to make them technically reproducible" (Pichler & Reiter 2021: 22).

Even in the abstract of their paper, Pichler and Reiter recognized the importance of operationalisation as a bridge between different disciplines:

> At the same time, operationalisation is the central link between the computer sciences and literary studies, as well as being a necessary component for a large part of the research done in computational literary studies. The advantage of a conscious, deliberate and reflective operationalisation practice lies not only in the fact that it can be used to achieve reliable quantitative results (or that a certain lack of reliability at least is a known factor); it also lies in its facilitation of interdisciplinary cooperation: in the course of operationalisation, concrete sets of data are discussed, as are the methods for analysing them, which taken together minimizes the risk of misunderstandings, "false friends" and of an unproductive exchange more generally (Pichler & Reiter 2021: 3).

Other scholars have recently tried to implement operationalisation in literary theory (Salgaro 2018; Alvarado 2019; Horstmann & Kleymann 2019; Gius 2019; Reiter *et al.* 2020; Weitin 2021, 55–57).[4] Their analyses represent attempts to demonstrate that the quantitative approaches of the Digital Humanities allow operationalisation of concepts in literary theory—that is, translation from a theoretical level to an empirical one. As Moretti showed by quoting Thomas Kuhn, numbers gathered without integrating them into a methodological framework "remain just numbers" (Moretti 2013b: 6). No laws of nature can be discovered by simply inspecting the results of a measurement, and measurement alone does not lead to new theories. For that, data must be interpreted. Once concepts are operationalised through quantitative analysis, data are produced that can inform qualitative research; in this way, a circular form of interdisciplinary research is created. Even the difference between *evidence* and *interpretation* can be overcome, because, as Jannidis and Lauer assert in the context of their stylometric analysis of German literary history, the "interpretations of the results of quantitative studies [...] are hermeneutic acts of sense making"

---

4 Others have tried to implement it in neighbouring disciplines such as history. For Sahle and Henny (2015: 113) "the historical sciences have been characterised above all by a contemplative hermeneutic practice ("reading—understanding—writing") ... [and] more quantitative approaches to historical research have always existed in the shadows." Although Emmanuel Le Roy Ladurie's famous prediction in 1973 that the historians of tomorrow would be programmers or would not be historians at all has not yet come true, the method of many contemporary historians has changed. For some, the historical research process involves the following steps: a) posing the question, b) operationalising, c) selecting sources, d) gathering information, e) analysing, and f) presenting the results (Sahle & Henny 2015: 113). To expose this method for historical research the two authors operationalised an understanding of "historians" in Wikipedia.

(Jannidis & Lauer 2014: 50). These operations are intertwined as the schema in Figure 1 shows.[5]

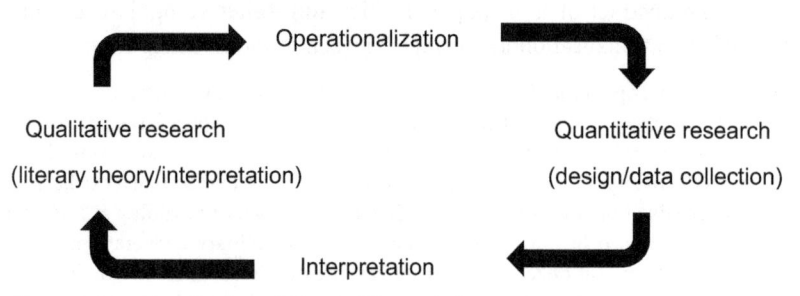

Figure 1: Operationalisation of Literary Theory (Salgaro 2018: 55)

The model above shows that a large amount of data, the "big data" of digitized texts, can act as a powerful incentive to research but that research itself cannot be "data-driven." The tools with which data are analysed always depend on a theory. I agree with Franco Moretti when he states: "If a theory is not there, clichés will take its place" (Moretti 2022).[6]

Contrary to expectation, operationalisation doesn't negate theories because, by "shifting focus from the remediation of *content* to the remediation of *ideas* (which have been developed to interpret that content), digital humanists may reconnect with the production of theory, an area in which the humanities and interpretive social sciences have developed expertise" (Alvarado 2019: 79).

Even though such important literary scholars as Moretti have argued for the combined use of quantitative and qualitative research in literary criticism, humanities scholars remain sceptical of such a method. Gerhard Lauer, editor of special issue of the *Journal of Literary Theory* on "Empirical Methods in Literary Studies" in 2015, made the alarming claim that "[a]lmost universally in literary theory, a sceptical perspective on empirical methods prevails" (Lauer 2015: 1).

---

5 Weitin (2021: 56) proposed a similar schema in which the passage I defined as "interpretation" is called "reconceptualization." Both concepts highlight the fact that empirical work always contributes to a deepening and refinement of theory.

6 In *Falso Movimento*, Moretti takes critical stock of his contribution to the "so-called quantitative" turn in the study of literature. On the one hand, he praises the contribution of the Digital Humanities which, by using the logic of measurement, illuminates the internal workings of literary systems, "a task towards which the hermeneutic tradition, with all its creativity, has never shown the slightest interest" (Moretti 2022). On the other hand, he denies the possibility of real collaboration between hermeneutics and quantitative studies. In his view, because of their conceptualizations of "form," "they can work alongside each other but cannot cooperate." Moreover, quantitative techniques such as text mining, topic modelling, and sentiment analysis neglect the social dimension of literature. In hermeneutics, "form is *a force, an act*," a way of shaping what exists; for quantitative studies, "form is a *finished product* to be measured with a cool head" (Moretti 2022).

The prevalence of more theoretical approaches in literary criticism has also been quantified in recent publications on stylistics (Fialho & Zyngier 2018: 332). Even if "empirical methods undoubtedly have their history and assured place in literary theory" (Lauer 2015: 2), only a few literary scholars have made use of them, often because of lack of competence. This situation is rapidly changing as the mass of data produced by digitization animates a revision of the status quo and a rethinking of the differences between empirical and theoretical approaches to literary studies.

In fact, the trend of operationalising the concepts of literary theories seems to be in continuous expansion. Empirical methods are widely used in literary criticism (Ajouri *et al.* 2013) to search for concordances and word frequencies, for example. Sandra Richter recognized, in computational literary studies, a tendency toward a "new rigor" (Richter 2020: 145). This branch of studies has helped literary studies improve the ways in which data are used in identification and explication, the accessibility and sustainability of data, methods of data analysis and data development from texts, and the visualisation of textual data (Richter 2020: 151–54). Textual data are determined with the help of procedures such as text mining, topic modelling (Ciula & Eide 2016; Weitin & Herget 2017), stylometry, network analyses, and the like.

Nowadays, larger humanities institutes often have a Digital Humanities centre, and many both national and supranational associations of Digital Humanities exist—the European Association for Digital Humanities (EADH) and the Digital Humanities association of Southern Africa (DHASA), for example. Consider, too, that the International Society for the Empirical Study of Literature (Internationale Gesellschaft für Empirische Literaturwissenschaft) was founded as early as 1987 and that, since 2013, a Max Planck Institute for Empirical Aesthetics has existed with a section devoted specifically to the study of language and literature. These scientific associations practice empirical research and put operationalisation at the basis of their work.

The implementation of operationalisation has pushed some scholars to reflect on the epistemological status of the Digital Humanities and on empirical approaches in literary theory. Literary scholars who use methods of the Digital Humanities include Matthew Jokers, who stated that literary methodology is "in essence no different from the scientific one" (Jockers 2013: 13). Surely in cases of authorship identification, literary theory can find comfort in the methods developed by the natural sciences.

Other scholars have expressed more nuanced positions. Jean-Gabriel Ganascia (2015), for instance, returns to the distinction between the "sciences of nature" and the "sciences of culture" proposed by Heinrich Rickert and Ernst Cassirer at the beginning of the twentieth century. According to these two German philosophers, the "sciences of nature" proceed by generalizing cases. They extract the general properties of objects and determine laws. By contrast, the "sciences of culture" proceed by understanding details and by observing individual instances and giving them meaning. This difference seems to mirror the distinction between quantitative and qualitative research expressed at the beginning of this chapter.

Ganascia believed that digital literary studies did not function as purely inductive sciences because they didn't aim to establish general laws. As part of the humanities, Digital Humanities examines the work of an author, a generation of writers, or a genre in order to understand these works and characterize their specificity. Unlike traditional literary scholars, digital humanists in literary studies make use of datasets that are automatically processed. Ganascia confirmed that "the use of computers in the humanities does not necessarily lead one to abandon theory. On the contrary, programs need to refer to well-defined theoretical frameworks on which they can bring pieces of material evidence to bear" (Ganascia 2015). For him, computer-aided methods could be seen as a continuation of traditional humanistic approaches.

Research has demonstrated that, in contrast to other disciplines in which the Kuhnian paradigm of sciences is in force, literary studies show the greatest respect for ideas developed in a remote past (Verdaasdonk & van Rees 1992). Aristotle's *Poetics*, for example, is still a point of reference for students and scholars. Problems pertaining to the nature of the literary text have continued to be tackled and formulated the same way for an extremely long time. For Verdaasdonk and Van Rees (1992: 142), literary studies appeal to a concept of literature and these concepts are always imprecise or ambiguous. They wrote, "a concept of literature fails to provide the criteria indispensable to a uniform and empirically verifiable application of the definitions it embodies" (Verdaasdonk & van Rees 1992: 143) and leaves much room for researchers to take subjective stands. These concepts are highly normative, and only "the skilled reader is thought to be able to do justice to a literary work" (Verdaasdonk & van Rees 1992: 151).

Consequently, an analysis never takes place as a testing of theory but rather as an exemplification of a concept of literature. Because decisions are made *a priori* regarding the features of literature that should be considered, with no clear and intersubjective phrasing of the nature of literature and without distinguishing between intrinsic and extrinsic features, it is impossible to determine that one concept of literature is more appropriate than another. As questions of literary theory are raised within the framework of a concept of literature, "the answers are entirely without descriptive status" (Verdaasdonk & van Rees 1992: 148). Based on this assumption, empirical studies of literature, such as the Digital Humanities or reader-oriented approaches, can contribute to the field because, along with their data, they bring descriptive elements from which literary theories can benefit. Moreover, the processes triggered by operationalisation often allow for a refinement of theory.

In this regard, the concept of style is a good example. As we have shown, style has always remained a vague concept in literary theory (Chapter 1). At the same time, stylistics has expressed a desire to use more quantitative methods to more closely approximate the experimental sciences. The combination of stylistics and stylometry seems to fulfil this desire by providing more descriptive elements to such concepts as authorial style or an epoch.

It is also important to consider the limitations of this practice. Operationalisation can answer some questions of literary criticism but not others. This study focuses on the potential of this approach while keeping its limitations in mind. Operationalisation cannot, for instance, answer questions such as: Is Schiller or Goethe more original or Why is Goethe more appreciated by readers than Schiller? It cannot do so because the concepts of originality and aesthetic appreciation are not sufficiently defined to allow such an analysis. Nor can operationalisation provide tools for questions that are too subjective in nature, such as Why does Dürrenmatt consider a story finished when it has taken the worst turn (*schlimmstmögliche Wendung*)? Or Why does he end his dramas in tragic or tragicomic ways?

Operationalisation can, however, provide suitable answers to the question Should Kleist be considered a romantic or a classicist writer? (Jannidis & Lauer 2014) or Do women authors write differently from men? (Weitin 2021: 8). Another question that could be tackled is "Did Molière and Corneille collaborate in the writing of *Psyché?*" (Cafiero and Camps 2022: 126ff). Such research can reveal that a novel like *Bekenntnisse einer schönen Seele: Von ihr selbst geschrieben/ Confessions of a Beautiful Soul: Written by Herself* (1806), supposedly written by Christine Unger, was, in reality, written by Friedrich Buchholz, an Unger collaborator (Weitin 2021: 106). Operationalisation does not always make it possible to gain such new knowledge. The first progress it yields is that it pushes researchers to refine concepts, as Gerhard Lauer and Fotis Jannidis cautiously suggest:

> We do not expect any dramatic new insights from this application; instead we seek to evaluate the method in terms of the knowledge we already possess. If, however, we can corroborate the existing scholarly consensus with this new computational method, then we will have succeeded in providing a firmer foundation for this knowledge, because we will have achieved the same result or similar results by two independent research methods. By the same token, if we can successfully and to a high degree confirm traditional knowledge with this approach, we can then—in cases in which the results do not corroborate previously held views—start to investigate and maybe even question traditional knowledge. (Jannidis & Lauer 2014: 33)

One of the added values of operationalisation is that it permits reproducibility—that is, it enables readers to prove that an error has occurred and that criticism is appropriate (Weitin 2021: 4). Because literary theory is a subfield of the humanities, it doesn't need to "progress" or seek "novelties" as the natural sciences do. Thus, the enhancement of a concept can be considered progress in and of itself.

2.3 Operationalization: A Case Study in "Familiarity with the Reading Device"

Another example of operationalisation of a literary value is familiarity with the medium used for reading. In the last twenty years, the ability to read literature on different devices has grown exponentially. Today, we can read on smartphones, tablets, computers, or e-readers. With a group of psycholinguists of the Freie Universität, we operationalised the concept of "familiarity with the reading device" to understand which media were favoured by readers and whether it was true that young readers, so-called digital natives, preferred digital media (Salgaro *et al.* 2020).

Marc Prensky (2001) introduced the dichotomy of digital natives/digital immigrants in order to describe a generational divide. According to him, "digital natives" were the "native speakers" of the digital language of computers and the Internet—the generations who were born into the digital world. So-called "digital immigrants," on the other hand, were those who started to use the language of new technologies at a later stage in life. Consequently, like all immigrants, they have experienced difficulties in adapting to new environments and always retain, to some degree, one foot in the past. Starting from Prensky's dichotomy, the aim of our operationalisation was to investigate whether the categories of digital natives and digital immigrants existed in the context of literary-reading habits associated with various supports (paper vs. onscreen) and to explore differences between the two groups.

Fifty-nine participants (thirty-seven women, twenty-two men) aged 18 to 70 were recruited in two German towns: Göttingen and Berlin. They were from different areas of Germany and from different backgrounds: students, workers, retirees, and people with and without academic training. The first part of the experiment required all participants to read various pieces of literature in printed books and on an electronic device (Salgaro *et al.* 2018). All participants read two short stories and two poems, one each in a printed book and on the Kindle reader (the order was randomly changed for each participant). At the end of the study, participants filled out a questionnaire concerning their reading habits and their age:

1. How many years have you been used digital texts for leisure reading?
   Answers on a 5-point scale: 1 (for more than 5 years)—5 (never)
2. How many books did you read last year for leisure?
   Answers on a 5-point scale: 1 (more than 20)—5 (none)

These first two questions served to split the sample into two groups (high familiarity vs low familiarity with digital reading) and focus on the digital-reading experience. To further explore group differences that resulted from familiarity with digital texts, we also presented an adapted form of the haptic dissonance scale (Gerlach & Buxmann 2011). Participants indicated their agreement with the following statements on a five-point rating scale (from 1: I strongly disagree to 5: I strongly agree):

3. It makes no difference to me whether I read a printed book or an e-book.
4. I find reading in digital formats cold.
5. An e-book is more technical and reminds me of work.
6. Reading an e-book feels more technically distant and not natural in my hands, thus I cannot establish a close relationship with the book.
7. Printed books for me have a pleasurable "odour."
8. I set a high value on the paper quality of printed books.

To test whether the two groups conformed to Prensky's categories, we compared their answers to other questions regarding reading habits and the use of digital vs. paper texts for leisure reading:

9. Do you prefer digital or printed books for your leisure reading?
   Answers on a 5-point scale: 1 (only digital books)—5 (only printed books)
10. Which medium better supports deep reading?
    Answers on a 5-point scale: 1 (only digital)—5 (only printed)

As a first step, we used the first item (familiarity with digital reading) to divide the sample into two groups: Thirty-three participants reported a high familiarity with digital texts for leisure reading (that is, for more than three years). The remaining twenty-six reported low familiarity as indicated by no use of digital devices or a use limited to two years or less. We also compared the ages of members of the two groups. The results showed no significant differences: $t(57) = 1.7$, $p = 0.10$. As shown in Figure 2, we identified young participants (those younger than 40) who reported lower familiarity (measured in time spent reading digitally in their free time) as well as older participants who reported high familiarity.

This outcome is striking because no homogeneous use of technologies for reading could be identified among younger or older people. In accordance with other studies, our findings seem to reject the metaphor of the "digital native"— that is, the idea that digital expertise is a generational or age-related issue. These

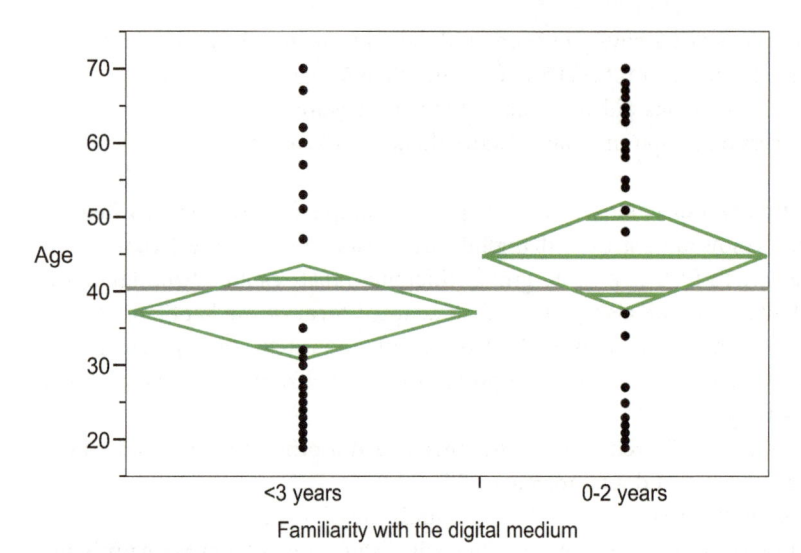

Figure 2: Responses to the Question "How many years have you used digital texts in your leisure reading?"

findings suggest that the dichotomy of digital natives/digital immigrants in reading behaviour (paper vs screen) is misleading. The inconsistency of the Prenskyian dichotomy with respect to preferred medium for leisure reading of literary texts is further revealed by the findings represented in the graphs below (see Figures 3 and 4). According to our results, subjects with both high and low familiarity with digital devices showed a stronger inclination for printed books in leisure reading because the latter allowed an active process of thoughtful and deliberate reading or "deep reading" (Wolf & Stoodley 2018) and supported critical analysis, reflection, and insight.

To explore the groups further, we compared whether both typologies of readers perceived differences between reading printed books and e-books. Readers with high familiarity with digital reading agreed more strongly that reading printed books did not differ from reading e-books, as shown in the t-test: $t(57) = -2.7, p = 0.009$.

Familiarity with the medium determined whether digital reading was perceived as "cold," "distant," or associated with work, and subjects in the low-familiarity group were more likely to report such perceptions (Figure 5). In other words, low-familiarity readers were unable to establish an emotional, close connection with texts in an e-book format. For literary reading, this is an important distinction because emotional bonding with fictional characters appears to be hindered by digital media. Gerlach and Buxmann (2011) described this lack of warm feeling as "haptic dissonance."

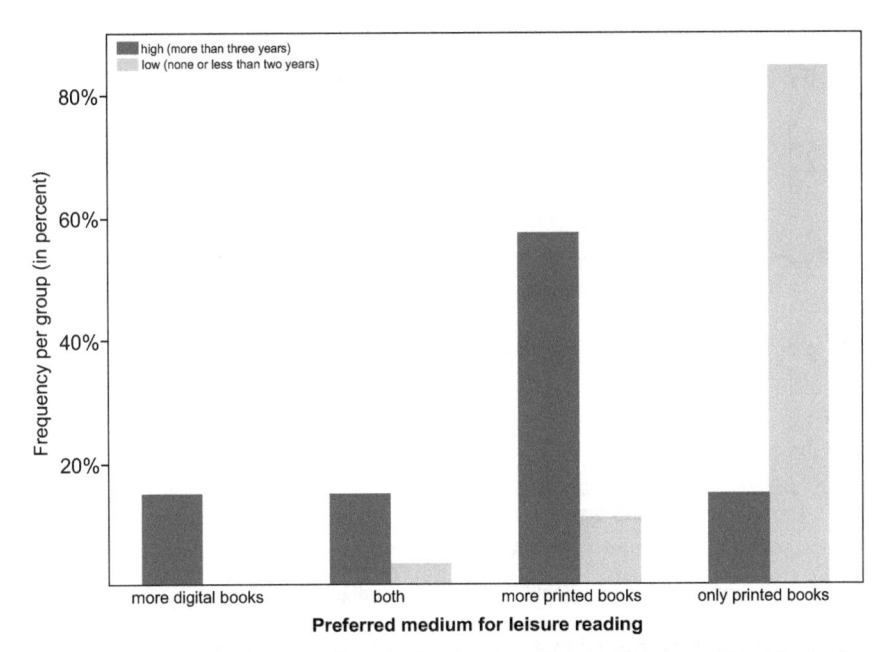

Figure 3: Responses by Group to the Question "Do you prefer to digital or printed books for leisure reading?"

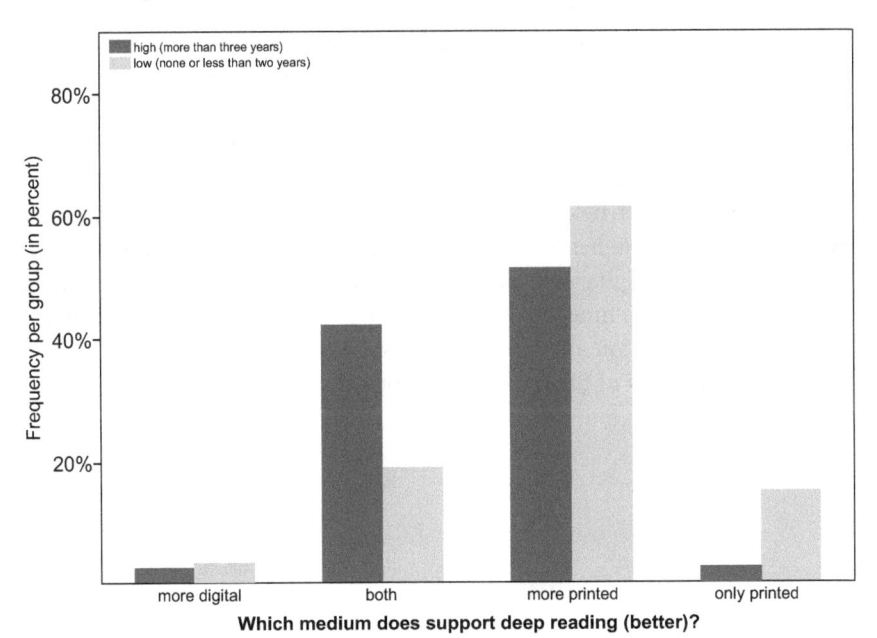

Figure 4: Responses by Group to the Question "Which medium better supports deep reading?"

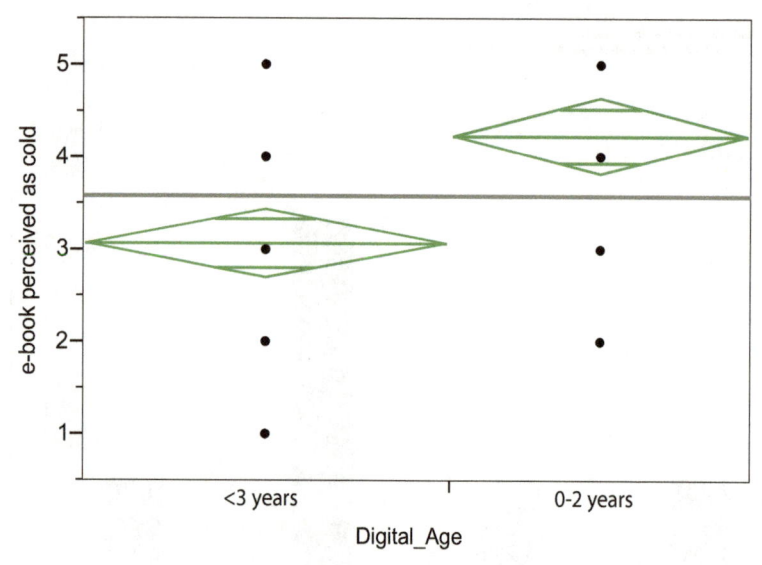

Figure 5: Responses to the Statement "I find reading in digital formats cold"

Overall, our results showed that familiarity with a reading medium was crucial to the quality of readers' experience. Haptic dissonance is a consequence of lack of familiarity with the digital medium. Along the lines of similar studies, our results seemed to indicate that the printed book still held an important position and that onscreen reading implied a kind of "digital inferiority" for some readers (Delgado *et al.* 2018).

The experiment described above demonstrates that operationalisation offers a unique and constantly expandable set of big data to contemporary literary criticism and to other fields. The balance between quantitative and qualitative research in literary studies is being changed by the digitization of literary texts and the creation of digital collections that can be investigated through statistical analyses. At the same time, the ways in which combining these approaches can lead to new information and innovative perspectives are becoming ever clearer. This will be the focus of the chapters that follow.

3. "Late Style" Put to the Test: Goethe's, Musil's, and Kafka's Late Works

In recent years, the concept of Late Style—the idea that the art produced during artists' and writers' final years is marked by a profound change in style with respect to earlier work and to the work of their contemporaries—has become fashionable (Leeder 2015; Zanetti 2012; Seidler 2010; Said 2006). Contemporary interest in gerontology and Late Style in the humanities is triggered by the aging of Western societies and declining birth-rates. Discourses that link creativity and age are not new, however, at least not in German culture. In fact, Stuart Taberner considered "lateness" a specifically German problem linked to the global aging crisis, on the one hand, and, on the other, to the fact that Germany sees itself as a "late-stage" nation (Taberner 2013).

3.1. Defining "Late Style"

In the mid-twentieth century, such important writers and philosophers as Hermann Broch, Gottfried Benn, and T. W. Adorno reflected on the relationship between aging and aesthetic style. Even earlier, in 1860, Jacob Grimm delivered a lecture "Rede über das Alter/On Old Age" (Grimm 2010), which may qualify him as the father of this reflection (Taberner 2013: 10). As McMullan and Smiles (2016: 38) have pointed out, "'Late Style,' invented by romantics, was reinvented by modernists." They noted that:

> The late-style trope takes from romanticism its emphasis on biography, subjectivism, the relationship between creativity and selfhood; from modernism it derives its interest in tradition, the avant-garde, abstraction, the subordination of self to epoch, the loss of linearity. Needless to say, these two understandings of creativity offer very different perspectives on the phenomenon. Their co-existence within the discourse of Late Style explains something of its flexibility, but also its critical instability. (McMullan & Smiles 2016: 12)

In German culture this concept seems particularly effervescent, and two terms capture the relationship between aging and style: *Spätstil* and *Altersstil*. Historical reasons may explain why discussion of "lateness" and aging seems to be a peculiarly German preoccupation (Leeder 2015: 17).

In his 1947 "Myth and Late Style/Mythos und Altersstil," Hermann Broch described "radical stylistic change" and "sharp stylistic break" in the creative output of such geniuses as Titian, Rembrandt, Goya, and Bach (Broch 1995: 213). What is interesting in Broch's definition of Late Style is the idea that the writer's vocabulary is reduced and becomes "abstract":

> What do all these very different examples have in common? All of them are characterised by a radical change of style and not merely by the development of directions taken initially. [This] sharp stylistic turn [...] can most aptly be described as a kind of *abstractionism* in which expression relies to an ever decreasing extent on *received vocabulary*, so that in the end only a few symbols remain of that original vocabulary, and expression makes increasing use of syntax alone. [T]herein lies the essence of abstractionism—in the increasing narrowing of the vocabulary and in the realm of expression through syntactic relations; thus in mathematics the vocabulary is reduced to nothing, while its system of expression is supported exclusively by its own syntax. (Broch 1995: 213)

Like Broch, Ernst Lewy also considered the "emphasis on the abstract" to be one of the main features of Goethe's Late Style (Zanetti 2012: 67). The final scenes of *Faust*, which are highly enigmatic, are an example (Broch 1995: 213). In his maturity, Goethe seemed to Broch to be a maverick. Because style, for Broch, was "the creation of a specific system of conventions for a specific epoch in history," the "late stylist" was "an artist who is not happy with the conventional vocabulary provided by his epoch" (Broch 1995: 214) and, as such, needed to take a position outside that constraint.

In his 1954 lecture, "Artists and Old Age/Altern als Problem für Künstler," Gottfried Benn similarly described the complex relationship between the aging artist and his era (Benn 1989). Although Benn claimed not to consider the physiology of aging, he provided a list of many geniuses who died at an advanced age, including Michelangelo and Titian:

> Titian 99, Michelangelo 89, Frans Hals 86, Goya 82, Hans Thoma 85, Liebermann 88, Munch 81, Degas 83, Bonnard 80, Maillol 83, Donatello 80, Tintoretto 76, Rodin 77, Käthe Kollwitz 78, Renoir 78, Monet 86, James Ensor 89, Menzel 90;-among the living ones: Matisse 84, Nolde 86, Gulbransson 81, Hofer, Scheibe over 75, Klimsch 84.
> Among poets and writers: Goethe 83, Shaw 94, 20 Hamsun 93, Maeterlinck 87, Tolstoy 82, Voltaire 84, Heinrich Mann 80, Ebner-Eschenbach 86, Pontoppidan 86, Heidenstam 81, Swift, Ibsen, Bjornson, Rolland 78, Victor Hugo 83, Tennyson 83, Ricarda Huch 83, Hauptmann 84, Lagerlöf 82, Gide 82, Heyse 84, d'Annunzio 75, Spitteler, Fontane, Gustav Freytag 79, Frenssen 82; among the living ones: Claudel 85, Thomas Mann, Hesse, Schröder, Doblin, Carossa, Dörffler over 75, Emil Strauss 87.

> There are fewer great musicians. I'd like to mention Verdi 88, Richard Strauss 85, Pfitzner 80, Heinrich Schütz 87, Monteverdi 76, Gluck, Händel 74, Bruckner 72, Palestrina 71, Buxtehude, Wagner 70, Georg Schumann 81, von Reznicek 85, Auber 84, Cherubini 82; among the living ones: Sibelius 88. (Benn 1989: 130)

The fact that so many artists lived to old age may be explained in two ways: from a sociological point of view, great artists need time to produce their work. From a biological point of view, Benn, who, in addition to being a poet, was also a doctor, hypothesized that the cathartic effect of art induced relaxation in artists that was beneficial to their health in the long run. He considered Late Style to be "a structural change compared to early work" (Benn 1989: 132). In addition, Late Style could assume different faces. For some artists, Late Style was more serene and transcendent or sometimes more autobiographical than the production of their youth or adulthood. In the case of Michelangelo, Late Style was expressed by "a rejection of his peculiar methods and techniques" and "of his role models" (Benn 1989: 135–136).

Theodor Wiesengrund Adorno, another eminent representative of German culture, dealt with Late Style, especially in relation to Beethoven (Adorno 2002). For Adorno, Late Style portrayed "in the clearest possible lines, the contradictions and flaws which cut through present-day society" (Adorno 2002: 391) and, in a posthumous publication, Edward W. Said (2006) picked up Adorno's main ideas, interpreting Late Style as discordance of the artist with his era, making him or her a figure of exile and anachronism.

Said interrogated the relationship between "bodily condition" and "aesthetic style" and considered the "momentousness of life, mortality, medical science, and health" (Said 2006: 3). He wondered how changes in the body, specifically aging, related to the forms in which artists processed and transformed those changes. Late in their lives, artists not only experience a flowering of creativity, they may also observe the past from a different perspective and make greater sense of their lives. This novel perspective can give artists the impression of "surviving beyond what is acceptable and normal" (Said 2006: 13). In so doing, they "problematize the conventions of 'timeliness' that underpin cultures that are themselves likewise advanced, that is, increasingly conscious of their own historicity" (Taberner 2015: 98).

Said (2006: 6) was not interested in late works "that reflect[ed] a special maturity, a new spirit of reconciliation and serenity" but rather in "the experience of Late Style that involve[d] a nonharmonious, nonserene tension, and above all, a sort of deliberately unproductive productiveness going *against*" (Said 2006: 7). As Said expressed it, "Late Style is in, but oddly apart from, the present" (Said 2006: 24). Writing along the same lines as Said, Karen Leeder considered Late Style to be the expression of a decisive break in the style of established and exceptional artists or writers in old age in favour of more peaceful, often more autobiographically inflected, sometimes primitive or child-like approaches (Leeder 2015: 6).

For McMullan and Smiles (2016: 11), Said's understanding of Late Style replicated the romantic understanding of the concept and its reinterpretation by the avant-garde. They commented that "the late-style trope takes from romanticism its emphasis on biography, subjectivism, [and] the relationship between creativity and selfhood; from modernism it derives its interest in tradition, the avant-garde, abstraction, the subordination of self to epoch, the loss of linearity" (McMullan & Smiles). In fact, Late Style re-emerged during modernism, at which point the traditional concept of artwork as perfection and totality came to an end (Zanetti 2012: 19–20). Sandro Zanetti (2012: 19–20) observed that the term "late work" itself appeared only at the beginning of the twentieth century along with such related terms as late work/*Alterswerk* and Late Style/*Spätstil*. The emergence of the term "late work" coincided with the decline of the classicist concept of a work of art, characterised by aesthetic coherence, temporality, and absolute autonomy.

The fact that this notion appeared in European culture some decades after the introduction and dissemination of the concepts of "childhood" (Key 2018) and "youth" (Pirro & Zenobi 2011) can be no coincidence. In Key's analysis, every child has a right to its childhood, which she defined as a period in an individual's early life that entailed no economic responsibilities. The right to childhood touched social issues as well, and Key was very critical of the existence of child labour on a large scale. The emergence of the concepts of childhood and youth had several repercussions. First of all, they split human life into phases with precise characteristics. In the cultural sphere, there were several movements, such as the avant-garde, that advocated the rights of youth in opposition to those of the "old" and "traditional." The year 1910 was striking for German cultural history because of the birth of the youth movement and the art movement, The Blue Cavalier/Der blaue Reiter. For Müller-Seidel, awakening and the youth cult were only one aspect of this movement; another was sympathy with age and decay (Müller-Seidel 1993: 120). In the same year, Thomas Mann published an essay on Fontane's late work. The contradiction and protest against the bourgeoisie can also be expressed in the work of old age. Expressionism, in fact, valorised the morbid, which is often associated with old age.

Said's definition of Late Style inspired several studies on artists' late works but also earned negative criticism. Robert Kastenbaum, for example, wrote that "'Late Style' is an illusion [...] which ignores the variety of processes and contexts in which creative works are produced late in life" (Kastenbaum 1985). Zanetti also warned against oversimplifying the concept (Zanetti 2012: 14–15; 204–05). Indeed, Kastenbaum criticized Said's generalization because, in Kastenbaum's view, Late Style was not a universal phenomenon, and every artist had a different stylistic trajectory. Gordon McMullan, similarly, expressed a trenchant judgement of the concept of Late Style which, for him, was not "a natural phenomenon," but a trope, "a critical construct" (McMullan 2016: 36). Given claims regarding the universality of "Late Style," McMullan considered it regrettable that interdisciplinary studies in literature, music, and the visual arts had rarely been attempted. He also highlighted the collapse of historical difference in the concept of Late Style and the lack of distinction between, for example, a specifically modernist and a pre-modernist Late Style (McMullan 2016: 34). Studies in art history by Elkins had already shown, however, that the "tripartism" of artistic production (youth, mature production, and late work) was already problematic because:

> The commonest phase sequence, the triad early, middle, and late style, gives rise nonetheless to several recurring problems, especially regarding the nature of the synthetic accomplishment that is recognized as a "late style." The first of these occurs when it is possible to doubt whether a "late style" has been established at all. Jackson Pollock showed signs of returning to a figurative mode but did not live long enough to develop that in a consistent practice. Are his figurative works signs of an incipient late style? [...]
> Secondly, some late styles do not seem to achieve sufficient syntheses of what went before or else synthesize in an uninspiring direction. It also happens that a late style might extend over so much of a lifetime that it overweighs the other two phases.
> Thirdly, an artist may be seen to "oscillate." Thus Panofsky (1971) proposed that Albrecht Dürer had no triadic sequence of style phases and no late style but "oscillated" between Northern (Germanic) and Southern (Italian) influences without being able to synthesize the two. His "late style" would therefore be a "latest" style. This is the clearest alternate theory to the triadic sequence, and its limited applicability demonstrates the pervasive power of the concept of triadic personal style. (Elkins 2003)

In reaction to these discussions, later contributors to the literary theory of Late Style offered more precise outlines of the category. For Zanetti, the author of an insightful monograph on Late Style, *Avantgardismus der Greise? Spätwerke und ihre Poetik* (2012), late works or *Spätwerke* were not merely literary texts that came later in life, after other production, but texts that changed perspectives regarding what had been written and published before. He recognized five features of Late Style: (1) a work that referred to another one; (2) a literary text that continued an earlier one; (3) a change in work methods; (4) work produced after half the artist's creative career had passed; (5) work produced when the end of the career was foreseeable. Not all five criteria needed to be met in order to distinguish a *Spätwerk* from an *Alterswerk* (Zanetti 2012: 55). Rather, what characterized a *Spätwerk* was a double temporal orientation, an internal dialectic that determined aesthetic quality. For example, a *Spätwerk* referenced an earlier work and, at the same time, was open to the future, implying the survival of the present moment (Zanetti 2012: 8–9).[7]

Zanetti argued that Late Style often appeared when an author produced serial texts or revised a former version of a text, one example of which could be Goethe's *Faust: Der Tragödie zweiter Theil* (1832), which referenced an 1808 *Faust*. In the late production of an author we might, surprisingly, recognize a sharp break—a "Greisen-Avantgardismus"—as Thomas Mann named it. Consequently, late works were a continuation, an expression of survival but also of a new beginning (Zanetti 2012: 8). When he was older, Goethe initiated discussion of his Late Style by exposing a rupture between his early and later works in the comments he made about his own work. Ernst Lewy, in his *On the language of Old Goethe/Zur Sprache des alten Goethe* (1913), described for the first time the main characteristics of Goethe's Late Style: epigrammatic concision, a preference for the unusual and for neologisms, and a tendency toward the symbolic and didactic. From these initial definitions, Zanetti accompanied the reader through the main discussions of Late Style in the twentieth and twenty-first centuries. Interestingly, Zanetti placed the concept in dialogue with such important abstractions of literary criticism as Kristeva's "dialogism" and "intertextuality" and Harold Bloom's "anxiety of influence" (Zanetti 2012: 215). For Zanetti, Late Style hid exactly this duality: openness to previous works by the same author but, at the same time, resistance to influence and to the anxiety of becoming different (Zanetti 2012: 231). Alongside other concepts born in the time of modernism, such as literariness (Salgaro 2018b) and style (Herrmann *et al.* 2015), Late Style shared a moment of rupture with tradition that was typical of modernist understandings of literature.

3.2. Methods and Aim

In combining literary theories on and analyses of Late Style with stylometric analysis of the Late Style of three important German authors of different epochs —Johann Wolfgang Goethe, Robert Musil, and Franz Kafka—several theoretical and methodological shortcomings become obvious. Of these, the definition of the concept of style is the most complex. Indeed, it is debatable whether the understanding of style in literary theory and in the Digital Humanities is equivalent. As discussed in Chapter 1, many bridges can be built between the concept of style in stylistics and stylometry, though this is also an empirical question. A truly interdisciplinary approach, such as the one employed here, combines the qualitative approach of literary analysis with the quantitative ap-

---

7 With reference to earlier works, late works can be "a) Follow-up works, b) Swan songs, c) Commemorative works, d) New approaches, e) Staging of works" (Zanetti 2012: 322).

proach of stylometry. This transdisciplinary approach may help resolve controversies regarding the existence of Late Style and determine whether it can be detected by quantitative methods. The method necessarily requires operationalising the concept of Late Style, which can then be tested.

For authors like Said or Broch, Late Style involves a double deviation—from the style of the early work of the author and from the style of contemporary writers. The first deviation may be termed an "internal" deviation, because the stylistic break is internal to the style of a single author; and the second "external" because the gap is between the style of an author and that of contemporary works by other authors. For Goethe, Musil, and Kafka, we combined internal and external analyses together with quantitative and qualitative methods (see Rebora & Salgaro: 2018):

1. In the "external" analyses, we compared the style of the author to reference corpora of contemporary authors and assessed relative deviations from them. Because we were dealing with huge corpora, we used solely quantitative measures based on computed frequencies, relations, and distributions of features and relevant statistics, which are typical of distant reading.

2. In the "internal" analyses, we compared the early, middle, and late works of the same author. In this case, we also employed an operational description of the Late Style of our three authors by a relevant literary critic. This (qualitative) identification may refer to linguistic features at the level of characters, lexicon, syntax, or semantics. Quantitative methods attempt to complement and potentially to confirm, with a different approach, the fine-grained analysis of literary hermeneutics. Our aim was not to oppose but to combine the two methods and overcome typical misunderstandings and shortcomings of the interdisciplinary dialogue.

The category of Late Style is not new in stylometry. As Jan Rybicki (2017) showed, stylometric distances have proven to be very sensitive to changes over time, and David J. Hoover (2014) used them to analyse Henry James' Late Style. In a 2018 study, Jonathan P. Reeve (2018) tested the category on a wide corpus, limiting his focus solely to the internal perspective (i.e., he compared the early and later production of individual authors).

We extended the analysis to the external perspective, broadening it beyond distance measures and word frequency. We therefore adopted methodologies that focused on the entire vocabulary and its semantic aspects: from Zeta analysis, which aims to identify words that are significantly over- or underrepresented in a specific author's works (Schöch et al. 2018) to word-class analysis, by which a text can be mined based on pre-compiled dictionaries to evaluate dominant semantic areas (Tausczik & Pennebaker 2010). For example, the occurrences of a group of words related to the concept of "lateness" (such as "old," "late," and "last") can be counted to evaluate how much a text is dominated by that concept. Of course, word-class analysis can adopt much more sophisticated approaches that involve natural-language processing, statistical estimates, and machine-learning techniques, but the simple "word count" method has also proved quite successful when dealing with issues of literary theory (Jockers 2014). In addition, this approach can reach aspects of the text that traditional stylometric methods do not fully grasp.

More in general, it is worth noticing that statistical approaches to the study of style cannot be limited to a single calculation or set of techniques because the field remains in flux and may and should be shaped by the needs of traditional stylistic research.

3.3.   First Case Study: Johann Wolfgang von Goethe

The decision to start our analysis of Late Style with Goethe was inspired by the major theoreticians of Late Style who, whether in the case of Benn, Broch, or Said, all cited Goethe's late works as paradigmatic cases of Late Style (Zanetti 2012, 61–70; Sampaolo 2009). Goethe is emblematic of the artist who, in his mature years, found an Olympian detachment from his contemporaries and his tormented youth. Goethe was also chosen to test and refine a methodology that could be expanded to other authors. The large availability of digitized texts by Goethe and of critical studies of his work offered an opportunity to verify the supposed distinctiveness of Goethe's late production from multiple perspectives, bringing together a variety of approaches and techniques.

The first, necessary component for any computational textual analysis, however, is a well-structured corpus. Representativeness of corpora (Leech 2007) is a quite dated—but still extremely relevant—issue in Digital Humanities. In particular, testing literary theories requires the definition of a corpus that reflects the main characteristics of the literary scene for the period chosen (i.e., it should be sufficiently extended but also well-balanced in terms of genres, geography, and time). In the case of Late Style, the temporal component becomes even more relevant. Samples must be dated with extreme accuracy in order to make both internal and external comparison possible.

We followed the indications of Herbert and Elisabeth Frenzel (Frenzel & Frenzel 1985: 200–295) in selecting a corpus of work by Goethe's contemporaries, ultimately choosing the most representative works from Sturm und Drang, Classicism, and Romanticism. Plain text versions were downloaded from the online digital libraries Zeno and Project Gutenberg-DE. We downloaded thirty-nine of Goethe's works from the Project Gutenberg-DE corpus. Following indications by Eder (2013), all texts shorter than 5,000 words were excluded because stylometric tools don't work well with short texts. Based on a periodization that is generally shared by Goethe scholars, we split our corpora into three sub-selections:

1. Young selection, corresponding to works published before 1776 (Sturm und Drang);
2. Middle selection, corresponding to works published between 1777 and 1808 (Classicism);
3. Late/old selection, corresponding to works published after 1809 (late works).

The late phase of Goethe's production is also characterized by a detachment from Romanticism (Eichhorn 1971: 31–32). As in all scientific approaches, and especially in empirical studies, we were forced to make decisions to conduct the analysis: in this case, the distinction between "juvenile," "middle," and "old" style was not made by us but in the research work we have discussed to this point.

a)   First Approach: Stylometric (Network) Analysis

Following the indications of Evert *et al.* (2017), we chose Cosine Delta distance and the 2,000 most frequent words as the best-performing features for stylometric analysis. Results of the internal analysis, obtained by using the Force-Atlas2 algorithm on the Gephi platform (for details, see Eder 2017), are shown in Figure 6.[8] Groupings (evidenced by the different colours of nodes and borders) were automatically determined by the modularity function, as described by Rybicki, Biernacka-Licznar & Wozniak (2018).

A group of late works (identified by the tag "Old") is isolated on the upper part of the graph. This caesura between Young and Late Style, however, is contradicted by at least two factors. First, a work from the Middle selection (*Novelle*) is located in this area. Second, two late works (*West-Eastern Diwan/West-östlicher Divan* and *Faust, zweiter Teil*) are grouped with the Middle section.

The results of the external analysis are shown in Figure 7. To reduce complexity, two colours were used, and Goethe's works are always represented by green. As is evident, there is no clear separation between Goethe's late works and those of other writers published in the same period. On the contrary, a group of texts by Kleist (the cluster of pink nodes isolated on the left side of the "Old" section of Figure 7) is most clearly separated from the rest.[9]

---

8 For an intuitive interpretation of the graph, all nodes (i.e., Goethe's works) might be considered as planets in a gravitational system in which stronger attractions correspond to shorter stylometric distances. As a consequence, the node closest to most of the others will be the most central, while the farthest will be the most peripheral.

9 This result is in line with the stylometric analyses already performed by Jannidis and Lauer (2014).

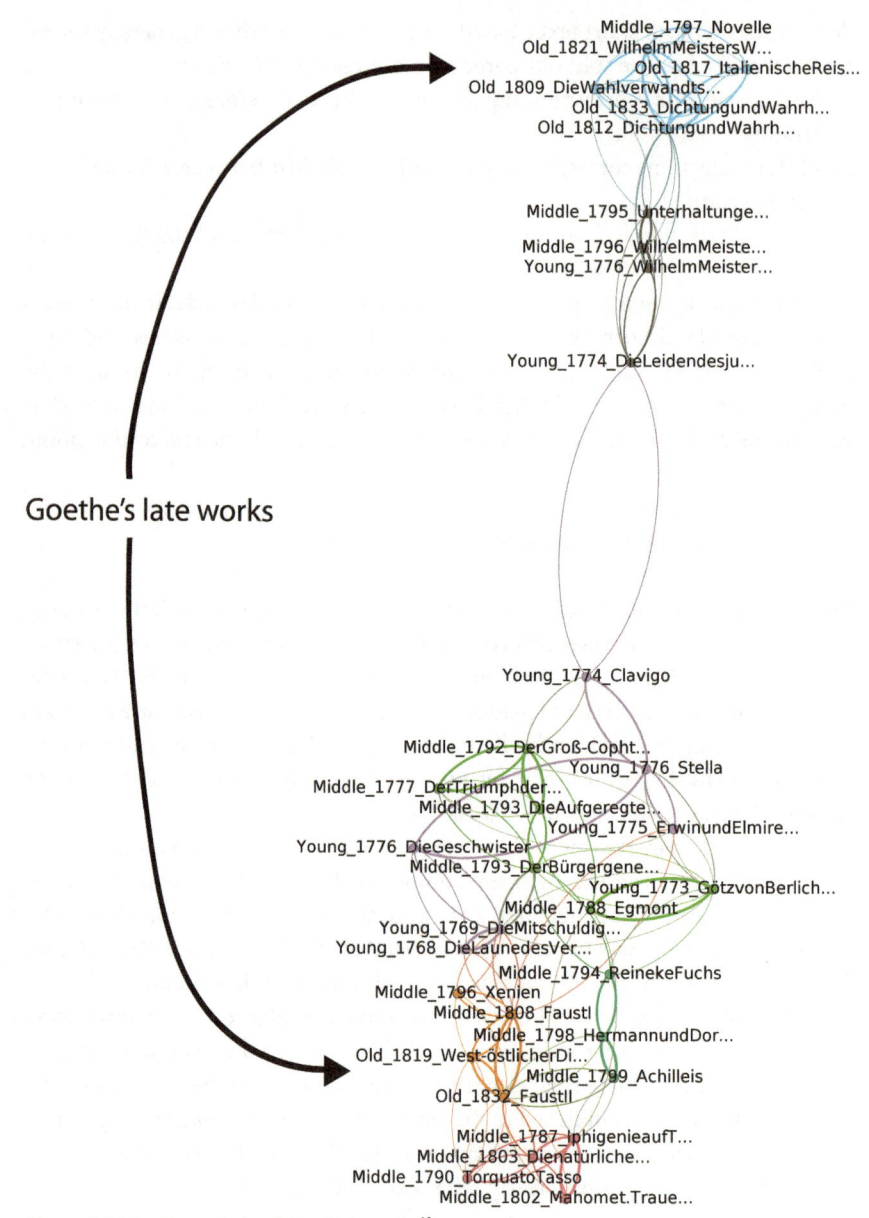

Figure 6: Network analysis of Goethe's works[10]

10 All the graphs in this chapter are by Simone Rebora and were already published (Rebora and Salgaro 2018).

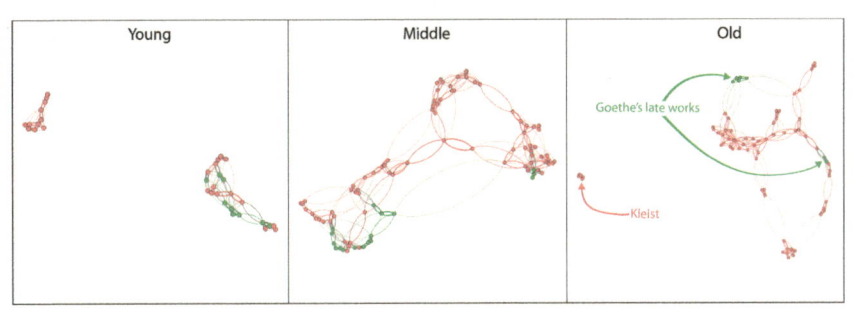

Figure 7: Network analyses of Goethe's works (green) and their contemporaries (pink)

b)   Second Approach: Zeta Analysis

To confirm these results with a different method, we chose Zeta Analysis as implemented by Craig and Kinney (2009).[11] This method offered an opportunity to reduce the selection of features to a group of words peculiarly over- or underused by an author, moving beyond the threshold of most frequent words. To generate the final graphs, we adopted the *Markers* method of the *oppose* function in the R package Stylo (Eder *et al.* 2016).[12] All parameters were set to their default values, apart from slice length, which was set to 3,000 words (Hoover 2013). Results of the internal analysis are shown in Figure 8.

The clear separation between the Old and Young areas seems to confirm the peculiarity of Late Style. Partial intersections between temporally closer selections (Young and Middle and Middle and Old), however, suggest that this phenomenon

---

11 The approach is quite straightforward: (1) given two groups of documents, each document is split into a number of segments of equal length; (2) for each word-type in the documents, the proportion of segments in which it appears is calculated (separately for each group); (3) the two values are subtracted. In a real case scenario, suppose that we would like to calculate the Zeta Value for the word *Licht* in Goethe: (1) the first group of documents will be composed of works by Goethe, the second by an ample selection of works by other authors; all documents will be split into 3,000-word-long segments; (2) the proportion of segments in which the word *Licht* appears is calculated both in the Goethe sub-corpus (suppose it will be equal to 0.65) and in the other authors (0.15); (3) the Zeta Value for the word *Licht* in Goethe will thus be 0.65–0.15 = 0.5 (indicating that it is overrepresented in Goethe). All values will be between –1 (indicating underrepresentation) and +1 (indicating overrepresentation).

12 The *Markers* method positions each text segment in a two-dimensional space by adding all positive Zeta Values for the words that appear in it (Y coordinate, also defined as "markers") and all negative Zeta Values (X coordinate, "anti-markers"). As a result of this procedure, segments tend to appear in two separate areas of the graph (upper-left side for the first group of documents; bottom-right side for the second group). The actual strength of the distinctiveness of words, however, is what determines whether the two groups will be fully separated or will partially overlap.

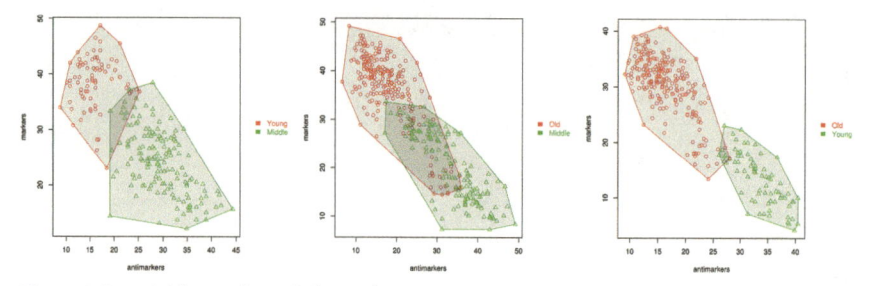

Figure 8: Zeta Analyses of Goethe's Works

may depend upon the chronological evolution of style, as demonstrated by Eder (2017) and Rybicki (2017). Quite surprisingly, the external analysis showed that Goethe's late texts were more connected to works by his contemporaries than were earlier ones (Figure 9), contradicting once again the supposed isolation of Late Style supported by Hermann Broch and Edward Said.[13]

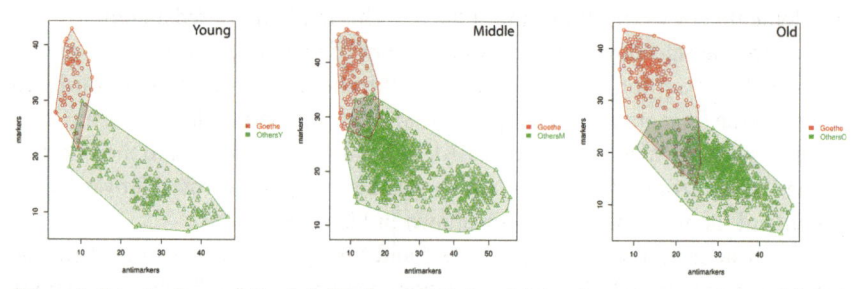

Figure 9: Zeta Analyses of Goethe's Works and Works of Other Contemporaneously Published Authors

The substantial inconclusiveness of these analyses, while hinting at the possible inconsistency of the category of Late Style (at least, in the case of Goethe), suggested the need for a different methodology more directly focused on the semantic aspects of the text.

c)   Third Approach: Semantic Analysis

Erich Trunz's essay, "Goethes Altersstil," first published in 1954, is one of the main studies of Goethe's "Late Style." Trunz distinguished three phases in Goethe's career, the last of which was characterized by strong symbolism and a

---

13 See the "Old" section of Figure 9. The red circles in the lowest positions represent 3,000-word excerpts from *West-östlicher Divan* and *Faust, zweiter Teil* (the same works that were already separated in Figure 6). These overlap with excerpts from Achim von Arnim, Bettina Brentano von Arnim, Jean Paul, and E. T. A. Hoffmann (represented by green triangles).

tendency toward totality (Trunz 1990: 139). Following Trunz, Goethe's "Young" work was inspired by Sturm und Drang and his mature works by the great masters of world literature. In contrast, Goethe's Late Style was completely unique:

> In his youth, Goethe had seen the representational nature of things, the uniqueness of the here and now; in his classical period, he linked related phenomena into a series and sought the type and the law; in old age, this view of the lawful gains a new dimension: everything becomes a symbol. In the last phase of his life everything ephemeral points beyond itself, becomes a "parable" of a supreme, imperishable world. (Trunz 1990: 139)

We see these changes of attitude in works like *Pandora* (1808), *Faust* II (1832), or the *Journeyman Years/Wilhelm Meister's Wanderjahre* (1821). In his mature works, then, the category of time recedes in order to emphasise the archetypal. In *Pandora* (1808), the mythological figures Prometheus and Epimetheus become representatives of the *vita activa* and *vita contemplativa*. The personal and subjective is distanced by generalising it into a case, a type.

As Trunz noted (1990: 144), these late works have "no relationship to contemporary poetry and have no model in the wide field of world literature." Trunz identified four conceptual symbols as representatives of Goethe's Late Style: (1) light and (2) totality as symbols of the divine; (3) the eye and (4) the cloud as symbols of humankind's position between finiteness and infinity:

> Goethe's poetry was always rich in images and symbols, but it is only in old age that this symbolism takes on such a variety that it becomes a great web of symbolic images. The light is the symbol of the divine, the colour means the reflection of the primordial light on earthly things, the eye is a symbol of man's position between light and matter; the earth is the material, rigid, unspiritual; the cloud becomes the symbol for the fact that matter can become lighter and lighter until it finally flows into the ether and returns to the Creator's hand (Trunz 1990: 141–2).[14]

Based on the examples Trunz provided, we extracted and stemmed[15] a series of words connected to these four semantic areas and calculated their frequency in the three sub-sections of Goethe's works. The results confirming Trunz's intuition, with the four semantic areas always dominant in Goethe's late production.

---

14 In *Pandora* we find most of these elements, for example:
  - light ("Flow thou, air and light, away from my face/Ströme du, Luft und Licht, Weg mir vom Angesicht!");
  - eye ("In the young man's eye I may see the tear; In the old man's eye it disfigures. Good man, do not weep!/Im Jünglingsauge mag ich wohl die Träne sehn; Des Greisen Aug' entstellt sie. Guter, weine nicht!");
  - cloud ("Then I looked up, and on the cloud already floated/Images of the gods, colourfully crowded, in the breeze/Da blickt' ich auf, und auf der Wolke schwebten schon/Im Gaukeln lieblich Götterbilder, buntgedrängt").
15 Stemming is a procedure that automatically extracts word roots, making it possible to identify (most of) their morphological variations. We stemmed the wordlist using the R package *SnowballC*.

To expand this analysis to work that is contemporaneous with Goethe's, we used a software package that functions with the same logic as in the previous experiment but does not depend upon categorizations of a single literary critic. The Linguistic Inquiry and Word Count software (hereafter, LIWC; see (Tausczik & Pennebaker 2010), more generally adopted in psycholinguistics and sentiment analysis (Liu 2015), offered an opportunity to expand semantic areas to one hundred.[16] For an explanation of these areas, which are represented by sometimes cryptic labels, see the explanation provided by Wolf *et al.* (2008) in Table 2.

LIWC Category	Label	Sample Lemmas
3rd person (general)	Other	sie, er, deren
Reference to others	Othref	deine, jemand, uns
Prepositions	Preps	als, bis, von
Present	Present	hilfst, isst, läuft
Pronoun	Pronoun	ich, wir, sie, dein
Social processes	Social	äußern, Begegnung, Kinder
Space	Space	abseits, breit, gegenüber
2nd person (general)	You	du, dein, dir
Article	Article	eine, das, dem
Communication	Comm	ablehnen, sprechen, Verhandlung
1st Person (singular)	I	ich, mir, mein
Occupation	Occup	Schule, Arbeit, Leistung
1st Person (general)	Self	ich, wir, mein
Affect Words	Affect	glücklich, hässlich, lächeln
Cognitive Mechanisms	Cogmech	abgrenzen, deshalb, wissen
Past	Past	gestern, hieß, sprach

Table 2: Semantic areas (Wolf *et al.* 2008)

We structured our experiment in two phases. First, we isolated the eight LIWC categories in which the comparison between Late and Young/Middle Goethe showed the highest divergences; second, we calculated the frequencies of the same categories in the work of other authors. Figure 10 shows that, in five of these categories, Goethe's path diverged diametrically from the approach taken by the authors of other contemporary, published works. In the other three categories, the difference appears less significant, though the variations are consistent with

---

16 LIWC's functional logic is even simpler than that of the other adopted software package. LIWC works on a series of multilingual dictionaries in which each word is connected to various semantic areas (such as "Social Words" and "Cognitive Processes," "Seeing" and "Hearing," "Space," and "Sexuality," to reach a maximum of over 100 categories). LIWC simply counts the words for each semantic area and calculates overall proportions in each text. The German dictionary is introduced and described by (Wolf *et al.* 2008).

those found in Goethe's work. Unlike previous methods, our analysis clearly demonstrated the "contradictory, alienated relationship," as Said termed it (Said 2006: 13), between Goethe's Late Style and his environment. In addition, the sharp decrease in the "Social," "Other," and "You" areas confirmed the widely held interpretation that Goethe's late works were more abstract and detached.

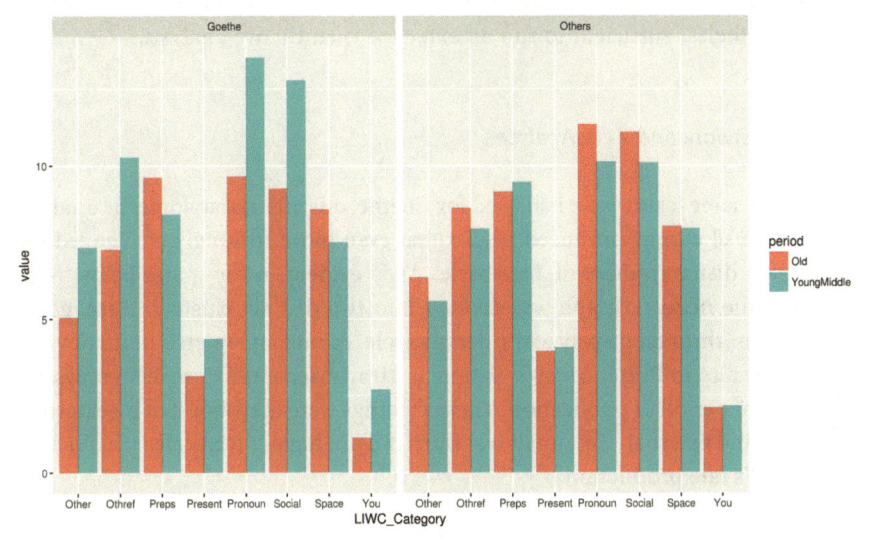

Figure 10: Frequency of Most Distinctive LIWC Categories in Goethe's Work and in the Work of Other Contemporaneously Published Authors

3.4. Second Case Study: Robert Musil

As soon as the methodology showed its effectiveness, we were able to include other authors in our analysis. Because of copyright issues, we were not able to incorporate truly recent works, an issue that interfered with the setup of the external analyses that demand ample and representative corpora. We therefore limited our focus to the first decades of the twentieth century and selected two of the most important representatives of German literary modernism: Robert Musil (1880-1942) and Franz Kafka (1883-1924).

The Musil corpus was extracted from the Klagenfurter digital edition (Amann *et al.* 2009)—that is, Musil's digitized opera omnia. By applying a temporal subdivision suggested by the Klagenfurter edition—1906-1917 for "Young" production; 1918-1927 for "Middle" production; and 1928-1942 for "Late/Old" production—we generated twenty-three samples of texts. Collections of short stories such as "Posthumous Papers of a Living Author"/"Nachlaß zu Lebzeiten" were segmented into sub-parts using the date of first publication of each story as a reference point. As for Musil's contemporaries, we selected the texts hosted by the KOLIMO online database (Herrmann & Lauer 2017). Out of the 42,694 entries in the database, 6,100 provided a date of first publication; of these, 875 fell between 1906 and 1942. Once again, copyright limitations interfered with the representativeness of the corpus: 470 works are included in KOLIMO for the period 1906–1917, but they decrease to 130 between 1928 and 1942. Our sample was nonetheless sufficient to run an extensive quantitative analysis.

a)   Network and Zeta Analyses

Using the same features we had used for Goethe, our internal stylometric analysis on the Musil corpus produced results that even more strikingly challenged the supposed distinctiveness of Late Style. As is evident in the graph below (Figure 11), the network graph was divided into two distinct clusters. Here, genre rather than chronology played the decisive role. From a stylometric point of view, as the results indicate, Musil's fiction is clearly separate from his essays regardless of period of publication. These findings were corroborated by external-network and external- Zeta analyses which did not highlight any clear distinction for Musil's late production.

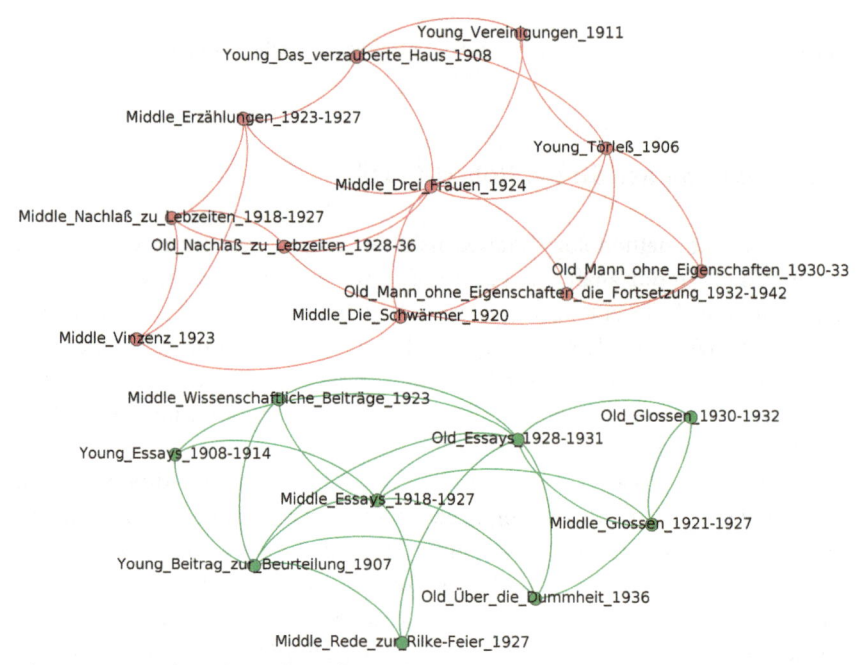

Figure 11: Network Analysis of Musil's Works

b)   Semantic Analysis

Robert Musil is not traditionally mentioned in considerations of Late Style (Zanetti 2012: 109ff). In an essay in which he discussed writers' both finished and fragmentary late works, Hans Blumenberg mentioned Musil (Blumenberg 1997: 165), describing Musil's unfinished novel, *The Man Without Qualities/Der Mann ohne Eigenschaften* (1930), as condemned to be the author's last because it contained obstacles, created by the author himself, that kept it from being completed:

> But there are also works that have been condemned to fragmentation and yet have come to the last place through solid completion. These are those which, according to their subject matter and claim, in their procedure as well as in their contempt for form, cannot be thought of as other than contingently aborted, as interrupted: Monuments to some kind of excess in the powerlessness to even come close to satisfying it. Musil's *Mann ohne Eigenschaften* is unimaginable as a completed work of art; or, insofar as it is conceivable, would be solely at the mercy of unsatisfactoriness and lapsed. The reasons may be good or bad, especially aesthetically questionable—they make sense only as obstacles to finding an end, which the author has created for himself, even if they appear as unintentional by-products of an enormous, oversized, life-time-demanding concept. The incomplete state of Musil's fragments documents our helplessness in determining even the direction in which a whole could have come together. (Blumenberg 1997: 165)

Nevertheless, a quality in Musil's writings is typical of Late Style. The last chapter of the first part of his immense novel, *Der Mann ohne Eigenschaften* (1930) is entitled "The Reversal/Die Umkehrung," and Walter Fanta, the scholar who contributed fundamental studies on the genesis of the novel, defined the shift from the first to the second book of the novel as "the great passage" (Fanta 2000: 391). Claudia Monti has also focused on this passage, recognizing two different styles in the first (1930) and second books (1932).

In Monti's view, the first book was characterized by what Musil called "the tree of violence," which was replaced in the second by "the tree of love" (Monti 1995: 71). The "tree of violence," a lifestyle and intellectual approach mostly inspired by Ernst Mach and Friedrich Nietzsche, was expressed through the destructive intellectual behaviour of the protagonist, Ulrich, who criticized such essential constructs of Occidental thinking as identity and causality. In contrast, "the tree of love," inspired by German romanticism, claimed universal analogy and connectivity and found its climax in the love between Ulrich and his sister, Agathe. Both conditions could be observed in Musil's texts through descriptions of Ulrich who, under the sign of the "the tree of violence," was impassive and isolated but empathic and affectionate under the sign of "the tree of love." This emotional reversal, from a convex to a concave condition, was inspired by experiments on "optical inversion" by the Gestalt psychologist Erich Moritz von Hornbostel (Monti 1995).

Monti recognized the same schema described in the novel *Der Mann ohne Eigenschaften* in the short story, "The Blackbird"/"Die Amsel" (Monti 2000: 236ff), which led us to date Musil's Late Style to 1928 when that story was published. "Die Amsel" is the ideal spur for a discussion of youth and adulthood in Musil, both because it tells of the meeting between two childhood friends called A1 and A2 and because the two meet in adulthood to discuss their past and their current lives. Bound in their youth by a religious upbringing that they later recanted in favour of materialistic belief, A1 and A2 were nonetheless fundamentally different: A2 was bold and fearless in his youthful outbursts while A1 was more cautious and calculating, and those distinctions would lead them to choose divergent paths in life. Like Ulrich, the protagonist of *Der Mann ohne Eigenschaften*, A2 rejects a stable and fixed identity because he considers it an artificial construction. He perceives that his adult self no longer has anything in common with the big-headed, blond-haired youngster he once was, and he has no need to fix his identity through memories like those who take pleasure in being photographed to remind themselves of where and how they lived.[17] A2 wants to escape from a constricting life such as the one Musil effectively describes in the metaphor of anonymous and depersonalised Berlin flats:

> The kitchens and bedrooms look outwards and downwards on all this; they lie close together like love and digestion in the human anatomy. On floor upon floor, the conjugal beds are stacked one on top of the other; since all the bedrooms occupy the same space in each building—window wall, bathroom wall, and closet wall prescribe the placement of each bed almost down to the half yard. The dining rooms are likewise piled up floor after floor, as are the white-tiled baths and the balconies with their red awnings. Love, sleep, birth, digestion, unexpected reunions, troubled, and restful nights are all vertically aligned in these buildings like columns of sandwiches at an automat. In middle-class apartments like these, your destiny is waiting for you the moment you move in. (Musil 1987: 130)

Monti effectively showed how the path taken by A2 paralleled that of the protagonist of *Der Mann ohne Eigenschaften* to the extent that the former can be considered a miniaturisation of the latter. Both A2 and Ulrich take a holiday from their lives to find their rightful place in the world. Maternal love in "Die Amsel" and sisterly love in *Der Mann ohne Eigenschaften* allow the two protagonists to recover their "lost self-love/verlorene Selbstliebe" and establish a close, intimate relationship with the world. For both, this path is indicated by encounters with

---

17 "For I can assure you that I don't like to dwell on myself, nor as so many others do, to stare smugly at photographs of the person they once were, or delight in memories of what they did in such and such a place at such and such a time; this sort of savings bank account of self is absolutely incomprehensible to me. I am neither particularly sentimental, nor do I live for the moment; but when something is over and done with, then I am also over and done with that something in myself" (Musil 1987: 139).

childhood friends. The fourteenth chapter of *Der Mann ohne Eigenschaften*, entitled "Jugendfreunde" describes the complex relationship between the two childhood friends, Ulrich and Walter.

An encounter with a blackbird, which, in reality, turns out to be his mother, induces A2's transition from the "tree of violence" to the "tree of love." In the latter, his boundaries dissolve and his being fills the surrounding space:

> Then I experienced a magical state; I lay in my bed like a statue on the lid of a sarcophagus, and I was awake, but not like during the day. It is very difficult to describe, but when I think back, it is as though something had turned me inside out; I was no longer a solid, but rather something sunken in upon itself. And the air was not empty, but of a consistency unknown to the daylight senses, a blackness I could see through, a blackness I could feel through, and of which I too was made. (Musil 1987: 132)

After three experiences of this spatial and bodily inversion in which "something has turned him inside out," A2 returns to his childhood home where he decides to live with the "mother blackbird." He muses that there the "hardness that had encompassed me melted away instantaneously" (Musil 1987: 142).

Monti's thesis regarding the evolution of Ulrich and A2 is based on a refined close reading of passages in which they are the protagonists. Such a technique, although very careful and shrewd, cannot be applied to Musil's entire corpus precisely because of the limits imposed by human cognition. This corpus contains a fragmentary novel of several thousand pages, *Der Mann ohne Eigenschaften*, a text that some readers have called a "monster." This is where operationalisation comes in, allowing us to translate Monti's reflections into an operation. Following her indications and quotations from *Der Mann ohne Eigenschaften* and "Die Amsel," we created distinct semantic areas for "the tree of violence" and "the tree of love," the latter of which characterizes Musil's Late Style (Table 3):

The Tree of Violence	The Tree of Love
Convex	Concave
Violence	Love
Sharp	Soft
Narcissism	Altruism
Lack	Fullness
Apathetic, cold	Welcoming, warm, compassionate

Table 3: "Tree of Violence" and "Tree of Love" Semantic Areas

Once again, quantitative analysis confirmed Monti's stylistic analysis, though LIWC analysis did not produce results as significant as those for Goethe. In the eight most distinctive categories in "Late" Musil, only two showed a slight counter-tendency with regard to the vocabulary used by Musil's contemporaries (see Figure 12). These results can be interpreted to mean either that Musil's late production does not fit into the more general category of Late Style or that the method we used could not adequately capture the specific nature of Late Style.

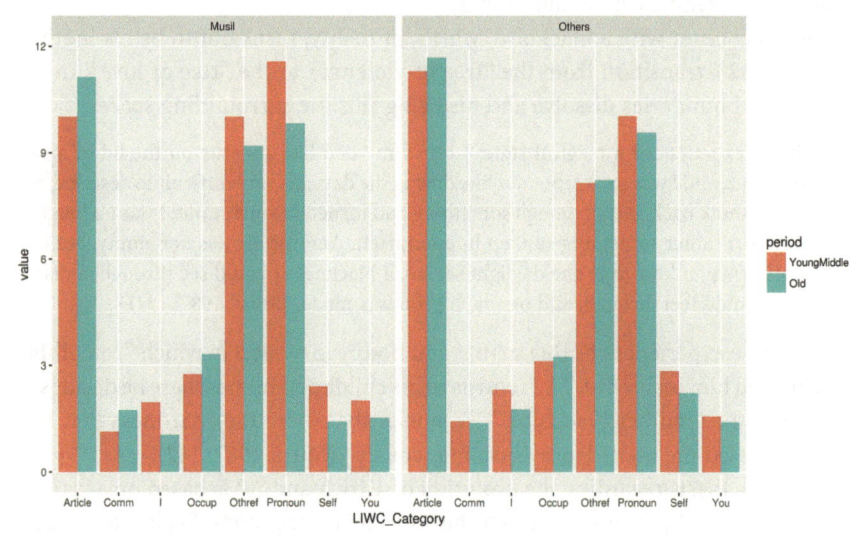

Figure 12: Frequency of most distinctive LIWC categories in Musil's works and in the work of authors published contemporaneously

3.5. Third Case Study: Franz Kafka

a)   Semantic Analysis

Franz Kafka (1883–1924) can be considered an exceptional case of Late Style due to the young age at which he died and the circumstances under which his novels were published. In his monograph entitled *Der späte Kafka: Spätstil als Stilsuspension/Late Kafka: Late Style as Style Suspension* (2013) Malte Kleinwort remarked upon three main features of Kafka's Late Style: references to earlier works, a peculiar form of tentativeness, and a poetics of asceticism (Kleinwort 2013: 10). While the majority of Kafka criticism dates the beginning of his Late Style to 1917, Kleinwort dated it to 1922 (Kleinwort 2013: 12), largely because, in 1921, Max Brod published his biography, *Adolf Schreiber: The Destiny of a Musician/Ein Musikerschicksal*, which Kafka read enthusiastically and which, in Kleinwort's view, had a pivotal impact on Kafka's late phase (Kleinwort 2013: 59).

Kleinwort argued that the biography of Schreiber influenced Kafka in four ways: it encouraged him to look retrospectively through his writings, to focus on the relationship between artist and impresario, to develop asceticism as a feeling for art, and to adopt reservation as a style of writing (Kleinwort 2013: 13). We can observe the poetics of reservation and asceticism in the loss of subjectivism and dramatization in Kafka's late works, including *A Hunger Artist/Der Hungerkünstler* and *Josephine the Singer, or the Mouse Folk/Josefine, die Sängerin oder das Volk der Mäuse*, in which Adolf Schreiber became a model for the characters (Kleinwort 2013: 59). It was not only music that became an important issue in Kafka's Late Style, because Schreiber had been a composer, but so did music's opposite—"the non-musical, silence and mere sound, noise, or tone" (Kleinwort 2013: 62).

Music is said to have a community-building power as is evident in the novel *Amerika/Der Verschollene* and in the short story "Josefine." In the writings of Kafka, however, very special cases of music and noise can be found. The peculiar whistling of the singer Josefine, for example, but also the buzzing of the telephone in the novel *The Castle*.

> Our singer is called Josephine. Anyone who has not heard her does not know the power of song. There is no one who is not carried away by her singing, an even greater tribute because we are not, in general, a music-loving race. [...] I have often thought about what this music of hers really means. For we are quite unmusical; how is it that we understand Josephine's singing or, given that Josephine denies that to us, at least think we understand? The simplest answer would be that the beauty of her singing is so great that even the most insensitive cannot be deaf to it, but this answer is not satisfactory. If it were really so, her singing would have to give one an immediate and lasting feeling of being something out of the ordinary, a feeling that from her throat something is heard that we have never heard before and which we are not even capable of hearing, something that Josephine alone and no one else can enable us to hear.... So is it singing at all? Is it not perhaps just a piping? And piping is something we all know about, it is the real artistic accomplishment of our people, or rather no mere accomplishment but a characteristic expression of our life. (Kafka 1988: 360–61)

Taking Kleinwort's qualitative analysis as a guide, we determined that the following semantic areas were typical of Kafka's Late Style (Table 4).

Semantic areas (as mentioned by Kleinwort)	Sample lemmas
The artist	Kunst, Künstlertum
Music	Musik, Konzert
The unmusical	Schweigen, Geräusch, Summen, Zischen, Rascheln, Pfeifen
Disrespect of the audience	Ungeschicklichkeit, Unfertigkeit
The poetics of asceticism	Schlichtheit, Einfachheit
Self-destruction of the artist	Selbstkritik, Selbstzerstörung
Loneliness in the metropolis	Einsamkeit, Fremdheit

Table 4: Semantic Areas of Kafka's Late Style

Kleinwort himself mentioned all these semantic areas and many related words. For every semantic area proposed by Kleinwort, we created a corpus of related words, for example: Music, non-musicality, silence, loud, noise, sound, humming, rustling silence, musician, musician/music, concert.

The aim of this operationalisation was to grasp the occurrence of these terms in Kafka's works. We extracted the corpus for the analysis from the KOLIMO database: twenty texts by Kafka and 564 contemporaneous texts by other writers. Following Manfred Engel and Bernd Auerochs (Engel & Auerochs 2010), we set the threshold between early and middle production to 1913. Our results (Rebora & Salgaro 2018: 28) confirmed, for the most part, Kleinwort's interpretation: the most striking matches were for the semantic areas of "asceticism" and "not music," while only "loneliness in the metropolis" showed a sharp decrease in "Late" production. Here is a list (Table 5) of the operationalised lemmas related to music in Kafka's works:

	young	middle	old
Musik	15.24	6.92	23.04
Schweigen	21.78	19.03	38.87
Laut	74.04	53.19	23.04
Geräusch	6.53	6.05	29.52
Klang	13.07	14.70	7.92
summen	4.36	0.43	2.88
rascheln	0.00	0.43	1.44
Stille	17.42	19.03	24.48
rieseln	0.00	0.00	1.44
lauschen	0.00	0.43	0.00
hören	54.44	59.68	64.07
zischen	0.00	1.73	11.52
Zischer	0.00	0.00	1.44
pfeifen	6.53	3.03	2.88
Ohr	43.55	25.95	23.04
horchen	0.00	6.92	17.28
Lärm	37.02	19.89	27.36
Melodie	8.71	1.73	3.60
Zuhörer	4.36	2.16	2.16
Musikant	0.00	0.43	0.72
Musiker	0.00	0.00	2.16
musizieren	0.00	0.00	0.00
Schweigsamkeit	0.00	0.00	2.16
Gesang	2.18	4.76	7.92

(Continued)

	young	**middle**	**old**
Gesänge	0.00	0.43	1.44
klagen	13.07	6.92	12.96
singen	19.60	3.46	2.88
still	47.91	54.05	59.75
klingen	0.00	2.16	2.88
piepsen	0.00	0.43	0.72
Ton	6.53	16.87	12.24
Töne	0.00	1.30	0.72
Konzert	0.00	0.00	1.44

Table 5: Operationalised Lemmas Related to Music in Kafka's Works

Moreover, external LIWC analysis of Kafka proved as efficient as it had for Goethe. Among the eight categories that showed the highest variance in Kafka, six were in counter-tendency to the characteristics of works of other contemporaneously published writers (see Figure 13). Among these was an increase in cognitive activities (indicated by the label "cogmec"), which may be in line with the increased abstractness of Kafka's late production. Following the results of the above described three case studies, semantic analysis appeared to be the most efficient method—though it is not infallible—for measuring "Late Style."

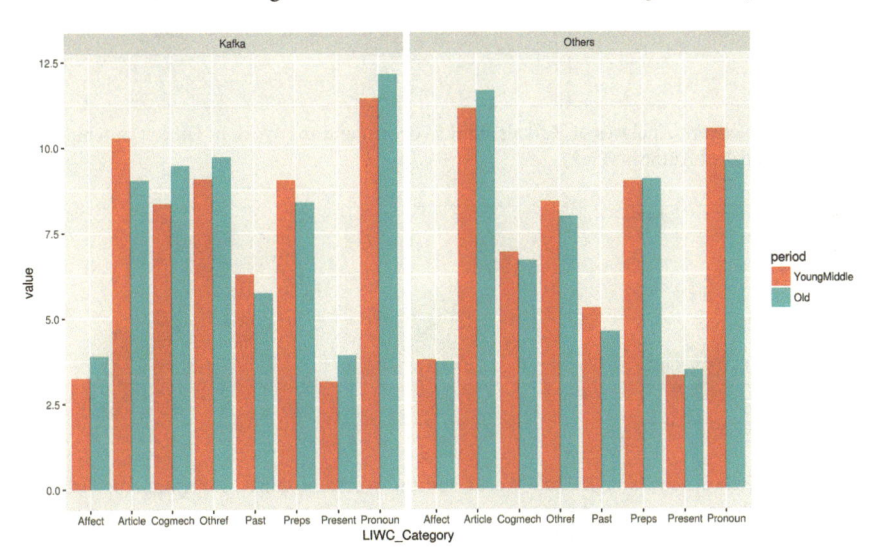

Figure 13: Frequency of the Most Distinctive LIWC Categories in Kafka's Work and in the Work of Other Contemporaneously Published Authors

b)   Network and Zeta Analyses

The success of semantic analysis is counterbalanced by the failure of the other two, more purely stylometric approaches. Internal network analysis showed that the "Early" period—and not the "Late"—distinguished itself most strikingly. This discovery was confirmed by an external analysis in which Kafka's four early works were clearly isolated from the rest. In addition, while "Middle" and "Late" works were not as strongly separated, they remained peripheral in the system (see Figure 14).

External Zeta analysis seemed most inconclusive because, in all three periods, no overlap existed between Kafka's work and work published contemporaneously by others; rather, these two categories occupied widely separated areas of the graph (see Figure 15). This result confirmed the much discussed "uniqueness" of Kafka's style, however, though they did so independently of the period in which they were composed, as Herrmann (2018) demonstrated with very similar methods.

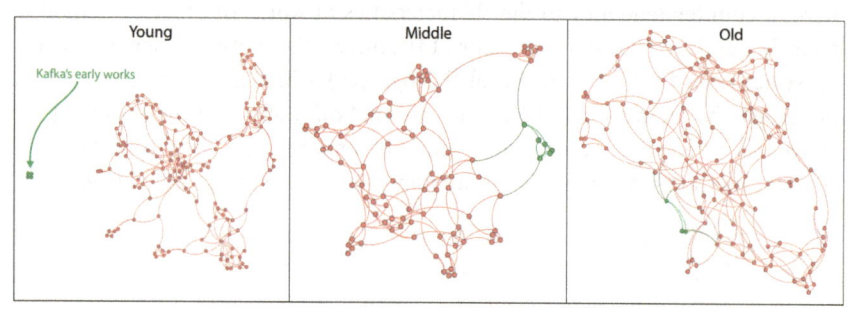

Figure 14: Network Analyses of Kafka's Works (Green) and the Work of Other Contemporaneously Published Authors (Pink)

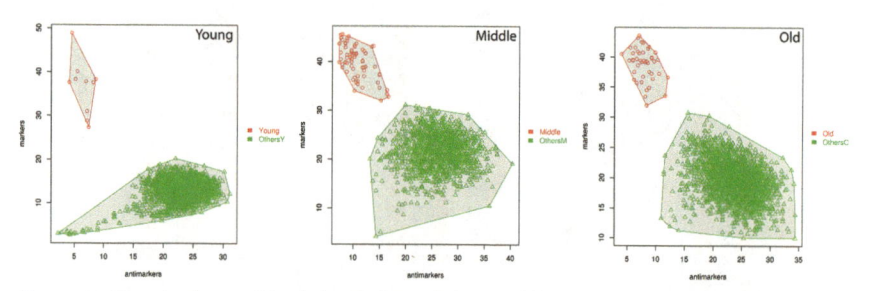

Figure 15: Zeta Analyses of Kafka's Works and the Works of Other Contemporaneously Published Authors

Zeta-analyses are very powerful stylometric tools that permit the extraction of the most used and most avoided words from a corpus of texts. If the corpus consists of an author's texts, we can extract such information as the most frequently used words or recognize the lexical preferences evident in an author's vocabulary. If we are dealing with concepts, we can try to reconstruct the author's poetics, philosophy, or ideology. At the same time, these analyses also make it possible to highlight the deviation from everyday language that both stylistics and stylometry have made the basis of their research. By way of example, Table 6 shows the words most or least used in the Kafka corpus.

PREFERRED WORDS	Zeta		AVOIDED WORDS	Zeta
obwohl	1		Gott	-1
freilich	0.9035604461		bereits	-0.6946373802
etwa	0.6857952349		selber	-0.6744455152
völlig	0.5669487644		indem	-0.655852003
öfters	0.5561669824		beiden	-0.5997372882
manchmal	0.5372450227		fuhr	-0.5419253955
zumindest	0.5128903715		Sonne	-0.5417027625
offen	0.4241506293		hab	-0.4957564451
besonders	0.4006579894		Mann	-0.4721080433
gerade	0.3826729858		nachdem	-0.4435171487
scheint	0.3719695616		Land	-0.437614356

Table 6: Kafka's Preferred and Avoided Words

3.6.   Late Style in Stylometry and in German Culture

It is impossible to draw definite conclusions from the results of these preliminary studies. The aim of this study was to combine two research methods—the qualitative analysis of literary criticism and the quantitative analysis of stylometry—to study the phenomenon of Late Style. In analysing the late works of three representative writers of German literature from different historical periods, Goethe, Musil, and Kafka—and in comparing those texts both to the writers' early work and to the texts of their contemporaries—we produced results that were as multifaceted as is the concept of style. The reasons for this manifold outcome may be several. As a theoretical matter, Late Style may not be a universal category, as some scholars have suggested (Kastenbaum 1985), but rather a tendency that can be observed in the study of single authors (Zanetti 2012: 204). In a certain way, we can confirm McMullan's perspective that Late Style "was established as a given, as a hallmark of genius, and as a transhistorical phenomenon" (McMullan 2016: 36).

On the methodological level, the results of our research underscore the necessity of pairing quantitative and qualitative measures on style, confirming the methodological approach described in the first chapter of this book. Late Style seemed confirmed by our internal studies on semantic areas and through LIWC measurements,[18] but it appeared unsupported by such traditional stylometric methods as network analysis and Zeta analysis, as shown below (Table 7).

	Network analysis		Zeta analysis		Semantic analysis	
	Internal	*External*	*Internal*	*External*	*Internal*	*External*
Goethe	red	red	red	red	green	green
Musil	red	red	red	red	green	red
Kafka	red	red	red	red	green	green

Table 7: Internal and External Analyses in Goethe, Musil, and Kafka (green dots represent the methods that were successful in identifying Late Style; red dots represent those that failed)

This may be because the phenomenon of Late Style is more evident on the semantic level than on the level of vocabulary or syntax. From this perspective, Late Style could be the result of the direction a writer takes toward the end of life more than of the involuntary use of a particular vocabulary. However, it should also be noted that many of the words identified by our semantic analyses are quite common. What differs from stylometry is the way in which these words are analysed (by focusing on more general categorizations, instead of fine-grained frequency patterns). LIWC categories such as "Article," "Prep[osition]s," and "Pronoun" are what Pennebaker termed "little words" that play a determining role in identifying psychopathologies and aging (Pennebaker & Chung 2014: 25–26). It may be, in summary, that Late Style is more a natural consequence of aging than it is the revolutionary stylistic break hypothesized by Broch and Said. Or

---

18 Note that the LIWC analysis, while it adopts a typically "distant" and "unsupervised" perspective, requires confrontation with the analysed author to identify distinctive categories. Consequently, it may be considered a middle way between close and distant approaches in the study of literature.

perhaps we should distinguish between theoretical innovators and experimental innovators, as psychologist Adam Grant did in his book *Originals* (Grant 2017). According to Grant, theoretical innovators tended to generate original ideas at a young age, but experimental innovators like Mark Twain and Robert Frost needed more time to generate new ideas based on their accumulated experiences.

These multifaceted results may confirm Reeve's claim (2018) that Late Style is not measurable—at least, not through most frequent words. Reeve asks provocatively, "Does Late Style exist? Do novelists exhibit a well-defined and distinctive stylistic shift as they reach old age, artistic maturity, or both? (Reeve 2018: 478). Such a reflection also offered Reeve the opportunity for operationalisation. To determine whether the concept of Late Style was more than just anecdotally true, he used new techniques of computational stylometric analysis to determine whether writer's late works were statistically dissimilar from the rest of their corpus (Reeve 2018: 479). He generated a corpus that included three of the novelists Said cited at length—Marcel Proust, Thomas Mann, and Jean Genet—as well as nine novelists from the nineteenth and twentieth centuries whom he chose for their prolificacy and digital availability: Charles Dickens, Joseph Conrad, Ernest Hemingway, Henry James, Walter Scott, George Meredith, Willa Cather, Arnold Bennett, and Mary Augusta Ward.

From each of these works, he took two samples that were then vectorized to 500-dimensional vectors according to their top 500-word frequencies. The aim of the stylometric analysis was the so-called "distinctiveness score" of a novel by determining the distance of the vector from the mean in five-dimensional space. A late work included in the corpus that showed a high distinctiveness score could be called an example of Late Style. Reeve's results disconfirmed Said's thesis on Late Style, as the example of Thomas Mann's texts show: The samples with the highest distinctiveness scores were from such early works as *Der Kleine Herr Friedemann* and *Tristan*. The samples displaying the least distinctiveness came from *Doktor Faustus*, the very work Said cites as an example of a distinctive Late Style (480). The same was true in the case of Marcel Proust's work, whose early style shows a stronger signal than his late: Proust's last published work, *Le Temps Retrouvé*, which Said cites as an eminent example of Late Style, obtained the lowest distinctiveness scores, while Proust's first work, *Du Côté de chez Swann*, is the most distinctive.

Another issue concerns the rupture inherent in the category of Late Style. What does it mean that Kafka differs more than Musil does from other early-twentieth-century writers, as Figure 15 seem to suggest? And how can we measure the rupture conceptualized in many deviance theories of literary style (Herrmann *et al.* 2015; Salgaro 2018b)? Once again, semantic analyses were revealing. Only in relation to a specific vocabulary, suggested by literary critics and by LIWC categories in our experiments, were we able to find internal and external differences with reference to style. Late Style seemed to emerge only after a reference model was established and not in relation to vocabulary as a whole. What is amazing, in any case, is that these software programs were able to grasp the "Kafkaesqueness" of Kafka.

From this perspective, the main problem in the application of stylometry is that the concept of *style*, which is so difficult to pin down, lends itself poorly to any kind of operationalisation. This has been highlighted by the question of Late Style, the inexistence of which, from the point of view of stylometry, depends mainly upon the fact that critics have often used it as a label to describe a phenomenon that occurs more on the level of thematic choices than stylistic preferences.

For Adorno, "late works are the catastrophes in the history of art" (Adorno 2002: 567). Late works are sometimes also an occasion to look back at the catastrophes of history, and, as we know, German history was particularly dramatic during the twentieth century. This is the position expressed by Stuart Taberner, who explored the topic of old-age style in well-known authors of the twentieth century, primarily Günther Grass, Christa Wolf, and Martin Walser, with an excursus on Ruth Klüger included in the chapter on Christa Wolf (Taberner 2013). His study offers a useful reminder of the position of the authors of that generation in the cultural identity of post-war Germany. Taberner believed that "old age style fashions life review in such a way as to confront individual shame that stands in for the collectively felt shame of the generation 1945 after the Holocaust" (Taberner 2013: 195). In contemporary German society, the German post-war author locates himself "in, but oddly apart."

As is typical for Late Style, Grass, Wolf, Walser, and Klüger represent significant inner cultural differences in German society. Günther Grass, for example, was the voice of the centre left, while Martin Walser held more conservative positions and sought a space in which to escape shame for the crimes of the German past. Martin Walser's late novels defy conventions of timeliness in relation both to their depiction of an "asynchronous" intimacy between elderly men and young women and especially to their aesthetic modes (Taberner 2015: 99). They express a rage against both the indignity of corporeal aging and against elderly bodies relegated to the margins of a society that is obsessed with youth and appearance. Walser imposes an attitude of *Entsagung* (renunciation) on these fictional figures which, for late-period Goethe, was the perception that he was becoming "historical even to himself" (Taberner 2015: 106). The same *Entsagung* characterizes Walser's speeches, writing, and other engagements with Germany's public life. In the cases mentioned, late works are a way of creating distance from a traumatic event and from collective trauma and allowing these matters to be processed by intellectuals and the German people.

All in all, the important questions raised by literary theory and by critics of Late Style confirmed the necessity of revisiting the concept of style through stylometry. We put operationalisation at the basis of our work by employing a mixed method in which direct confrontation with critical theory and focus on single case studies is merged with the techniques of Digital Humanities and distant reading. This approach could be expanded to other authors if appropriate corpora were available.

4. An Anonymous Erotic Novel and a Children's Book: Felix Salten

A few years ago, we performed an experiment in which we asked subjects to express the semantic proximity of words in a pair (Salgaro 2015). In this study, 107 subjects were asked, "Do you think the two words are very related or not related at all?" and they then rated that relationship on a scale from 1 to 7. To cite just one example, recalling perhaps the most famous oxymoron in German literature, we also used the pair "black" + "milk." Our results showed that synaesthesias and personifications were judged to be more semantically distant than were oxymora.

If we were to repeat the same experiment with genres of literature, we would probably find great similarities between the genres of the Künstlerroman (the artist's novel) and the Bildungsroman. Animal stories and fairy tales should appear in this cluster as well because their animal protagonists share an anthropomorphic nature. In this hypothetical experiment, the two fictional genres likely to appear at opposite poles are children's literature and the erotic novel. At first glance, nothing appears more incompatible in terms of content, tone, and "ideal audience." This chapter concerns an author who, in all likelihood, devoted himself to both genres, which, on closer inspection, reveal similarities. If these similarities can be perceived not only by humans but also by computer analysis, we are faced with a new case of operationalisation.

4.1. When Attribution of Authorship Becomes a Legal Case: The Mutzenbacher Novel

The writer in question is Felix Salten, the author of the world-famous children book that served as the basis for the Disney classic, *Bambi*, and allegedly also the author of a very different novel, *Josefine Mutzenbacher oder die Geschichte einer Wienerischen Dirne von ihr selbst erzählt* (published in English as *Josephine Mutzenbacher or the Story of a Viennese Whore as Told by Herself;* Salten 1967), published in Vienna in 1906. The novel opens with a fictitious preface by a hypothetical editor who introduces the author and protagonist of the story, Josefine Mutzenbacher, a prostitute who lived in Vienna and Klagenfurt from 1852 to 1904. Before her death, according to the preface, she delivered the manuscript of her memoir to her doctor, and the editor "corrected only linguistic [and] stylistic errors," substituting only "the names of renowned personalities that Josefine named in her memories" (Salten & Farin 1990: 38).·

The first chapter of the fictitious memoir introduces a framing story in which Josefine looks back on her tumultuous life "without regret" (Salten & Farin 1990: 39). She even recognizes that, thanks to prostitution, she "was educated" and "in touch with distinguished and erudite men" (Salten & Farin 1990: 39). What follows is a detailed, naturalistic, first-person narrative of her depraved life from the age of five to fourteen. During her childhood, she had sexual intercourse with a multitude of adult men and ended up becoming a prostitute. Josefine supposes that, in her whole life, she had had sex with an "army" of around 33,000 men.

Since its publication, the Mutzenbacher-novel has been celebrated by writers and critics for its literary quality despite its erotic content. According to Farin, Ernst Klein defined it "a masterpiece ... that should be put at the peak of the [entirety of] modern literature" (Salten & Farin 1990: 467–68). The writer Friedrich Torberg celebrated *Josefine Mutzenbacher* as "an accurate description of the milieu and the manners of Vienna at the turn of the century" (Salten & Farin 1990: 30), and Ulrich Weinzierl called it "a piece of prose with artistic status" (Salten & Farin 1990: 27). In 1969, two important representatives of German and Austrian literature praised the text: the authoritative critic Hellmuth Karasek wrote that "no pornographic book that I know describes in such a pervasive manner the side-products of the act that is so common within humanity" (Salten & Farin 1990: 9). Karasek highlighted the literary features of Josefine Mutzenbacher, including the grotesque parodies of Viennese society (Salten & Farin 1990: 14–15), and hyperbolic descriptions, exaggerations, and puns have also been noted. Karasek stressed the linguistic peculiarity of the novel's style in which the use of Viennese dialect or slang is more effective in rendering descriptions of sexual activity than is the terminology employed in more "cultivated" language (Salten & Farin 1990: 16).

In 1969, the experimental writer, Oswald Wiener, wrote that the author of *Josefine Mutzenbacher* should "be re-evaluated and [the author's] position in the history of literature reconsidered" (Salten & Farin 1990: 362). Wiener, along with other critics, highlighted the realism of the novel, along with its avoidance of hypocrisy or social criticism. Like Karasek, Wiener believed that the realism of *Josefine Mutzenbacher* was bolstered by the author's use of many words in Viennese dialect, especially in the descriptions of scurrilous experiences, which he considered the best "code" to convey the secret life of the Viennese suburbs with its "unmentionable lasciviousness" and common prostitution (Salten & Farin 1990: 361–461). He further noted that the novel's unity relied upon its depiction of eroticism, which is "anti-social, outside the rational communication, and a real anarchy" (Salten & Farin 1990: 363). As a result, Wiener added a glossary of Viennese sexual vocabulary to his essay (Salten & Farin 1990: 365–462), noting that the novel used "Viennese erotic expressions which accounted for more or less 40%" of the work (Salten & Farin 1990: 465). As one example, in a single sentence Josefine used three different vulgar expressions to mean "to have sexual intercourse": "vögeln, pudern, stemmen sie mich" (Salten & Farin 1990: 123). The example shows that the style of the novel is characterized by redundancy and that the protagonist's vocabulary is crass and characteristic of Viennese slang.

Despite its aesthetic qualities, *Josefine Mutzenbacher* is surely pornographic (Ruthner *et al.* 2019: 39–41). It was also a commercial success: some 150,000 paperback copies were sold, two sequels were published, and it was widely reprinted, translated, and filmed (Salten & Farin 1990: 25). Sexual activity dominates not only the plot but the dialogue as well. Even during sex, the characters talk to each other endlessly. According to some critics, it is not so much the sexual act that is central in the novel, but rather the characters' discussion of desire that triggers the sexual act. The male wish to physically penetrate another body parallels the longing to know women's secret desires and thoughts (Liebrand & Börnchen 2019). According to Dietmar Schmitt and Claudia Öhlschläger (1994: 251), the novel's protagonist not only aims for expiation through her "confessions"—to her father, her priest, and to various other characters—but also tries to make explicit the language of a desire that can't be expressed in words. Thanks to its explicit language, some contemporary scholars consider Josefine Mutzenbacher an anticipation of feminist assertions of women's right to orgasm (Ruthner *et al.* 2019: 274); others have named it "Austria's most (in)famous piece of child pornography" (Ruthner 2011: 101).

From the very beginning, Felix Salten, a pseudonym for the Jewish writer Siegmund Salzmann (1869–1945), has been the main candidate for the authorship of *Josefine Mutzenbacher*. In his youth, Salten belonged to the Jungwien movement, whose members included such iconic writers of Austrian literature as Hugo von Hofmannsthal and Arthur Schnitzler. Farin reports the hearsay that *Josefine Mutzenbacher* may have been the product of a bet among Jungwien writers to see who could write the best pornographic novel (Salten & Farin 1990: 520). The influential journalist and thinker, Karl Krauss, suspected Salten of being the novel's author and, after the publication of *Bambi*, he nicknamed Salten the "deer sodomite" (Salten & Farin 1990: 469ff). Salten's friend and contemporary, Arthur Schnitzler, confirmed the rumours about Salten's authorship of *Josefine Mutzenbacher* when he wrote in his journal, "Probably

Salten" (Salten & Farin 1990: 29). From the beginning, most critics recognized *Josefine Mutzenbacher* as a masterpiece, though many argued whether Salten would have been capable of crafting such a work (Eddy 2010: 114).

Schnitzler himself was victim of these rumours. Because he had published a scandalous theatre piece (*Reigen*, 1900), he was also considered a potential author of the book. Farin reports that, in 1909, the German Anonymen-Lexikon, edited by two employees of the Vienna University Library, mentioned both Felix Salten and Arthur Schnitzler as potential authors of the novel while, in the 1911 edition of the Anonymen-Lexikon, only Salten was named (Salten & Farin 1990: 513). In Paul Englisch's 1927 History of Erotic Literature, as a consequence, he directly identified Arthur Schnitzler and Felix Salten as potential authors. Both denied writing the novel. In 1931, Englisch expressed another hypothesis that I have tested with Simone Rebora (Rebora & Salgaro 2022): Felix Salten wrote two-thirds of the novel but refused to accept the fee offered by the publisher and was replaced by the journalist, Willy Handl (Salten & Farin 1990: 512).

Even Stefan Zweig was involved in this mysterious case of authorship attribution. On one occasion, as he and Salten were discussing famous authors who had written bawdy stories, Salten mentioned Goethe's work, and Zweig brought up Mark Twain's story about the English court of Elizabeth I. This seemed for Zweig a good occasion to ask Salten about his alleged authorship of *Josefine Mutzenbacher*:

> [Salten] smiled mysteriously and said: "If I deny it, you won't believe me, and [if] I admit it, you'll think I am teasing you. So…" and he shrugged. To me this was a badly disguised admission. Knowing Salten well, I realized he'd have become very angry at being asked such a question unless he *was* the author. (Salten & Farin 1990: 515)

Salten was considered by his peers the main candidate for authorship because he had written a short story entitled Mutza, whose protagonist was also called Josefine Mutzenbacher. Salten, however, denied authorship again and again (Salten & Farin 1990: 518; 521).

The crucial steps of the long and complex history of the debate about the authorship of *Josefine Mutzenbacher* are summed up in a miscellany edited by Michael Farin (Salten & Farin 1990) that included not only early reviews and feedback from authors and critics but also extracts from the records of the three legal proceedings in which the novel was involved. The first began in 1970, when the German Federal Department for Youth-Endangering Media considered the novel "bawdy," and many copies were confiscated (Salten & Farin 1990: 529–44). The second legal proceeding was initiated in 1986, when Felix Salten's heirs took legal action against the publishing house Rogner & Bernhard with the intention of receiving royalties from the work of the presumed author of the novel, their ancestor. Third, in 2014, when the digital version of the book was published on the internet, the Berlin Prosecutor's Office considered *Josefine Mutzenbacher* and decided that safeguarding artistic creativity was more important than protecting children and youth (Ruthner *et al.* 2019: 224–25). The authorship question has extended to such issues as freedom of press and artistic creativity (Ruthner *et al.* 2019: 195–225).

The rumours of Salten's authorship propagated without evidence until, in 1976, Salten's heirs asked the publisher Rogner & Bernhard for royalties from *Josefine Mutzenbacher* (Salten & Farin 1990: 522). Ten years later, on 5 June 1986, the heirs took legal action and introduced five pieces of evidence to demonstrate that their ancestor had written the book: First, on 12 June 1973, Fritz Peter Molden, a journalist for the Neue Freie Presse, stated that a former collaborator of Felix Salten, Adolf David, had revealed himself as the typist of the manuscript of *Josefine Mutzenbacher*. For this work, Salten had paid David 1,000 krones, and David had promised Salten his professional secrecy. After Salten's death, however, he felt exempted from his vow.

Second, an expert analysis by literary scholar Fritz Hochwälder emphasized the close relationship between Felix Salten and Karl Kraus and noted that Kraus, in an article, had publicly declared that Salten was the author of Josefine Mutzenbacher (Salten & Farin 1990: 524).

Third, Lily Schnitzler, Arthur Schnitzler's daughter in law, declared under oath in September 1986 that, according to her own family and to Felix Salten's daughter, the book was without any doubt authored by Salten.

Fourth, Gertrud Schattner, Salten's former secretary, declared under oath that Felix Salten had confessed to being the author of the novel (Salten & Farin 1990: 525).

Fifth and finally, Arthur Schnitzler, who was a close friend of Salten's, identified Salten as the probable author of the novel, as mentioned earlier. According to the lawyers, Molden's and Schattner's testimonies were deemed inadmissible because they did not satisfy the burden of proof.

On 19 May 1988, the District Court of Munich rejected the Salten heirs' lawsuit because the copyright of *Josefine Mutzenbacher* had expired, and the work had been in the public domain since 1956. When the novel was published in 1906, according to German law, the term of protection for an anonymous works was fifty years. The heirs contested the verdict without result.

Murray G. Hall recapitulated the attribution history started by Michael Farin and updated it with the most relevant findings up to 2015 (Hall 2019; 2015). Salten's heirs continued unsuccessfully to search for an edition of *Josefine Mutzenbacher* published before 1956 that mentioned Salten as the author of the work. Their lawyers suggested stopping the legal action because there was no clear evidence—no letters or manuscripts, for example—of Salten's authorship.

The trial failed to dispel doubts about the authorship of the novel that had been attributed to many writers over the previous hundred years. The following is a list of the conflicting authorship attributions in chronological order:

Author	Attribution	Publication date	Bibliographical reference (Salten & Farin 1990)
Ernst Klein	F. Salten or A. Schnitzler	1908	467
Michael Holzmann/ Hanns Bohatta	F. Salten or A. Schnitzler	1909	504
Hugo Hayn/Alfred N. Gotendorf	Ernst Klein	1914	505
Bernhard Stern-Szana	F. Salten	1921	506
Karl Kraus	F. Salten	1923	469
Anton Kuh	F. Salten	1924	476
Paul Englisch	A. Schnitzler or F. Salten	1927	507
Leo Schidrowitz	F. Salten, last chapter by Willy Handl or Fritz Freund	1929	511
Paul Englisch	F. Salten, last chapter by Willy Handl	1931	511
Oswald Wiener	Uncertain	1969	361
Jürgen Kolbe	Uncertain, but suggests A. Schnitzler	1969	487
Hellmuth Karasek	Uncertain	1969	13
K.H. Kramberg	F. Salten	1969	482
Oswald Wiener	Uncertain	1970	464
Urs Widmer	Uncertain	1970	21
Klaus Pinkus	Uncertain, but not F. Salten	1970	521
Ulrich Wenzierl	Uncertain	1985	29
Michael Farin	Ernst Klein	1991	Weichinger 1991
Murray G. Hall	Ernst Klein	2015/2019	Hall (2015; 2019)

Table 8: Attributions Overview of the Mutzenbacher Novel

From this overview we can extract several hypotheses, most of which are based on hearsay. The author of the novel could be one of the writers of the Jungwien movement or the ending of the novel may have been written by a different author. While conjecture about the authorship of the novel began shortly after its publication, questions regarding its final pages are more recent and were brought up for the first time in 1991 (Ruthner *et al.* 2019: 15): Michael Farin and Murray G. Hall have suggested that the true author of *Josefine Mutzenbacher*, was Ernst Klein, a writer, journalist, and translator. Under the pseudonyms Fedor Essée and Richard Werther, he wrote such pornographic novels as *Geschichten von der Birkenrute/Tales from the Birch Rod* (1910) and *Der Skandal von Graz oder der nackte Ball: Enthüllungen aus den Geheimnissen einer österreichischen Provinzhauptstadt/The Scandal of Graz or the Naked Ball: Revelations from the Secrets of a Provincial Austrian Capital* (1907). This hypothesis seems more credible because, from the point of view of genre and content, there is continuity between these texts and *Josefine Mutzenbacher*.

As his main documentary evidence of Klein's authorship, Michael Farin quoted a review by Klein (writing as Richard Werther) that appeared in a journal called Blätter für Bibliophilen: Bibliographie der Sexualwissenschaft in 1908 (Salten & Farin 1990: 467–69). To corroborate his thesis, Farin carried out a stylistic analysis, about which Robert Weichinger later concluded that "the comparative stylistic analysis between *Josefine Mutzenbacher* and the erotic novels of Ernst Klein, written under the pseudonym Richard Werther, close, for Michael Farin, the eternal discussion on the authorship of [*Josefine Mutzenbacher*] in favour of Ernst Klein"(Weichinger 1991). Hall shared Farin's opinion (Hall 2015; 2019), noting that Klein's review seemed like a voluntary disclosure by the hidden author of *Josefine Mutzenbacher*. He further believed that the writer of Klein's review (as Werther) was an intimate connoisseur of the novel, insisting that it was absolutely clear that "Felix Salten is not its author" (Hall 2015). Hall also noted the "many serious arguments which plead for the anonymous authorship of Ernst Klein" (Hall 2015: 160), though he did not mention specifics. Klein had, however, stated, in his review, that *Josefine Mutzenbacher* should be put "at the peak of modern literature."

The issue of authorship is not the only mystery surrounding this novel. The stylistic break in the last third of the novel suggests the hypothesis that the concluding section was drafted by a different author. The novel ends with Josefine's first day as a prostitute and culminates in an orgy that involves Josefine, Zenzi, and Karl. In one of the typical puns in *Josefine Mutzenbacher*, Karl's penis is named "a helper in time of need" (Salten & Farin 1990: 287). After the description of sexual intercourse among the three, a stylistic shift takes place at the level of content and narrative. While the previous section consisted of Josefine's inner monologues or her dialogues with sexual partners, the last part of the novel consists of a dialogue between Zenzi and Josefine, who comment on their past and on episodes introduced earlier in the novel. For example, they report the relationship between Zenzi and Rudolph, who had been together for eight years by that point. Rudolph was first Zenzi's mother's lover and began a relationship with Zenzi after her mother's death.

The final part brings a change in narrative focus as well: while the first part is focused on Josefine's experiences in the present, in the last part she explains and comments on episodes recounted earlier in the novel. Zenzi explains, for example, that Rudolph pushed her to have sex with Josefine's father, the owner of the flat in which they lived, in order to avoid paying the rent (Salten & Farin 1990: 295). In contrast, her actions in the first two-thirds of the story were genuine and spontaneous without this kind of causal thinking.

The narrators' tone also changes. Zenzi comments ironically on her life by defining Rudolph, who is much older than her and her pimp, as "a good teacher" (Salten & Farin 1990: 292). In the final section, Josefine speaks about her life as a prostitute at the point at which she began to accept money for her "services" and could financially help to support her father. While the novel is amoral in its first part, the final pages are suddenly moralistic. Josefine, who always had acted spontaneously, now describes attempts to avoid syphilis (Salten & Farin 1990: 305). She even tries to justify her way of life by extracting from her vast experience with men a philosophical maxim: "All men do the same. They lie above, we lie below" (Salten & Farin 1990: 306).

At this point, the reader has the impression that the author wants to wrap up Josefine's childhood memories and express the moral of the story, though such a moral attitude is absent from most of the novel. In contrast, Beverley Eddy wrote that this change of style was not convincing evidence for Salten's authorship: "Part of the argument here is the novel's break in time and tone, an argument that is greatly weakened by the fact that Salten frequently included breaks in his novels, often occasioned by a death and generally signalling a change in the protagonist's behaviour over time" (Eddy 2010: 119). Based on these stylistic observations, and noting that the final paragraph seemed different from the rest of the novel, Eddy opined that it was "difficult to believe that anyone other than Salten composed anything but the final paragraph" (Eddy 2010: 120).

In 1987 Paul Katzenberger, the former head of the Max-Planck-Institute for patent law, was asked by Salten's heirs to provide an expert opinion on the Mutzenbacher issue in the legal action they had started. In a letter of 28 October 1987, he suggested a computer-based text analysis to foster the argument for Salten's authorship (Hall 2015). As I explained in Chapter 1, these tools were not refined enough to answer such questions at that time, though today such questions could be operationalised. Simone Rebora and I have implemented Katzenberger's advice by adopting a mixed-method approach to try to solve the question of the authorship of the Mutzenbacher novel (Rebora & Salgaro 2022).

4.2.   Operationalising the Quest for the Author of the Mutzenbacher Novel

As we have shown in previous chapters, stylometry functions, at its core, through the comparison of texts. Consequently, a corpus of works representative of the style of the candidate authors is the first and most important element of an analysis. In the case of *Josefine Mutzenbacher*, this so-called training set was defined by selecting works of the seven candidate authors to create a corpus that included texts written by Felix Salten as well as by Arthur Schnitzler, Hermann Bahr, Peter Altenberg, Hugo von Hofmannsthal, Ernst Klein, and Willi Handl. The rationale behind the selection of the texts was the desire for consistency with respect to the genre of *Mutzenbacher*. To make texts comparable, we selected mainly fiction (novels, short stories, and theatre pieces) by the seven authors.

The text of *Josefine Mutzenbacher* was downloaded from Project Gutenberg, which offers free access to the digital versions of a wide selection of out-of-copyright books. For Felix Salten, we selected the twelve texts hosted by the German version of Project Gutenberg, Projekt Gutenberg-DE. Because Ernst Klein and Willi Handl are rather forgotten authors, we bought their books on the antiquities market and manually scanned them with the Transkribus platform, which uses a machine-learning algorithm to extract text automatically from images (Kahle *et al.* 2017). We manually corrected all identified errors. The rest of the corpus, including texts by Schnitzler, Bahr, Altenberg, and Hofmannsthal was collected from the KOLIMO corpus (Herrmann & Lauer 2017). KOLIMO is an acronym for Korpus der Literarischen Moderne, a collection of literary texts written around 1900. An overview of the selected titles is provided in Table 9.

Author	Number of texts	Publication years	Genre	Number of words	Source
Arthur Schnitzler	40	1890–1931	Drama, short story, and novel	777,234	KOLIMO
Felix Salten	12	1905–1940	Novel	421,000	Projekt Gutenberg-DE
Hugo von Hofmannsthal	18	1892–1923	Drama, short story, and fictional letter	203,656	KOLIMO
Hermann Bahr	4	1897–1922	Novel, drama, and essay	203,482	KOLIMO
Ernst Klein	3	1915–1923	Novel	169,377	OCR
Peter Altenberg	195	1896–1919	Prose sketch and fragment	92,276	KOLIMO
Willi Handl	1	1920	Novel	52,441	OCR

Table 9: Composition of the Corpus Prepared for Stylometric Analysis

All stylometric analyses were performed using the functions of the R package Stylo, which enables efficient application of Burrows' Delta and its numerous variants (Eder *et al.* 2016). These tools, which are used to compute the most frequent words (MFW) of a text and corpus, are firmly established within stylometry. The frequencies of the MFW in a specific text set determine a distance measure which establishes the similarity or distance of each text from every other text in the corpus. To maximize the reliability of stylometric results, we used a multi-methodologic approach that combined different methods by weighting their efficiency (in fact, all methods were first of all tested on texts of known authorship).

Before running the analyses, we split all texts of the candidate authors into 5,000-word segments, which is the minimum length for reliable authorship attribution. This procedure produced between 10 and 155 measurements for each author. The results of the analyses are presented in Figure 16, which shows the percentage of attributions for each candidate.

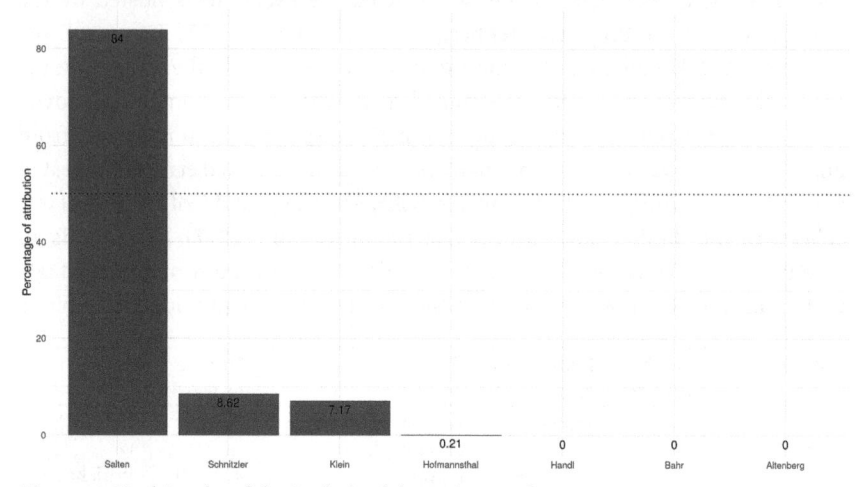

Figure 16: Final Results of the Analysis of the Entire Novel

As the length of the bars shows, Salten clearly dominates in the attribution, followed distantly by Arthur Schnitzler and Ernst Klein. This result seems to confirm the dominant hearsay on the authorship of the novel among scholars: the author of the scandalous *Josefine Mutzenbacher* was also the author of *Bambi* (Eddy 2010: 309–24). Though this claim had never been confirmed, whether from documentary research or in legal proceedings, the utility of stylometry in cases of authorship attribution becomes clear. Our conclusions were supported by a curious coincidence as well: in a separate cluster analysis run on the non-split corpus, *Bambi* clusters closely to *Josefine Mutzenbacher* as Figure 17 brings to light.

It is not uncommon to find analogies between literary texts and children's literature. In a similar cluster analysis, Berenike Herrmann found similarities between Kafka's style and that of two authors of children's books, Johanna Spyri and Agnes Sapper (Herrmann 2018). Despite these intriguing results, various questions remain regarding the Mutzenbacher novel. Some critics have stated that the novel was not written by a single author. To operationalise the question "Was the novel written only by Felix Salten?" we adopted another tool offered by

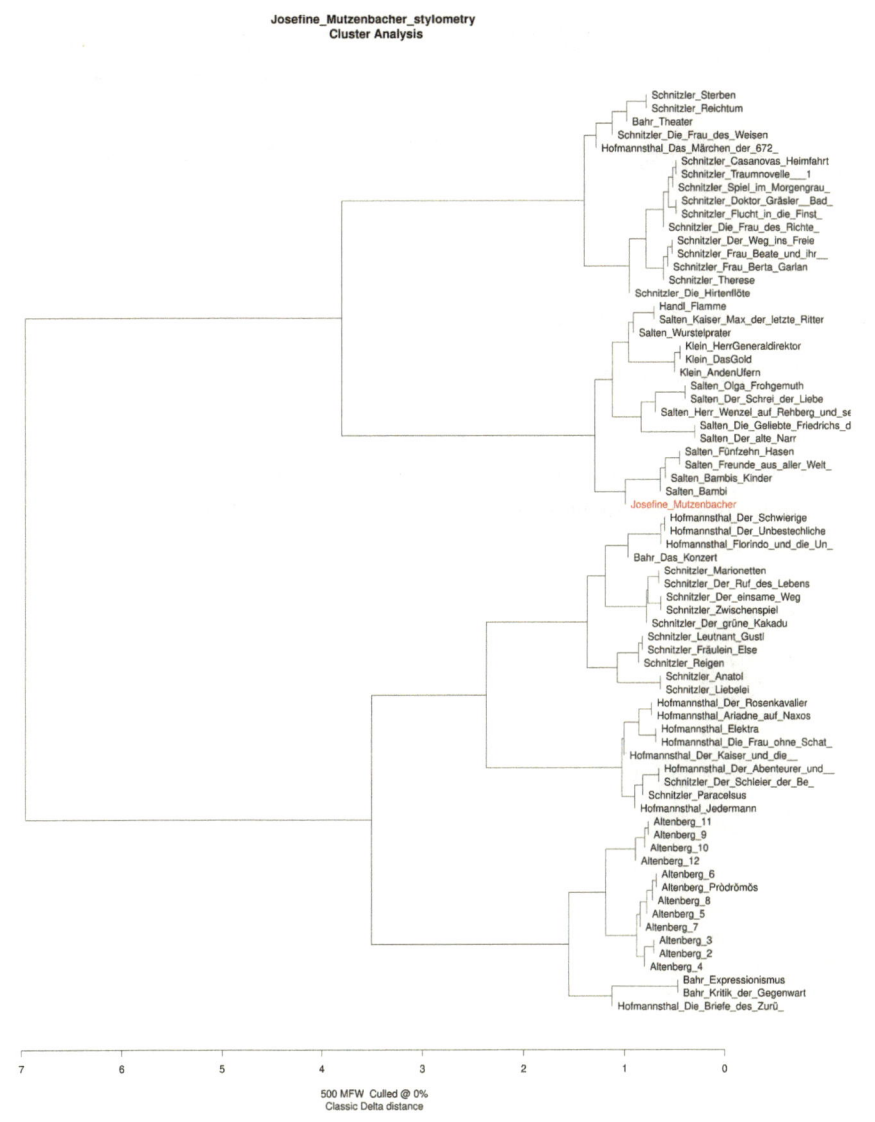

Figure 17: Dendrogram Showing the Close Connection between *Bambi* and *Mutzenbacher*

the Stylo package called the "rolling Delta" procedure (Eder 2015), the goal of which is to analyse authorship through the course of a text, verifying in particular if there are any significant breaks in style that could indicate multiple authors. Figure 18 shows that the "rolling Delta" applied on *Josefine Mutzenbacher* produced a significant outcome.

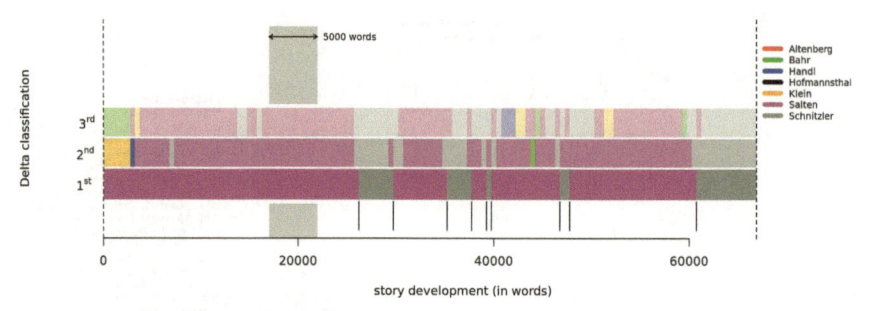

Figure 18: Rolling Delta Analysis of *Josefine Mutzenbacher*

While Salten is confirmed as the most probable author of the novel, the software classified a few short passages in the middle and a longer passage at the end of the novel as bearing Schnitzler's stylistic footprint. To solidify this result, we repeated the stylometric procedure used for the entirety of the novel on its ending alone. The above-described analyses were simply repeated, generating the results shown in Figure 19.

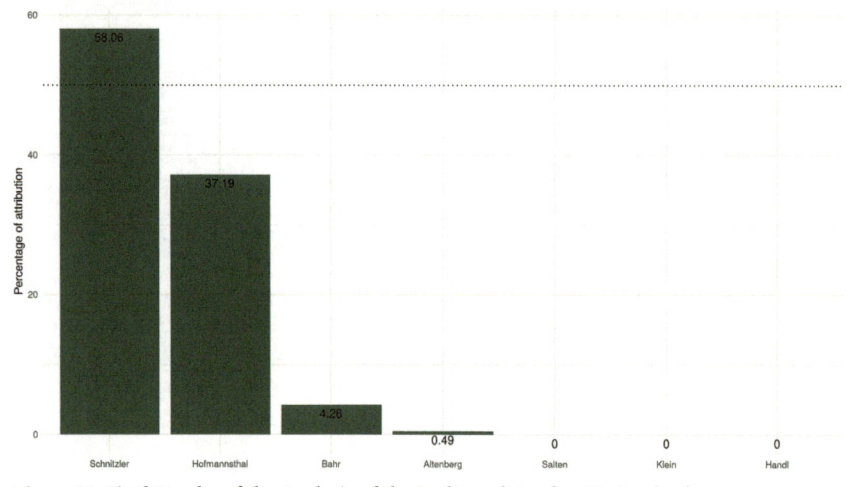

Figure 19: Final Results of the Analysis of the Ending of *Josefine Mutzenbacher*

In contrast to the entire novel, it was not possible to identify a candidate who clearly dominated the others, as Figure 19 shows. Hofmannsthal and Schnitzler share the highest number of attributions, with a slight dominance of the second. The proof of these results via the "impostors" method finally excluded the attribution to any of the candidate authors. As an example, the attribution to Schnitzler alone oscillated between 27% and 39% (Rebora & Salgaro 2022: 17–18).

This result suggests that the ending of *Josefine Mutzenbacher* is close both to the overall style of Hofmannsthal and to a few passages by Schnitzler but can't be attributed to either of them. A possible, still unchecked hypothesis, is that the publisher Fritz Freund himself, who was not able to come to an agreement with Felix Salten and was in need of money, finished the novel. In 1906 Salten wrote a letter to his publisher that began with the words "Dear Mr. Freund: Here at last are the long missing sheets. I would still like to speak with you about the ending" (Eddy 2010: 120). This passage serves as another indicator of Salten's authorship and suggests that the author and his publisher may have had some disagreement on the conclusion of the novel or on their collaboration.

A more detailed stylistic assessment of the results shows that the texts closet to *Josefine Mutzenbacher* are the novella, Leutnant Gustl, and the theatre piece, *Reigen*. The proximity between *Josefine Mutzenbacher* and *Reigen*, which was translated into English with the title *La Ronde*, is given by its topic: *Reigen* is a controversial play based on ten sexual encounters in Vienna between pairs of lovers. These lovers come from different social backgrounds: the whore, the soldier, the poet, the count. Strangely enough, the play was published in 1903 by Wiener Verlag, the same editor that published *Josefine Mutzenbacher* in 1906. The links to *Leutnant Gustl* are based on its formal aspects. The novella reports the stream of consciousness of the soldier, Gustl, who loses his pride and plans a suicide. During these suicidal thoughts, he remembers his love story. The inner focalization and the topic of love surely link *Leutnant Gustl* and *Josefine Mutzenbacher*. But they are also similar linguistically as the use of words from Viennese dialect makes clear.

4.3.   The Voice of Animal Instincts in *Bambi* and in *Mutzenbacher*

As the dendrogram in Figure 17 shows, *Bambi* and *Mutzenbacher* are closely connected. Even if critics have highlighted the analogies between the Mutzenbacher novel and Salten's other fictional writings (Eddy 2010: 115–18), the proximity between an animal story and a pornographic novel is surprising and needs further investigation. The first to acknowledge this similarity were Dietmar Schmitt and Claudia Öhlschläger who found that *Josefine Mutzenbacher* and *Bambi* share five common elements (Schmitt & Öhlschläger 1994).

First, both novels are attempts to capture life through narration: "In [*Bambi*], animals speak; the pornography [of *Josefine Mutzenbacher*] gives voice to the animal instincts of men" (Schmitt & Öhlschläger 1994: 240). Thus, in *Bambi*, animals, as bearers of an undeniable instinct, speak the language of nature; in *Mutzenbacher*, human bodies speak the inarticulate language of lust and the flesh.

Second, both novels strive to overcome a stage of civilization and culture that is understood as the loss of an original natural condition. In Josefine's dialogues, there is no hypocrisy; the characters simply satisfy their lust with whatever is available to them. In this inverted utopia, men and women are equally lustful. It is a "fairy tale from nature" (Eddy 2010: 119). Paradoxically, Josefine's sexual romps in the Viennese suburbs can be considered an expression of her natural state, while her business transactions in the city are a corruption of civilization. In both novels, Salten identifies the natural state—whether in the country or in the forest—as a nostalgic condition of innocence in opposition to the corruption of urban society (Eddy 2010: 119).

Third, two language rituals are used in both novels: the riddle and the confession (Schmitt & Öhlschläger 1994: 249). Josefine's confession to her father is an act of linguistic penetration, which leads to a physical one; it produces a desire to control knowledge, leading to sexual domination of the daughter. Riddle and confession constitute a game of revealing and concealing truth in Bambi as well, and the enigmatic words of the deer prince identify him as the guardian of secret knowledge. The elder's authority over Bambi is expressed in their first meeting:

"What are you calling for?" the old stag asked severely. Bambi trembled in awe of the elder stag and did not dare to make any answer. "Your mother hasn't got the time to spend on you now!" the elder continued. Bambi was completely cowed by this imperious voice, but at the same time he felt admiration for it. "Can't you be by yourself for a while? You should be ashamed of yourself!" Bambi would have liked to say that he could be by himself perfectly well, that he had often been by himself, but he said nothing. He did as he was told and became terribly ashamed. The elder turned round and left him (Salten 2020).

Fourth, both Salten's *Bambi* and *Josefine Mutzenbacher* attempt to tell the story of an individual as a totality—but in different ways. Whereas Salten's story of Bambi's life is structured in cycles, the adventures of Josefine Mutzenbacher are structured in a series. In *Bambi*, the development of the young deer takes place within natural annual cycles (spring, summer, autumn, winter), life cycles (birth-death), and social cycles (peace, struggle) (Schmitt & Öhlschläger 1994: 241). This cyclicality is recognizable in the ending of *Bambi* as well, at which point the encounter with the elder is repeated, this time with Bambi as the elder who gives suggestions and educates the other deer:

Before they understood what was happening, Bambi was standing there before them. Speechless, they stared at him. "Your mother does not have the time now," Bambi told them sternly. He looked in the little one's eye. "Can't you be by yourself for a while?" The little one and his sister remained silent.

Bambi turned away, slipped into the nearest bush and disappeared, even before two of them could understand what had happened. He walked on. "I like that lad ..." he thought. "Maybe I'll meet him again when he's a bit bigger ..." He walked on. "And the little lass," he thought, "she's nice too ... that's what Faline looked like when she was a child." He walked on and disappeared into the woods. (Salten 2020)

Fifth, *Bambi* and *Josefine Mutzenbacher* are family stories whose protagonists are children undergoing education. As socialization stories, they recount the path from childhood through adolescence to adulthood (Schmitt & Öhlschläger 1994: 253). Bambi's development takes place as a transition from the maternal order to the paternal-symbolic order. The patriarchal order in Salten's novels that Schmitt and Öhlschläger described is synthesized in the naïve wisdom Mutzenbacher extracts from her rich life-experience: "All men do the same. They lie above, we lie below" (Salten & Farin 1990: 306).

Another could be added to the similarities listed above. The "natural condition" that so many critics recognize in both *Bambi* and *Mutzenbacher* is one that we also find represented in fairy tales such as those of the Grimms, and talking animals are only one of their shared features. Unlike the Grimms, Salten did not sweeten descriptions of the sexual, violent conditions of childhood (Zipes 2006; Tatar 2003). Several references to an "unspoken" that only adults understand can be uncovered in *Bambi*, and similar passages can be found in *Mutzenbacher*:

> "Please, my love," he said, "please … don't call to me when we're apart … never call to me again …! We can look for each other until we find one another … but please, don't call to me as … your voice is something I can't resist." (Salten 2020)

Linguistic correlations can be identified as well because both stories portray the conditions of childhood. The author of the Mutzenbacher novel tried to reproduce spoken language as closely as possible and was attracted by pre-logical, infantile expressions of an authentic and primary dimension, as exemplified by Josefine's juvenile adventures (Blumesberger 2006: 26). In *Bambi*, we can appreciate the mimicry of infantile speech whose main feature is redundancy, for example in this dialogue between the fox and the dog:

> "Leave me alone …" he began to say. "Leave me alone …." He spoke quietly and imploringly. He was very dull and disheartened.
> "No! No! No!" the dog threw back at him in a malevolent howl.
> "I beg of you …" said the fox, "I can't go any further … I've had it … just let me go … let me go home … at least let me die in peace …"
> "No! No! No!" the dog howled.
> The fox begged him even harder. "But we're related …" he lamented, "we're almost brothers …let me go home … let me die among my own folk … we … we're almost brothers … you and me…."
> "No! No! No!" the dog said excitedly. (Salten 2020)

As Michael Maar has observed, Salten's style reveals itself through small recurring patterns, mannerisms, preferences, tics—for example, Salten's excessive use of punctuation marks in the dialogues (Maar 2021: 505). To underpin his stylistic observations, Maar cites two examples, one from *Bambi*:

"We'd better stop talking about things like that," said the first leaf.

"Yeah, we'd better leave it," the other replied. "Only ... what we going to talk about now then?"

They became silent, but after a short time resumed the subject. "Who d'you think's going to be the first of us to go down there, then...?"

"It won't be for a while yet," the first reassured him. "Let's just think about how beautiful it used to be, how wonderfully beautiful! When the sun came out and burned us so hot it seemed we'd just swell up with all the good health it gave us. Remember? And then there was the dew, early in the morning ... and the lime trees, wonderful nights ..."

"The nights are horrible now," whined the second. "They never seem to come to an end."

"We can't complain," said the first leaf gently, "we've lived longer than so many others." [...]

"Well, thank you," the second leaf whispered, feeling quite touched. "I'm not sure I believe you ... well not everything ... but thank you for it. You are so good to me ... and you always" "have been ... it's only now that I'm starting to understand how good you've always been to me."

"Oh, stop it now," said the first, and became silent himself. He could not talk anymore because he was upset. (Salten 2020)

For comparison, Maar quotes a passage from *Mutzenbacher* in which he focuses only on punctuation:

Oh my god ... this is good ... I like that ... slowly we have time.

Rudolf ... I'm coming...

And Zenzi whispers: Ah ... fuck me ... make a child with me ... yes ... bite my nipples ... bite my nipples ... Rudolf ... fuck me ... fuck me. (Maar 2021: 506)

His conclusion: "only one and the same author distributes ellipses in the dialogue with the evenness of a salt shaker" (Maar 2021: 506). Maar's examples chosen are symptomatic of the use of ellipses in infantile speech. Suspension points are, indeed, a means of expressing something that one does not know or cannot say. In the quotation from *Bambi*, the leaves are discussing "What happens to us after we've fallen?"—that is, death. They don't know what death is and neither does Bambi. In the case of *Josefine Mutzenbacher*, the suspensions are a way to express sexuality which, for her as a child, is an unknown dimension. In this case the ellipses can also be the way to censor what the writer cannot express with words so as not to offend public decency.

What is surprising is that the observations made by Dietmar Schmitt, Claudia Öhlschlager, and Michael Maar based on "close reading" can be confirmed, with a completely different method: stylometry based on "distant reading." While the correlations found by literary critics are based on content similarities or textual details such as punctuation that can be picked up by the naked eye, stylometry focuses on the recurrence of the most frequent words. We can recognize this very easily in the list of the 100 MFW of *Josefine Mutzenbacher*.

1–10	11–20	21–30	31–40	41–50	51–60	61–70	71–80	81–90	91–100
und	in	sich	ihm	Zenzi	Vater	Rudolf	mehr	Schweif	wollte
ich	so	s	noch	dann	eine	nach	bei	Mund	Frau
er	das	es	nur	hatte	wenn	hand	uns	Brust	Herr
die	mit	dass	auch	den	ihr	aus	einmal	ihre	liess
sie	war	an	ist	schon	seinen	Mutter	nein	nichts	Ekhard
der	auf	was	da	hat	im	immer	dir	dich	gleich
mir	den	ein	sagte	als	vor	kam	voegeln	fragte	einem
mich	aber	ja	wir	wieder	hab	mein	einen	meinte	dabei
nicht	du	von	dem	ganz	sein	doch	na	Schwanz	man
zu	wie	ihn	jetzt	meine	seine	hast	gut	Bett	weil

Table 10: The 100 Most Frequent Words in *Josefine Mutzenbacher*

As is obvious, most of the words in this list are function words—pronouns, conjunctions, prepositions, or articles, for example—which have little lexical meaning on their own and are used to express grammatical relationships. In contrast, content words (proper names or nouns that name objects, adjectives to indicate the attributes of objects, verbs that refer to actions, and adverbs to indicate the attributes of actions) have semantic content and contribute to the overall meaning of a sentence. The first three columns of the most frequent words in *Josefine Mutzenbacher* consist only of function words: the first content word is "sagte," which means "said," at position 38. In the following columns are other common verbs such as "hatte/had" (44), "kam/came" (68), "fragte/asked" (88), "meinte/meant" (89), and "wollte/wanted" (92). Because *Josefine Mutzenbacher* is a memoir, all the verbs are in the past tense. This also explains why "Ich/I" is the second most used word in the novel, but the first names of and nouns referring to the protagonists are not among the most frequent words: "Zenzi" (41), "Vater" (51), "Rudolf" (61), "Mutter" (65), and "Ekhard" (95). This shows that the comparison of the different corpora was based on function words, which are independent of the semantic dimension expressed by content words. We can find confirmation for this circumstance in the ranking of words related to sexual vocabulary which have an eminent importance in an erotic novel. The German words for penis, "Schweif" and "Schwanz," occur only at positions 81 and 89 and "vögeln" ("fuck") only at position 77. The primacy of the sexual dimension is highlighted by the keyness analysis in Figure 20. It compares the frequencies of single words in a text with those in a larger reference corpus. Thus, the reference corpus words acts as a statistical norm against which the vocabulary of the analysed text may be contrasted. The output is a list of words that deviate from that reference corpus and expresses the keyness of a text. The latter is closely related to the notion of "aboutness," which is the understanding of the main concepts and topics discussed in a text or corpus. Keyness therefore provides a representation of important concepts in a certain cultural or linguistic framework.

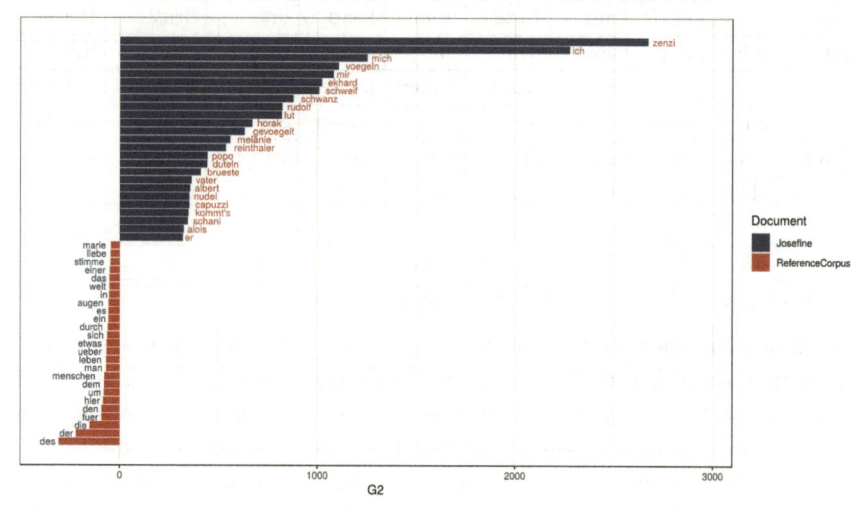

Figure 20: Keyness Analysis of the Mutzenbacher Novel and the Reference Corpus

For the Mutzenbacher novel, keyness analysis extracted not only the names of the protagonists (Zenzi, Ekhard, Schani) but also the text's sexual vocabulary ("vögeln," "gevögelt," "kommt's") and terms for the related anatomy ("Schweif," "Schwanz," "Popo," "Brüste," "Nudel"). None of these words appears in the reference corpus published by other writers.

The stylometric analyses in this chapter show their pliability and their dual relationship to literary interpretation and theory. On the one hand, stylometric analysis allows a satisfactory answer to the question of who wrote *Josefine Mutzenbacher*. On the other, the data that emerged during the analysis give rise to new questions about the author of the novel's ending and the proximity between the Mutzenbacher novel and *Bambi*. This potentially inexhaustible circularity between theory and experimentation, which we expressed in our model on the "operationalisation of literary theory" (see Figure 2 in Chapter 2), makes operationalisation a valuable methodological resource for current literary criticism.

5.   Sentiment Analysis in Twitter: Felix Meimberg's Twitterature (2011)

For some time, the world after the extinction of the human being has become a common focus of reflections on the "posthuman." Rosi Braidotti, whose work concerns "life after the individual, the species, death" (Braidotti 2014), is one of the eminent theorists of the field. In Braidotti's view, the posthuman is not a new category, but it challenges traditional models of life, economy, the body, and society. The classical ideal of the human being as the "measure of all things" was epitomised during the Italian Renaissance by Leonardo da Vinci's Vitruvian Man, the representation of an ethical, aesthetic, and intellectual ideal. In the development of that ideal, the Enlightenment glorified the rational abilities of the human subject.

According to Braidotti, the crisis of the "human," and of the "humanism" based upon it, is only partially connected to rapid technological development. As early as the sixties, the human "ideal" was knocked off its pedestal and deconstructed by philosophers such as Jacques Derrida and Luce Irigaray (Braidotti 2014: 32–33), who reconfigured this supposedly natural ideal as an historical construct and, consequently, as contingent. The ideal human had also taken on characteristic traits—"white, European and beautiful"—which, from Braidotti's perspective, make him appear to be the "macho of his species." Moreover, though supposedly characterised by moral perfection and the ability to reason, the behaviour of this ideal human throughout history (colonialism, the Holocaust, and Hiroshima, to name only a few examples) had been questionable.

Today, ethical issues can no longer be ignored in a world dominated by robots and artificial intelligence, Braidotti affirms, going on to ask who should be held morally responsible for these powerful and ubiquitous "artificial" beings: the engineer, the programmer, the manufacturer, or the operator? (Braidotti 2014: 52). The distinction between machine and human, between nature and culture is no longer guaranteed. Hardware and the biological body are networked via interfaces (Braidotti 2014: 155). In such a world, intersubjectivity no longer takes place only between people, and interactions between humans and machines and among humans in virtual dimensions is increasingly common. In this context of "empathy in computer-mediated communication" (Pinotti 2011: 170), physical presence is replaced by an avatar.

Nanotechnologies, biotechnologies, computer science, and the cognitive sciences are trying to explore this new world scientifically. Through biotechnologies, humans can intervene in the genomes of humans and other living beings. The laboratory-produced sheep Dolly is a prime example. These scientific achievements are implemented on a gigantic scale by late capitalism and used to exploit both nature and other human beings.

This new historical phase, according to Braidotti, demands a "post-anthropocentrism" in which life is no longer seen as the right of a species. Life is to be considered not only as human life *qua bios*—life lived in and with the world—but as *qua zoë*, which includes both human and non-human life (Braidotti 2014: 68). In this perspective, death takes on a different meaning, representing a "continuum" in which *bios* and *zoë* are intermingled (Braidotti 2014: 146). Braidotti considered it necessary to extend the fundamental rights of humans to all other living beings, and she has demanded an "embrace that unites the different species" (Braidotti 2014: 93). In fact, the Anthropocene, characterized by human ideals, is proving to be both self-destructive and a mortal danger to the planet. The predatory schemes of capitalism have led to the climate crisis and to doubts about the sustainability of human life.

5.1. Posthuman Scenarios in Reality and Fiction

Braidotti's radical analysis set the anthropological background for Florian Meimberg's unique contemporary literary work, *Tiny Tales: Sehr kurze Geschichten—Auf die Länge kommt es an/Tiny Tales: Very Short Stories—It's the Length that Matters* (Meimberg 2011). These are texts that originated on the Internet, or more precisely on Twitter, and only later found their way into book form and published by the prestigious editor Fischer. In Meimberg's collection of stories, in the compressed form of the 140 characters of a Tweet, adventurous journeys through space and time take place, but the result is almost always the same: a tragedy or the downfall of humanity. Here, antediluvian and post-apocalyptic scenarios alternate to show readers the fragility of their existence.

The theme of the annihilation of humanity—both an attraction and an aberration for audiences in Braidotti's view (Braidotti 2014: 72)—has been popularised in film and literature and has been a popular theme of dystopian literature since the second half of the twentieth century (Kermode 2000). John Christopher's *The Death of Grass* (1956) and Brian Aldiss's *Greybeard* (1964) are earlier examples, but the theme is taken to extremes in *Tiny Tales*. A perpetual sense of impending tragedy is best evidenced by three texts from *Tiny Tales*, which describes a poisoning, a poison gas attack, and a suicide bombing:

> "Guess who's back!" the little note said. Pete dropped the fortune cookie. He froze as the arsenic entered his bloodstream.

> The bubbles floated over the Champs-Elysees. Many passers-by smiled with emotion. The poison gas spread slowly and over a large area.

> The suicide belt weighed heavily. He whispered a prayer and stepped onto the balcony. St. Peter's Square was full. The 50,000 pilgrims cheered him. (Meimberg 2011: 88)

For Braidotti, creating distance from the *bios*-centred life to reach the *qua zoë* requires "a kind of alienation and repositioning" (Braidotti 2014: 96), the best means for which is a "strategy of alienation" and an "active deterritorialisation." This dis-identification opens new paths and new interpretations. Meimberg's minimalist narratives are likewise characterised by a deterritorialisation into an unknown space-time dimension.

Meimberg's micro-scenarios, however, invoke other models related to new understandings of time. Once such model in the digital world has been explored by Douglas Rushkoff's 2013 *Present Shock: When Everything Happens Now.* Digital technologies have changed society's perception of time such that the present, what is "going on now," occupies the centre of the horizon. This extreme focus on the now has had consequences on our cognitive system, which no longer allows us to follow linear reasoning, make plans, build or reconstruct lengthy narratives in history, or focus. We live a "present shock" Rushkoff says (2013: 4), in which time becomes a technological matter. The shock is a consequence of the dissonance between our digital identities and our analogue selves.

Today's society has thus freed itself from the tyranny of the past; it is no longer in our memory, whether individual or collective, but has been handed over to computers as information where it is stored with billions of other bits. The "now" that dominates this way of life is not the one that is presently experienced, but the one that has just passed and is publicized in the social media (Rushkoff 2013: 6). Twitter is one of the protagonists of this new global behavioural scheme; it presents itself as the social network that registers "everything that is going on":

> Narrativity and goals are surrendered to a skewed notion of the real and the immediate —the Tweet, the status update. What we are doing at any given moment becomes all-important—which is behavioristically doomed. For this desperate approach to time is at once flawed and narcissistic" (Rushkoff 2013: 6).

Digital time thus replaces chronological time, and digital time rushes on because the digital universe is always up to date with breaking news, trends, emails, posts to read (Rushkoff 2013: 73–74). These inputs strain our ability to concentrate and urge us to focus on something that happened elsewhere and else "when" (Rushkoff 2013: 86; Gazzaley & Rosen 2016).

Digital time is non-linear, disembodied, and associative. Our sense of time thus becomes dependent on the media that provide a constant flow of information. Rushkoff, however, has emphasized again and again that the chronological now and the digital now of Twitter do not correspond: what is "now" for Twitter is, strictly speaking, already past (Rushkoff 2013: 142). The time travel that is so characteristic of Meimberg's narratives appears to Rushkoff to be a social phenomenon, which has been called "digiphrenia," the tendency of media and technologies to be simultaneously active in multiple places on the web. "Phrenia" refers to a disturbed mental state in which physical presence and ubiquitous digital presence do not harmonize, and it is therefore a digital pathology as well (Rushkoff 2013: 75).

But other elements of Meimberg's poetics find explication in Rushkoff's model. "Overwinding" (Rushkoff 2013: 7) is described as the tendency to squeeze large periods of time into much smaller ones, as can be seen in many *Tiny Tales*. "Apocalypto" perhaps best describes Meimberg's apocalyptic visions; Rushkoff describes it as "a belief in the imminent shift of humanity into an unrecognizably different form" (Rushkoff 2013: 245). These apocalyptic visions of "the collapse of civilization due to nuclear accident … or SARS epidemic" offer an exit from the precarious world of "present shock" (Rushkoff 2013: 247). According to Rushkoff, these tragic narratives, which closely resemble the doomsday myths of religions, are an escape route from the endless tension of the digital present. One symptom of "apocalypto" would be TV series like *The Walking Dead*, which relocates humanity to a zombie world where it is forced to ask fundamental questions about human life. Other dystopian visions prophesy the replacement of biological beings with artificial ones and the danger that technology will take on a life of its own and become an enemy of humankind.

Time travel, deterritorialization, and the dissolution of distinctions between past and future in a digital present are not only contemporary phenomena, but are themes and narrative strategies found in Meimberg's texts. As mentioned, these texts often describe a dystopian or tragic vision of the future from which our present appears as an historical past. This creates an alienation effect, as Anne-Rose Meyer (2014: 166–69) has reflected in her categorization of the temporal paradoxes that Meimberg plays with in *Tiny Tales*. In fact, Meimberg's micro-stories seem to blur the boundaries between future and present. The poetics of *Tiny Tales* seem to have the same code as the computer programs we write today: they are written in the present, but they contain a formula that prescribes the future.

5.2. The Function of Titles in *Tiny Tales*

The title of Meimberg's collection, *Tiny Tales: Very Short Stories: It's the Length That Matters* is strikingly redundant. Even in the original German version, "tiny tales" appears in the title in English; and, in English, "tiny tales" are simply short stories. Because of the brevity of Meimberg's texts, which have the maximum length of a tweet (140 characters), Carmen Pförtner defined them as "espresso-type stories" (Pförtner 2011). The definition of Meimberg's "tiny" stories is not just duplicated but even tripled in the title, which repeats the concept by emphasizing that "length matters." In contrast to the supposed focus on concision, this title is strikingly long; it could even be defined as baroque.

Meimberg's oxymoronic repetition is not accidental, as the structure of the collection's seventeen chapters makes clear. "Beginning" is the title of the first chapter, and the book comes to a close with a sixteenth chapter, "End." The title of the second chapter Lie is answered by "Truth" in the ninth. The fifth chapter is "Life," which is semantically opposed to "Death" in the fourteenth. Other semantic oppositions include "happiness" and "misfortune," "hatred" and "love," and "error" and "deception." The secondary literature has already pointed out the circularity of these titles (Nicoli 2016: 108).

The title of a literary text always directs readers' expectations. The complex structuring of the book and chapter titles in *Tiny Tales* shows that the reader's expectations—and surprising those expectations—play a prominent role. In addition, the titles seem to anticipate how they may be received by the public— surprise, deception, and error, e.g. In his preface to the collection, Sasha Lob emphasizes "What if the most important ingredient to a story were not the story itself? But rather what it triggers in us?" (Meimberg 2011: 7).

The extremely compact structure of *Tiny Tales* directs the reader's attitude (Meyer 2019: 236–40). In order to build the reader's expectations in these micro-texts, only to then systematically disappoint them, Meimberg conjures a familiar theme, motif, or story. In cognitive and narrative research, this is called a "frame," a term introduced to narratology by Umberto Eco to mean a stereotyped structure. To explain the concept of the "frame," Eco used the "supermarket" as an example: the reader must know that supermarkets sell food and not cars (Eco 1979: 80), for example, which is a presupposition of familiarity. Meimberg's poetics of decontextualization and semantic shift allows readers to see things anew. Familiar elements are constantly transposed into new contexts and, thus, are alienated, affecting the reader's cognition by dissolving fixed associations and enabling a change of perspective. This strategy is particularly striking when Meimberg refers to well-known historical figures, celebrities, familiar stories, or myths from world literature or the Bible because he affects the reader through familiarity and the satisfaction that comes from recognition.

Directly proportional is the effect of surprise at the moment when these familiar references are placed in an unexpected context or light. The surprise effect of Meimberg's Tweets can be empirically assessed as well. We tested the feedback of seventy-seven readers to eleven of Meimberg's Tweets, and the main reaction was surprise and a feeling of being lost (see Chapter 7).

Meimberg's texts often describe time travel to suggest that past and future are open dimensions, and their narratives reveal a process of objectification of the "not-yet," the utopian or possible reality. In the narratives, elements are assembled, and their combination allows possible, meaning utopian or dystopian, realities to emerge.

5.3. Travels in Time and Space

As Braidotti's and Rushkoff's analyses have foreshadowed, our posthuman digital age demands a new understanding of space-time characterized by deterritorialization, alienation, and dissolution of past and future in the digital present. Meimberg's work, born in the digital dimension of the Internet, reflects this mobility. Two forms of travel in *Tiny Tales* epitomize this new world of experience: the first is travel in time (through time machines or time jumps). The second is travel in new dimensions (in space through spaceships or through diving capsules or robots). Time machines and time jumps appear many times in the collection (Meimberg 2011: 12; 21; 97; 136; 172), just as do space shuttles (Meimberg 2011: 73; 92; 97) and diving capsules (Meimberg 2011: 56; 97).

Both forms of travel result in the alienation of common categories. Eurocentric and anthropocentric perspectives are shaken, and posthuman, non-anthropocentric points of view are described. Often, an inversion of conventional categories blurs the boundaries between human-non-human (Meimberg 2011: 55), civilization and barbarism, life and death, inside and outside (Meimberg 2011: 59). The crossing of cultural boundaries and the crisis of human civilization can be observed in Meimberg's conspicuously frequent evocations of cannibalism (Meimberg 2011: 25; 65; 128) and incest (Meimberg 2011: 22; 154; 156).

Probably the most intriguing text on the subject of the time jump of this collection is the following:

> With the Macintosh 128k under his arm, he stepped out of the time machine. "Time for a revolution!" thought the young Steve Jobs. It was 1983. (Meimberg 2011: 12)

This text connects the Internet—the medium that introduced an epochal break in the understanding of time—to time travel. The "revolution" that the young Steve Jobs announces means not only a radical change in social conditions but also a turning, a movement around an axis. As this Tweet makes clear, the

Internet is the centre from which past and future are blended in a digital now. Past and future therefore lose their contours. In 1983, Steve Jobs could not have known that he would introduce a revolution; such a statement can be made only after the fact, and thus a time machine is required to bring these dimensions into contact. But the fallout of the Internet and technology on the characters in *Tiny Tales* is anything but idyllic. In fact, it can have disastrous consequences:

> Amid the shouts of the villagers, the two men were led to the scaffold. Piet hissed: "Shitty idea, the time machine." (Meimberg 2011: 136)

Technology has become dangerous, endangering the characters' lives. From the villagers' point of view, the two men belong to a future dimension, and technology changes the men's history and the history of the villagers by bringing them into contact. The past, then, is always open to intrusions from the future.

Time travel does not have to be mentioned explicitly in Meimberg's stories; in some texts, the reader grasps it intuitively because present time is viewed from the future. Thus, the reader experiences "alienation" because the present appears as an outdated and distant past. This change of perspective also forces the reader to rethink categories of "current" and "modern":

> The discovery sent the scientific community into a state of shock: In ancient times, there had been a primitive computer network. The "internet." (Meimberg 2011: 77)

The very core of our age and, so to speak, the native habitat of *Tiny Tales*, which was born on the Internet, is declared "primitive." These decontextualization of the present and of history both shock and amuse the reader, and Meimberg takes full advantage of such reactions in Tweets in which the alienated view of a future archaeologist takes in such modern technological status symbols as the iPhone (Meimberg 2011: 72), the iPad (Meimberg 2011: 54), the Internet (Meimberg 2011: 77), and cell phones (Meimberg 2011: 95). The humour in *Tiny Tales* was appreciated by the readers who participated in our experiment (see Chapter 7).

And as is typical of Meimberg's style, the punch line of the Tweet comes at the end—exquisitely, in the following example, in the last word. For a German reader in particular, the existence of a Third World War, after the Second has been so long and profoundly remembered and rehashed, is overwhelming news:

> "No, my dear." The old man smiled at his grandson. "The scar on the arm is from the Second World War. THIS one I got from the Third." (Meimberg 2011: 59)

Both the time and the space dimensions of the reader are confused. In the next Tweet, a still unknown technique is described that allows movement within the body of an unspecified living being. A diving capsule, usually used in the sea or in lakes, is within a body, a question of a spatial inversion:

> Slowly, the diving capsule floated through the murky darkness. Wordlessly, Maurice peered through the hatch. Soon they would reach the brain. (Meimberg 2011: 56)

In this way, the boundaries between both the inside and the outside and the human and the non-human are put to the test, sometimes humorously:

> "I leave my entire estate to my beloved Maja." The notary closed the document and looked around. Maja barked. (Meimberg 2011: 115)

The heiress is revealed to be a dog, and the punch line once again appears in the last word. Through this humorous anti-speciesism, the human perspective is definitely outdated, and anti-speciesism is, above all, a matter of perspective: world history is no longer seen through the eyes of humans, but of animals, aliens, computers, or unspecified "creatures" or "beings" (Meimberg 2011: 33; 55; 109). In this new posthuman habitat, a dolphin becomes the "crown of creation" (Meimberg 2011: 53) and a penguin "the dream woman" (Meimberg 2011: 158).

In some *Tiny Tales*, time and space dimensions are intertwined as figures from the past and the future appear simultaneously:

> Spaceships hung inert over the jungle. The ancient Mayan king tapped the alien lord on the shoulder. "All in. We're good to go." (Meimberg 2011: 89)

Mayans are an extinct civilization, and aliens are a potential posthuman civilization. In these three sentences, future and past as well as nature (the jungle) and culture (spaceship, Maya) are brought together. Playfully, these Tweets allude to such fundamental concepts of Western thought as culture and civilization (*Kultur* and *Zivilisation* in German) that have been discussed for centuries. While human and non-human culture seem to coexist peacefully in this Tweet, in others, human culture must clearly give way to posthuman culture. Human history is thus viewed and alienated not only from the inside but from the outside, losing its centrality and linearity in the process because it is placed in the context of other stories and timelines. It is in time travel that beings appear that are not known today, and alien creatures are among the most common characters in *Tiny Tales*, again forcing readers into an unspecified space-time constellation from which identity is called into question:

> The president strode through the hangar, eyeing the tanks holding the captured aliens. His chief of staff whispered, "They call themselves humans." (Meimberg 2011: 51)

From an alien's point of view, a human is indeed an alien. In this case, the context does not seem to be a peaceful one, and "hangar," "tanks," and "captured" point instead to a war scenario. Such dystopian scenarios are not uncommon in *Tiny Tales*, and technology often seems to be the cause of tragic circumstances: computers, Emails, USB sticks, cell phones, and hackers bring about tragedy in

Tiny Tales, as it is typical of dystopian literature (Marks 2017: 141–55). One of the "creators" of this reality, as historically documented, is Bill Rory Gates:

> The huge cyborg army marched toward the distant horizon. The steel creatures awaited new orders from their creator: Rory Gates. (Meimberg 2011: 15)

Bill Gates is called here, perhaps endearingly, by his middle name, Rory. For his creatures, he is *de facto* a father figure, but he also seems to be the commander of troops. By definition, a cyborg is a hybrid of biological organism and machine, and here they have been formed into an army. Here, the dystopian nature of Meimberg's narratives becomes apparent as current trends are taken to extremes, and scenes of war are no exception:

> "… significant works from the age of religious wars." The museum guide paused. "This one circa: 2078, The Battle of Google." (Meimberg 2011: 33)

The narrative perspective places the reader in the future, certainly after 2078. Not only is the present long gone, but the future (2078) has become a museum object, and Google, a corporation, is connected to the Wars of Religion. What is left behind is often a post-apocalyptic world in which cities like Los Angeles (Meimberg 2011: 16; 36; 46) or Hamburg (Meimberg 2011: 35) are destroyed, Manhattan (Meimberg 2011: 30) is under water, and Berlin has become an "island full of cannibals" (Meimberg 2011: 65). In these cases, nature seems to have taken revenge on technological progress by nullifying human culture.

5.4. Perfection on Social Media and As the Accomplished Time of Historical Facts

In his studies of *Tiny Tales*, Roberto Nicoli attempted what might be called a philological gesture, locating the texts in their original medium of Twitter. This is not only comprehensible from a philological perspective; it allows us to understand the connection of these texts to social media.

As we know, social media like Twitter are a screen onto which the narcissism of millions of users can be projected. Vacations, weddings, awards, feelings of success, and moments of happiness are displayed to feed the digital ego. *Tiny Tales*, while referring to these narcissisms, also plays with the values and views of society and, as the next text suggests, with the expectations and scenarios associated with marriage:

> Gently, he put the wedding ring on her finger. The moment was perfect. He touched her cheek. Rigor mortis had set in. (Meimberg 2011: 11)

The text opens with a classic frame of a marriage proposal with all the usual elements: the ring, the cheek, the romantic moment. Then comes the disillusionment, or rather the classic surprise finale, in which the adjective "perfect" stands out. The opening scene is, or seems, "perfect" because it promises the happiness of a love story. But happiness, as the last sentence conveys, is only a promise. As frequently happens in *Tiny Tales*, love and death co-exist (Meimberg 2011: 24). The word "perfect" and its variants occurs eight times in Meimberg's micro-stories. Here is another example from the same page:

> The doctors looked at him in silence. "I can't feel my legs," Edwin lied. The plan was going perfectly. His new life had begun. (Meimberg 2011: 11)

This text describes a new beginning for Edward. Change is brought about through Edwin's plan, which has progressed "perfectly." But the plan is not perfect. First, it is based on a lie in which Edwin states that he is paralyzed. This use of "perfect" forces us to doubt the typical positive connotations of this word. Indeed, perfect means not only "incredibly good," "excellent," but also, especially if we consider its Latin root, *perfectus*, something that has been accomplished or completed. Something perfect(ed), then, lies in a past that is strictly closed off from the present. It is precisely this perfection that causes Meimberg's narratives to waver. The perfect, completed fact is reopened and subjected to a new interpretation. In the example of Edwin and his doctors, the text encourages a reconsideration of the boundary between truth and lies, disease and health. That boundaries are at stake is shown in the next example as well:

> Sue stepped out of the shower. The water beaded over her flawless body. Today would begin. Day 001. Inside her, the processor core hummed. (Meimberg 2011: 13)

Here, substance is expressed by elements that reflect one of the society's highest values: female beauty. This flawless—that is, perfect—body is, in addition, naked because Sue is taking a shower. But Sue cannot be a specimen of female beauty because, as the "humming" of the processor signals, she is a cyborg or an automaton. Once again, the perfect situation is broken down, pitting basic categories like human and non-human against each other.

The rupture of perfection is a form of time travel as well. Meimberg's narratives break the sanctity of past and future by infusing possibility into these dimensions. They retrospectively alter stories or myths of the past or prospectively imagine events of the future. The triggers of these narratives are questions such as "what if?" By posting them, the course of history is changed or events are allowed to reach an unexpected outcome. What, for example, what would happen if the brain of a mafia boss were transplanted into a child? (Meimberg 2011: 94). What if Eve had rejected Adam? (Meimberg 2011: 26). What if Gutenberg had destroyed his invention? (Meimberg 2011: 15). What would Nostradamus have written down if he had talked to a "stranger from the future"? (Meimberg 2011: 26). What would modern times look like if Columbus had not set foot in America? (Meimberg 2011: 41). And how would the narration of the New Testament change if Judas had declined to betray Jesus because he did not consider his payment appropriate? (Meimberg 2011: 84). Meimberg also transforms well-known myths of the past:

> The king of Troy eyed the huge wooden horse. "Is that the best you can do, Agamemnon?" Smiling, he turned: "Ignite!" (Meimberg 2011: 102)

The wooden horse of Troy, according to the myth that has been handed down in Western history, is an example of cunning, a ruse devised by Agamemnon to conquer Troy. In the finale of Meimberg's mini-narrative, however, the cohesiveness of the myth, its perfection, is attacked by Meimberg's corrosive poetics, and its narrative is overthrown. Meimberg's poetics extend as far as the Bible:

> "Sorry. I have a boyfriend." Eva lied. She didn't like the guy right away. "Too bad," Adam muttered and disappeared back into the woods. (Meimberg 2011: 26)

The Old Testament Eve is given a contemporary ambience through the juvenile use of the English word "sorry" or the colloquial form for man, "guy." But the story gets a new twist.

Meimberg is not concerned with the content of the stories and myths he uses as models; he needs, as Warhol did in his silkscreens, only their aura. The most famous characters of the Grimm fairy tales—Hansel and Gretel, Little Red Riding Hood, and Mother Holle, for example—appear in *Tiny Tales*, and whether the foundation is a real personality, a fictional character, a myth, or a fairy tale is irrelevant. The aura can be that of a historical occurrence such as the bombing of Dresden which, in the distorted vision of Meimberg's tales, reoccurred in "November 2014" (Meimberg 2011: 52). Subverting historical and chronological order, the genius of Mozart is transformed into the genius of Dalí (Meimberg 2011: 108), and even a modern icon like Lady Diana can be invoked.

> "I've changed my mind. I'd rather stay at the hotel." Tiredly, she waved to the crowd. Then Lady Di disappeared into the elevator. (Meimberg 2011: 107)

What if Lady Di had not left the Paris hotel? If we could turn back time, perhaps she wouldn't have gotten into the car that was involved in the accident that killed her. Because our culture is full of stories and myths, Meimberg is spoiled for choice in the use of these materials.

For Meimberg, the Internet is not just an endless supply of stories and myths, it has become a second reality, a reality that lays claim to reality and is itself reality-creating. The facts and stories circulating on the Internet can become "alternative facts" on which a post-factual politics is based. That these terms are the subject of Meimberg's reflections is shown by titles such as "Truth," "Lie," "Error," and "Delusion." An author has a special function in this post-factual world:

> "Bonus number: 7," he typed. Then he closed the laptop. He loved being an author. In the living room, the television murmured: "Supplementary number: 7." (Meimberg 2011: 84)

An author who loves his work writes a text that foretells a media reality subsequently broadcast on television. This author in this example has probably written the script of a film or a TV programme, but an author can be more powerful as well:

> The author was crying. He had just let his main character die. Gently, he wrapped the body in a rubbish bag. (Meimberg 2011: 149)

The author has the power to create a character, but, as the example shows, also to let the character die. Here we have a metaliterary punch line. What triggers the reader's shock is not that the character dies in the text but that the author wraps the corpse in a rubbish bag—that is, wraps it in a real, physical sense. Boundaries between reality and fiction are blurred, as the emotional reaction of the author shows. If the Internet can assert alternative facts, then fiction and reality can lay claim to equality, and the author becomes a demiurge who can act on reality. In this context, we must not forget that Meimberg is a creative director and has used his creativity for advertising campaigns (Meimberg 2022). Advertising implies that texts and images can influence reality, which is the intended effect and, for Meimberg, advertising has affinities with literature (Meimberg 2011: 179). This influence can be seen in the following example:

> Tom opened the old book and began to read: "Tom opened the old book and began to read. He still had no idea that his death was near." (Meimberg 2011: 150)

Tom is reading a book in which he is the main character. His fate is prescribed but is hidden from him and, as is so often the case for Meimberg's characters, tragic. Thus fiction intervenes in the real fate of an individual, but it can do the same in historical fate:

> The End. His novel about the WTC attacks was finished. He closed the laptop, looked at the clock. It was almost midnight. It was 10 September 2001. (Meimberg 2011: 166)

Once again, a writer, in this case explicitly a novelist, is foregrounded. He finishes a novel in which the attacks on the World Trade Center are described, but his fiction prophesies the event with a day's notice. Historiography, as Hayden White has pointed out, follows a narrative structure (White 2000), but here history can even be considered a product of fiction. Our twenty-first century could therefore appear to be the product of a director, and at the change of scene Satan smiles:

"Cuuut!" The director's voice resounded across the set. "Perfect! Conversion to the next scene: 21st century." Satan smiled. (Meimberg 2011: 105)

5.5. Sentiment Analysis in Twitterature and on Twitter

The Internet is a global medium that has not only incorporated all other media but has given rise to a new reality. It is no coincidence that the media are one of the leitmotifs of Meimberg's collection (Meimberg 2011: 44; 63). Meimberg's texts are an example of Twitterature, a new genre that is a hybrid of two media and which has recently attracted the attention of literary critics (Freuler 2011; Drees & Meyer 2013; Kreuzmair 2017; Kreuzmair & Pflock 2020).

If one wants to do justice to this hybrid literature, Meimberg's "tales" must perforce be treated as Tweets. Tweets, according to their inventor, Jack Dorsey, respond to the question, "What's going on right now?". Nowadays, millions of people use social networks like Twitter to express emotions and opinions and to share views about their daily lives, and the content they create is focused on the present, on a feeling, on an experience or thought. Through online communities, the result is an interactive media that allows consumers to inform and influence others. Tweets thus diffuse a sentiment or a mood through language, hashtags, or emoticons.

This is why Tweets are combed by Internet companies to discover users' reactions to products and events (Kharde & Sonawane 2016), and so-called sentiment analysis, in its commercial application, attempts to capture positive or negative opinions. Sentiment analysis in Twitter can be defined as a process that automates the mining of attitudes, opinions, views, and emotions through Natural Language Processing (NLP), classifying them into categories like "positive," "negative," or "neutral." Today, the Internet provides a large repository of reviews and feedback on almost everything (on "rating culture" see Chapter 7), including products, political issues, and taxi, hotel, or restaurant service, and research has increasingly developed computational techniques to retrieve feedback or ratings on Twitter (Antonakaki *et al.* 2021). Here we are again in the familiar field of advertising for Meimberg.

In recent years, however, sentiment analysis has become a useful method in literary research (Rebora 2020a; Zehe *et al.* 2017) precisely because emotions have become such a pressing topic in literary studies. Not only can texts describe a wide range of emotions but readers' reactions to literary texts are highly charged with emotion, and they can be studied (Rebora 2020a: 215). Paul Ekman has reduced human emotions to seven basic types: joy, anger, disgust, fear, contempt, sadness, and surprise. In the case of Meimberg's collection of stories, sentiment analysis is suggested for an intrinsic reason: Two of the chapter titles in *Tiny Tales* are directly related to Ekman's basic emotions: "Fear" (Meimberg 2011: 63) and "Surprise" (Meimberg 2011: 72) name two basic emotions. In addition, two titles, "Happiness" (Meimberg 2011: 112) and "Hate" (Meimberg 2011: 82), are strongly related to the basic emotions "Joy" and "Anger." The title "Love" (Meimberg 2011: 152) does not describe a basic emotion in Ekman's terms, but it does indicate a high level of emotion. Sentiment analysis measures the statistical frequency of the vocabulary of these emotions in a text. We applied this method to *Tiny Tales* to test two hypotheses:

- Do the titles "Fear," "Surprise," "Happiness," and "Anger" correspond to the 'sentiment' of the texts in the chapters that bear them?
- How does the 'sentiment' of *Tiny Tales* differ from that of the Tweets posted during the same period on German Twitter?

The answer to the first question requires a sentiment analysis of the three chapters mentioned above in addition to Chapter 8, "Hate" (Meimberg 2011: 81). For this analysis we used "sentiart" (Jacobs 2019), a standard instrument for sentiment analysis in German corpora.

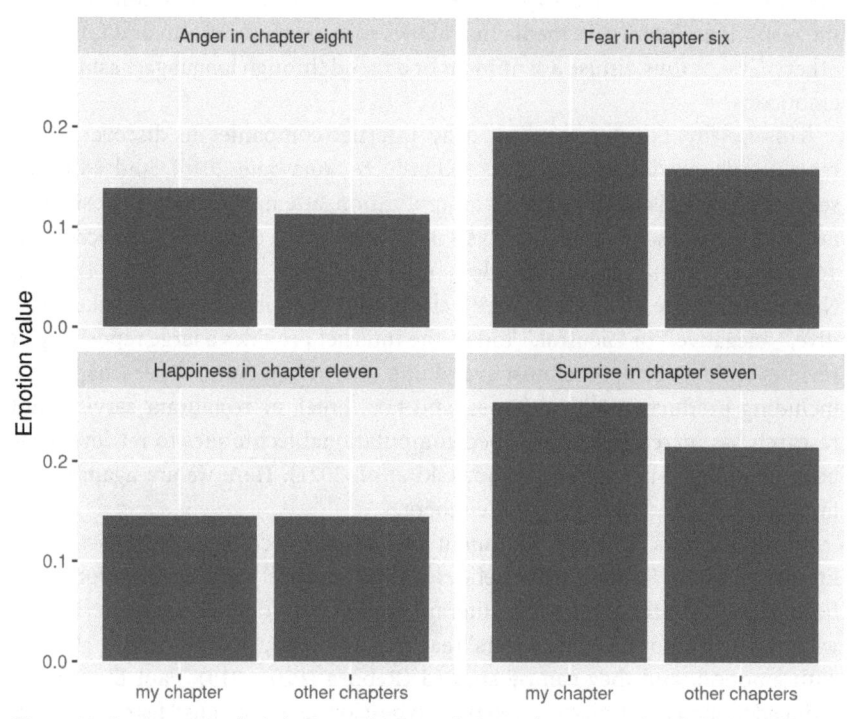

Figure 21: Sentiment Analysis in Four Chapters of *Tiny Tales* compared with the Sentiment of the Other Chapters

The results show that the base emotion indicated by each chapter title predominated in that chapter when compared to the presence of the same base emotion in other chapters. Our sentiment analysis revealed that Chapter 11 ("Happiness"), for example, contained more of the base emotion "Happiness," though the difference was minimal, an unsurprising finding in a collection of stories focused primarily on apocalyptic motifs and tragedy. The classification of Tweets within chapters also corresponded to chapter titling. Titles such as "Surprise" or "Fear" synthesized Meimberg's dystopian and alienating poetics and are guides for the reader. As other studies have shown, the emotions of readers and the sentiments of literary texts can be more-or-less attuned (Pianzola *et al.* 2020). Although this is interesting, Meimberg's texts are so short that the differences expressed in the graphs are not confirmed by statistical analyses of the p-value.

Having established the internal coherence of the collection, we wanted to explore whether basic emotions predominated compared to other texts through the use of external comparison. Research by Roberto Nicoli showed that Meimberg began posting his Tweets in October 2009, and his book was published in November 2011 (Nicoli 2013: 224), but we returned Meimberg's Tweets to their "natural habitat" by constructing a comparison with a corpus of Tweets in German from 2011. The corpus used contains one million Tweets and a total of 19,550,672 words.

Figure 22 shows the Affective-Aesthetic Potential value (AAP), which is to say the aesthetic/emotional potential of a text. We started with a very large corpus, which contained all German tweets from 2011. We then converted all the words in the corpus into vectors and calculated the distances between all the words and the sixty positive/negative ones to generate a "sentiment dictionary" in which each word was associated with a positive or negative value. We then took the Meimberg texts and assigned emotional values to each by counting the words and summing their values in the sentiment dictionary. The result with respect to *Tiny Tales* shows that their emotional valence is average.

The analysis of the Ekman's six basic emotions (excluding Contempt) yields more interesting results. As Figure 23 demonstrates, negatively charged emotions predominate and only Happiness is close to the average. The dystopian character of the mini-narratives in Meimberg's collection can also be seen in the vocabulary they deploy, as other studies have highlighted (Gius *et al.* 2020).

The results of the last graph show that Meimberg's collection of stories, as we have demonstrated in our hermeneutic approach, describes negative scenarios and uses the vocabulary necessary to do so. These results can be compared with those from automatic sentiment analysis on Tweets in German posted in the same time frame (Cieliebak *et al.* 2017).

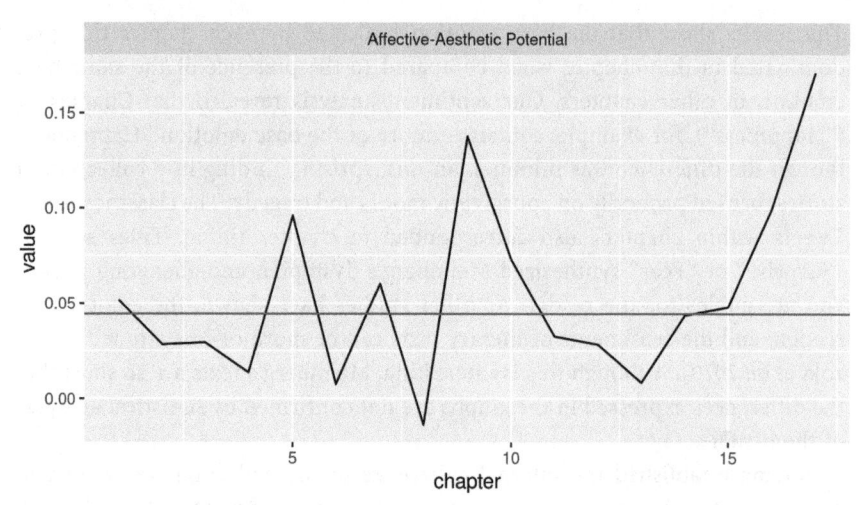

Figure 22: Affective-Aesthetic Potential of *Tiny Tales* Compared to the Sentiments of Tweets in German from 2011

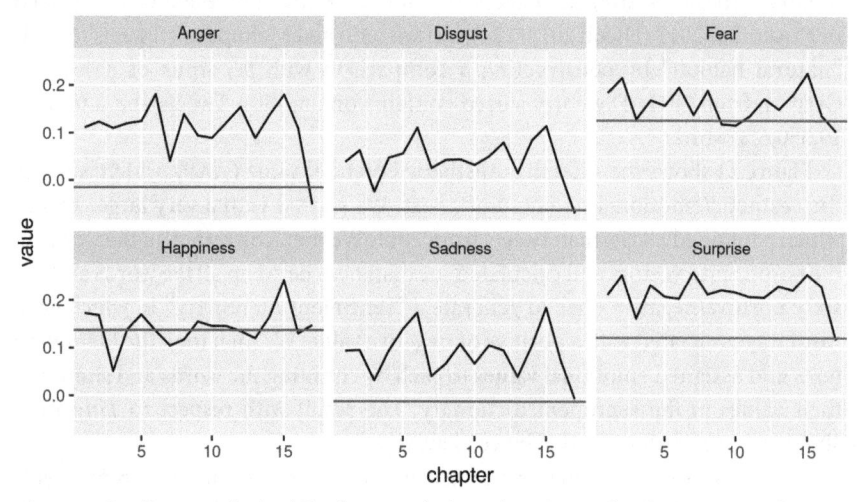

Figure 23: Sentiment Analysis of Six Chapters of *Tiny Tales* Compared to the Sentiment of Tweets in German from 2011

Meimberg's "tiny stories" are the manifestation of a "not-yet," the utopia of a posthuman world. In this vision, an atavistic human fear is realized: the extinction of humankind, the devastation of the earth, the annihilation of civilization. Meimberg's "worst possible" scenario surpasses classic dystopian literary themes by more than a little. The operationalization of our research questions permitted us to appreciate the main features of this contemporary dystopian literature in different ways.

6. Character Style and Emotions: Daniel Glattauer's Email Novel *Love Virtually* (2006)

Daniel Glattauer's novel, *Gut gegen Nordwind/Love Virtually* (2012), published in Germany in 2006, depicts the reality of virtual love through social media. At the beginning of the novel, the protagonist, Emma Rothner (known as Emmi throughout the novel), writes an email to cancel a subscription to a magazine published by the Like Publishing House. She receives a reply from a certain Leo Leike, who has received her message by mistake. This miscommunication, prompted by a typo, develops into a lively email exchange and an interpersonal relationship that is increasingly charged with emotion but which culminates in no real-life rendezvous. This love story cannot have a happy ending because Emmi is already married to Bernhard and is not ready to give up her marriage. Until the end of the novel, whether Leo exists as an actual person or is merely a computer program or an artificial intelligence remains unresolved. Closely related is the question of the reality and authenticity of his emotions.

Glattauer's *Love Virtually* is innovative at the formal level as well. It is the first email novel in German literature, and the love story between Leo and Emmi is depicted in 785 email messages. *Love Virtually* quickly became a bestseller and has been adapted several times for theatre and film, though fitting the novel into the genre of pop literature is difficult. Indeed, *Love Virtually* deals with fundamental questions of mediality, individuality, and corporeality, which have taken on new contours as a result of computerization and "virtualization," and has consequently been included in the canon of twenty-first-century literature and recommended as school reading (Hayer 2015). Thanks to the book's great success, Glattauer published a sequel in 2009: *Alle Sieben Wellen/All Seven Waves* (Glattauer 2009).

6.1. Virtual Reality Created by Computer-Mediated Communication

The secondary literature has examined the Internet-based communications between Leo and Emmi from several perspectives, but the "virtualness" of the relationship has not been sufficiently explored. The relationship between Leo and Emma is virtual because it is lived only on the Internet and because their email exchange requires a computer, thus becoming "computer-mediated communication" in the truest sense of the term. The computer not only facilitates communication between the characters, it "actively" participates in their conversation twice by sending automatic error notices from Leo. This makes it clear both that the computer is the medium of the love relationship and that it has the power to make the relationship impossible:

> *Ten seconds later*
> Subject: Delivery Status Notification (Returned)
> This is an automatically generated Delivery Status Notification.
> THIS EMAIL ADDRESS HAS CHANGED. THE RECIPIENT CAN NO LONGER RE-
> CEIVE MAIL SENT TO THIS ADDRESS. ALL INCOMING MAIL WILL BE DELETED
> AUTOMATICALLY. FOR ANY QUERIES, PLEASE CONTACT THE SYSTEMS MAN-
> AGER. (Glattauer 2012: 280)

The novel ends with this email written in capital letters. Symptomatic of the centrality of the computer in their relationship, Leo writes: "I never intended to get to know you more closely than the electronic exchange of letters makes possible." And it is not Leo but the computer that Bernhard defines as "the cosmos of [Emmi's] dreams" (Glattauer 2012: 231). Interestingly, even attentive readers often fail to notice that a computer also has its say in the novel; they only recognize three voices in the novel (i.e., Leo, Emmi, and Bernhard; see Wastl 2010: 77 and Kusche 2012: 148).

The computer is a medium that, in general understanding, transmits data and thus plays a crucial role as a channel for human communication. We are usually unaware of the channels that convey our communications, although unmediated communication does not actually exist. The human voice, but also the letter, the radio, and the television are media, and messages must always be communicated through a medium. Despite their tendency to remain invisible, media channels demand specific codes of interaction that change their consciousness and thinking of the communication partners. Leo is aware of the mediality of the email-writing process because computer-mediated communication, as a means for the transmission of emotions, is the subject of his research. This mediated writing process becomes a theme elsewhere in the text—for example, when Leo points out that Emmi's name is a sequence of hand movements on the keyboard: "I like writing Emmi. Left middle finger once, right index finger twice and, the rows above that, right middle finger" (Glattauer 2012: 110).

Emmi's and Leo's function as readers and writers in front of a screen becomes all the more relevant in light of the fact that the narrator's position otherwise remains empty in Love Virtually: no narrative entity directs the action, comments on it, or provides an external perspective on the characters (Kusche 2012: 147). Even a fictional editor of Emmi's and Leo's messages, traditionally a popular technical device to guarantee a consistent point of view in the multiple perspectives of the epistolary novel, is not present in Love Virtually. Rather, both the beginning and the end of the novel are produced by interventions of the medium and not, as is common, by the narrator: the beginning is marked by an informatic miscommunication, the finale by an automated error message sent by the computer itself.

Emmi's and Leo's relationship is virtual in a figurative sense as well because it takes place only at a distance and is consequently lived out in the participants' fantasies (Glattauer 2012: 20). Emmi requires a clear demarcation between her "real life" and the "other world" (Glattauer 2012: 130) of her virtual relationship with Leo. Because they never meet, their identity is based on the self-dramatizations of the writing process. Aware of this circumstance, they rename themselves "Fantasy Emmi" and "Virtual Leo" (Glattauer 2012: 104).

Emmi realizes that she has fallen in love with Leo through a written medium. Her computer-generated feelings may be a mistake, and the actual Leo hidden behind the emails may not be the man she thinks she loves. The computer-mediated communication of Love Virtually has spawned a new literary genre, the email novel, which has a noble ancestor in the epistolary novel.

Research has already shown the novel's proximity to the epistolary novel and to that genre's metalinguistic and metaliterary richness (Dupont 2014; Ketelsen 2009). For Schneider-Özbek (2011: 353), Glattauer is "attempting a modification of the genre [of epistolary novel] in light of technological innovations." Sabine Kusche (2012: 32), who convincingly defined the email novel as the "epistolary novel of the twenty-first century," showed the continuities and ruptures between the two genres. Significantly, the novel incorporates itself into this new genre; thus Leo once calls his writing partner, "Emmi the heroine in my email novel" (Glattauer 2012: 156).

It is above all the emails from Emmi's husband, Bernhard, that illustrate the distance between the email novel and the epistolary novel. Bernhard admits at the beginning that email is an unusual form of contact for him. He addresses Leo as "Dear Mr. Leike" (Glattauer 2012: 228), imitating a formal letter. He also reads his wife's correspondence on paper because Emmi has printed out the emails. Compared to the letter, writing in the digital age generally leaves no material trace: the emails do not make it possible to interpret the writer's handwriting nor to experience the odour of the paper.

The two main characters seem to be aware of their "virtual togetherness" (Glattauer 2012: 32). Their professional occupations provide them with the necessary background for this knowledge: Leo is a psycholinguist working on a study about the influence of email, and Emmi is a web designer. The Internet is relevant to them both professionally and privately: "We don't have faces…. We don't live in any particular time. All we've got is our computer screens" (Glattauer 2012: 20).

Emmi and Leo create a parallel universe for themselves that is a "virtual alternative" (Glattauer 2012: 131) to their everyday lives. It is, in fact, a "second life," similar to the successful platform of a few years ago on which participants' avatars could meet in a virtual dimension.

The temporal space in which they find themselves is virtual as well. The introductory email to the novel is the only one with a specific date, January 15 of an undefined year. All other messages are instead preceded by a temporal designation that allows no relationship to the everyday world: "Eight minutes later," "33 days later," "the next day" (Wastl 2010: 99–111). In their email exchanges, Emmi and Leo constitute a counter-world within a specific space-time. This "heterotopia" is separate from the writers' daily lives and stands as a virtual place in opposition to everyday life (Kusche 2012: 152–53). Both temporality and spatiality are virtual because, in contrast to traditional correspondence, spatial distance is irrelevant to the email exchange.

Their writing is no less a struggle with time: Leo and Emmi "write for the impossible present" (Gellai 2015: 153), attempting to reach the "now." In their messages, a paradoxical situation of lack of presence is created. Because they are pen pals writing and reading, they are simultaneously absent and present, near and far. Moreover, it is not possible for the email writer to experience and report an event simultaneously. Despite the simultaneity of digital communication, the writer's present never exactly matches that of the reader. Because the present is insufficient, the immediate future, which promises the (virtual) presence of the other, becomes "a magnet that ties the protagonists to their screens" (Gellai 2015: 156). Emmi and Leo, until the end of the novel, invent and anticipate a meeting that will never take place.

Their email exchanges, especially in comparison to traditional correspondence, are also characterized by speed, a shortening of response times, and the resulting desire for a response and acceleration of the exchange. Leo and Emmi discuss the matter of speed several times:

Four days later
Subject: Open questions
Dear Ms. Rothner,
Please forgive me for not having replied earlier, but my life is somewhat chaotic at the moment. You wanted to know why I wrongly assumed it had taken you no longer than twenty seconds to tell me about your "ei" mistake. Well, your emails seem to "effervesce," if I may be allowed to make this observation. I could have sworn that you were a fast talker and typist, a bubbly individual who cannot go about her daily business quickly enough. When I read your emails I can't detect any pauses. Both their tone and tempo seem to be bursting with energy—breathless, zippy, even a touch excited. (Glattauer 2012: 8)

In addition, Glattauer constantly changes the pace of the narrative, alternating long emails with short messages in an increasing narrative tempo. The style oscillates between that of a somewhat formal correspondence and the informal one of a chat. The rapidity of the "email quasi-dialogues," in which the time intervals between messages decrease, is characterized by the numerous ellipses typical of oral communication (Wilke 2007: 161–62). The impression of oral communication is reinforced as well by graphic and stylistic expressions that simulate the facial expressions and gestures of orality. Emmi "addresses" Leo with a capitalized: "LEEEEEOOOOO, ARE YOU THE-ERE????????" (Glattauer 2012: 33).

Because the protagonists are not always online, pauses occur in their communication, which Emmi experiences dramatically. She repeatedly expresses concern that Leo will cut off communication altogether and asks him to respond (Glattauer 2012: 33; 223; 234). Bernhard's email, on the other hand, leads to a narrative standstill and interrupts the flow of communication between Leo and Emmi.

Precisely because they live in a virtual spatiotemporal dimension, the central question for the protagonists in *Love Virtually* is that of identity and authenticity. From the beginning, they project wishful images onto one another that they can never confirm or refute because they never meet. The recipient of their emails thus becomes a surface onto which they can project wishful ideals. Programmatically, Leo states: "I'm constructing my very own Emmi Rothner" (Glattauer 2012: 34). For Katrin Schneider-Özbek (2011: 353), *Love Virtually* is about the "effectiveness of the word in virtual space." Apart from writing, all tactile, acoustic, and visual elements of perception are eliminated, and their projections and impressions can be neither confirmed nor denied. The identity of the writers therefore remains fluid and open until the end.

Even an appointment in a crowded café fails to bring clarity. On the contrary, Leo sees Emmi only as she is mirrored in the eyes of the Leo's sister, Adrienne, who has accompanied him to the café; Leo immediately identifies three possible candidates for Emmi among the visitors to the coffee shop, but Adrienne neither confirms nor negates them. They plan three encounters, none of which takes place, characterizing the last of these as a "blind date," (Glattauer 2012: 115; 225; 271). "You come in… It's dark," proposes Leo (Glattauer 2012: 271). A meeting in a dark room cannot, by definition, create clarity.

Despite their familiarity with digital media, Emmi and Leo can't see through the computer's influence on their relationship. Near the beginning, Emmi insinuates to Leo that he is using her for his studies on "email as a medium for conveying our emotions" (Glattauer 2012: 31). Leo informs her that he could create programs to force Emmi to take unwillingly part in his experiments (Glattauer 2012: 121). The very opacity of the medium would make such an experiment possible. With her doubts, Emmi may intuitively grasp what social psychologist Robert Feldman has shown in his experiments—that people are five times more likely to lie online than in face-to-face communication (Zimbler & Feldman 2011). Emmi's suspicions cannot be swept off the table until the end of the novel.

6.2.   The Fear of Disillusionment in Virtual Love Affairs

If a reader wanted to judge the love story of Leo and Emmi by the criteria of the everyday world, one question would come to mind: Why don't the two lovers meet? How can we interpret a love relationship that excludes the body? How is one to understand Leo's blunt pronouncement: "I really don't want to know what you look like," he says (Glattauer 2012: 225). As Bruno Dupont (2014: 196) has succinctly put it, "The main characters do everything in their power to get as close to each other as possible without stepping out of virtuality."

There are two potential answers to these questions. On the one hand, these characters seem to embody Denis de Rougemont's model of disembodied love in Western culture that he called "amour passion" (described in his monumental *Love in the Western World*; de Rougemont 1983). The love between Emmi and Leo stands in a glorious line of literary history whose famous characters include Tristan and Isolde and Romeo and Juliet. For de Rougemont, Tristan loves Isolde not as an "other," but only because he can nourish his own desire through her. He needs the obstacles that thwart the fulfilment of his love so that desire is prolonged and increased to the greatest possible intensity. It can be no coincidence, then, that Emmi defines her relationship with Leo as "some kind of virtual Tristan and Isolde" (Glattauer 2012: 244). From de Rougemont's perspective, Tristan and Isolde's self-boycott of their relationship could be explained as a realization of "amour passion."

Emmi and Leo, on the other hand, are very much rooted in the twenty-first-century present and show the behaviours typical of the compulsive Internet users who are their contemporaries. Bernhard describes Emmi's absentmindedness this way: "She sits in her room for hours on end, staring at the computer screen" (Glattauer 2012: 231). Her absentmindedness is typical of the "distracted mind," which has become common among frequent users of digital media (Gazzaley & Rosen 2016). Bernhard adds, "she has to make a real effort to hide her distraction from the children. I can see just what a torture it is for her to sit next to me now" (Glattauer 2012: 231). Emmi's focus on the computer takes all the charm out of reality.

Leo and Emmi's love, which fails in reality but finds its expression in "virtualness," could therefore also spring from a different cultural-historical model. Emmi seems to be a perfect example of the "cold intimacy" that Eva Illouz (2007) has defined as the typical form of love in the age of the Internet. Illouz drew her observations from singles and dating sites that have become a successful and profitable business. Users of these websites are asked to create a profile in which, based on introspection, they provide a psychological profile of themselves, including personal information, profession, hobbies, and physical appearance. In this self-presentation, users of singles exchanges must break their individuality into categories to test whether their values are compatible with those of a potential partner. This results in a "textualization of subjectivity"—that is, a way of describing the self through by means of visual representations and language. The resulting relationship is a disembodied textual interaction. Self-presentation on the Internet is aimed at an abstract, general audience. This is another reason why the same stereotypical descriptions are used over and over again, leading to the standardization of profiles. The logic of romantic love is turned upside down: rather than being characterized by the uniqueness of the beloved, as it once was, Internet love is characterized by the idea of abundance and the interchangeability of partners.

If, despite these limitations, a happy combination of the characteristics of potential partners is found on a singles exchange, another problem arises. According to Illouz (2007), virtual relationships incorporate a constant fear of disillusionment through confrontation with reality. This fear is not unfounded. In face-to-face communication, relationships are formed between interlocutors that mix physical and unconscious elements with knowledge about the individuals. The person's present experience is related to images and experiences of her or his past. In this process, the beloved person is idealized and perceived as unique. On the Internet, in contrast, the person is perceived through abstract categories and cognitions that are based on neither real nor past experiences. Acquaintances formed on the Internet are thus exposed to high "prospective" expectations, which prepare the best conditions for disillusionment.

Illouz's 2007 model of love in the digital age can easily be applied to Glattauer's novel. Emmi and Leo "textualize" their individuality through writing, and their relationship is consequently disembodied and dominated by language. In *Love Virtually*, the protagonists' bodies are replaced by bodies of signs, thus creating "illusions of love via email" (Glattauer 2012: 231).

Emmi and Leo are aware that their written self-presentations put them in competition with many other "textualized" Internet visitors, and they therefore try to impress one another with cultivated, even literary language. They are witty and rhetorically dexterous, as Emmi proves when she defines the "family idyll" as an oxymoron (Glattauer 2012: 183). As cultured and educated people, they despise "chat room drivel" (Glattauer 2012: 17) and the use of emoticons. They intend their use of language to set them apart from the masses of Internet visitors.

Along with others who are looking for a partner, as Illouz describes them, Leo and Emmi share above all a sense of panic about comparing the ideal produced by the Internet with reality. This fear is expressed obsessively, and Emmi writes at one point, "And I'm worried that I won't like the way you look" (Glattauer 2012: 39). Their fear of failure is so great (Glattauer 2012: 21; 41; 202) that their virtually-lived love affair does not even result in a meeting, as Leo dejectedly notes:

> With us it's different, Emmi. We're starting off at the finishing line and there's only one way to go: backwards. We're heading for massive disillusionment. We can't live the things we write. We can't replace all those images we've painted of each other. It'll be a disappointment if you hide behind the Emmi I know. And that's what you'll do! You'll be depressed if I hide behind the Leo you know. (Glattauer 2012: 203)

They try to get physically closer, for example by recording their voices on the answering machine, yet the projections in which they fulfil their wishful ideals do not seem able to satisfy them. Their real "flesh and blood" selves should be able to withstand these projections and not flee from them, but disillusionment is waiting around the corner, and Emmi's voice creates irritation in Leo. "I imagined you to sound quite different. Tell me, do you always talk like that, or did you disguise your voice?" (Glattauer 2012: 222). These are unsuccessful attempts of an approach that is not concretized.

Their projections are filled and nourished by sexual fantasies, but they remain quite limited for two adults, and, for Leo, Emmi is reduced to a fetish object with shoe size 37 (Glattauer 2012: 18). It is "computer sex, but again, without the sex or the downloadable pictures" (Glattauer 2012: 50). Emmi and Leo live by the motto: "Writing is like kissing, but without lips," and therefore "Writing is kissing with the mind" (Glattauer 2012: 108). The written body replaces the biological body.

The onomastics of the characters' names in *Love Virtually* has so far focused insufficiently on "virtualness." Emmi's given name, Emma, must inevitably be linked to Emma Bovary in the context of the Leo-Emmi-Bernhard love triangle. The name "Leo" seems to fit into this schema as well because Madame Bovary's first suitor is Léon Dupuis. Like Leo, Léon leaves his love object to pursue his studies abroad. Emmi's friend, "Mia," in Italian the feminine possessive pronoun "my," does belong to someone: She is Emmi's "puppet" whom Emmi manipulates and attempts to couple with Leo. At the same time, Mia's name is associated with Italian culture and Mediterranean flair, which keep popping up in the glamorous conversations between Emmi and Leo.

Leo's last name, "Leike," doesn't seem to allow connections to literary models but more to Internet practices. A "like" is, in fact, the typical gesture of approval of a message or image on social media. This link is additionally suggested because the "ei" of Leike in German is pronounced like the "i" of like in English. "Leike" thus becomes a contemporary Don Giovanni who seeks or grants recognition. For these fictional characters, beauty and appearance are important: "I like 1) to like. And I like 2) to be liked" (Glattauer 2012: 40). The beauty of several protagonists is depicted: Leo's sister is a model, Mia is an athlete, and Emmi is a "lively, sparkling, sassy, gorgeous young woman" (Glattauer 2012: 229) whom "so many men have worshipped and lusted after" (Glattauer 2012: 232).

But the habitat of this Don Giovanni of the keyboard is a virtual one, a world of words as his email address makes clear: woerter@leike.com (Glattauer 2012: 2) —"woerter" are literally "words" in German. Bernhard, Emmi's husband, who is firmly anchored in the everyday world, puts the reader on the right track when he writes to Leo,

> You're not palpable, Mr. Leike, you're not tangible. You're not real. You're just my wife's fantasy, an illusion of unlimited emotional happiness, an other-worldly rapture, a utopia of love, but all fashioned out of words. (Glattauer 2012: 228)

Björn Hayer has noted that the two men skirmish with unequal weapons because "the virtual imago of Emmi's avatar lover [acts] in reality without being physically present there" (Hayer 2015: 126).

If Leo's existence is language-bound, then the relationship between Leo and Emmi is hermeneutic in nature, realized in a boundless interpretation. As Glattauer writes, "We're trying to read between the lines, and soon I expect we'll be trying to read between the letters" (Glattauer 2012: 20). The characters' names, with their references to literary models and to the textual dimension of the Internet, show that Leo and Emmi's relationship is about computer-mediated words and nothing else. Emmi and Leo "text each other," as digital communication through the smartphone is called. They create a union through words, but the connecting element is an Internet server:

> Let's assume you feel there's more that connects us than our computer servers, and that it's not mere coincidence that we've become so caught up in each other. Do you think

you might not want to see me again, Leo? Might you not want to keep on writing to me, even from Boston? (Glattauer 2012: 268–69)

The virtual love market that Illouz described has meanwhile improved technologically, but its logic has remained the same. In partner search, the Internet is a screen on which characters stage themselves. The distance of this virtual world from the everyday world is problematized. Contemporary readers of *Love Virtually* cannot escape the problem of "virtualness" that the novel depicts because, like its protagonists, they live in a world dominated by the Internet and social media.

6.3.   The Style and Emotions of the Protagonists of *Love Virtually*

Whether Emmi and Leo correspond to actual, living individuals or whether they are as they describe themselves remain open questions. From a narratological point of view, *Love Virtually* includes four distinct fictional characters who communicate via email. The broader question is whether something like a "character's style" exists. This assumption that it does presupposes that the character's style is reflected in their use of words, and discernible stylistic differences in word frequencies could then be interpreted as a character's "individual style." Stylometric analysis can operationalise this question by observing whether each voice has a distinct writing style.

Burrows' 1987 monograph, *Computation into Criticism*, can be considered a landmark of stylometric works on character style. Burrows focused on the idiolect of characters in Jane Austen's novels—that is, the speech behaviour they demonstrated through vocabulary—and proceeded with the belief that the most common words, such as articles and prepositions, were the best indicators of literary characters' speech behaviours. Statistical evaluation of relative word frequencies, Burrows emphasized, made it possible to distinguish between Jane Austen's characters in a way that was appropriate to the subject matter (Burrows 1987: 4). In a later work, Burrows and Craig (2012: 292) stated that "Authors create characters who speak in distinctive voices: imagined beings, with their own styles of utterance," and characters can thus be identified by physical and bodily features but also by the way their speech expresses personality, age, and social background. Using stylometric analysis on Shakespeare's dramas, Burrows and Craig (2012: 293) tried to show that no contradiction existed between the author's writing style and the style of the characters he created.

Stylometric tools for detecting character style have been tested on a large number of literary texts. Hoover applied it to the Sherlock Holmes novels to see whether the distinctive voices of Holmes and Watson were a way of characterizing them (Hoover 2017); and Karina van Dalen-Oskam used zeta-analyses on the epistolary novel *Sara Burgerhart* (1782) to show that only a small number of the main characters displayed a distinct individual style (van Dalen-Oskam 2014: 448–50).

This question has been addressed more recently by Benjamin Krautter, who used stylometric analyses to explore whether the individual characters in a drama could be distinguished by the linguistic design of their speech alone (Krautter 2020). The analysis was based on a corpus of sixty German-language dramas written between 1740 and 1930 and extracted from the German Drama Corpus. Each author, including such canonical names as Gotthold Ephraim Lessing, Heinrich von Kleist, and Arthur Schnitzler, contributed three stage plays to the corpus (Krautter 2020: 308). Krautter divided characters' speech into segments. For each speech segment, the so-called nearest neighbour was determined—that is, the segment with the smallest stylometric distance or, in other words, the greatest similarity. If a speech segment and its nearest neighbour belonged to the same character, they were assigned to the class "character." If, on the other hand, the two segments appeared in the same act, they were assigned to the class "act." If neither applied, the speech segment was categorized as "other."

The results showed that the class "act" contained considerably more speech segments than did the other two classes, "character" and "other" (Krautter 2020: 315). Krautter's analyses suggests that that it is, above, all the co-presence of characters that creates stylometric similarity. Speech segments uttered in the same act (meaning that characters in this act were on stage together) seem to be characterised by comparable word frequencies. These results suggested a question to Krautter: Was the style of speech evident in the plays—i. e., the rhetorical design of the characters—more a matter of the thematic design of the dramatic action than something like character style (Krautter 2020: 319).

Because the results of research on character style are not univocal, we wanted to test whether differences in characters' personality, age, profession, gender, and values were reflected in specific linguistic choices. In *Love Virtually*, in fact, the Bernhard's, Emmi's, and Leo's emails show different writing styles as well as specific use of such rhetorical figures as neologisms. The three characters likewise express a different familiarity with and propensity for digital media (Glattauer 2012: 228). Using stylometric analyses, we sought to answer whether Glattauer distinguished his characters through a unique linguistic design.

Our operationalisation can be summarised in four steps: First, we separated the mails written by the various characters in *Love Virtually*. Second, we performed a stylometric analysis on a sample of texts taken from the emails of Emmi, Leo, Bernhard, and the computer. Third, we performed a sentiment analysis on the same sample of texts. The last step was the comparison of the results of Steps 2 and 3.

If the individual character segments were most similar to each other in a stylometric cluster analysis—that is, if they are grouped in proximity on their own branch in the dendrogram—that could be taken as a quantitative argument for a character's distinctive speech. Whether the "voice" of a character is distinctive, then, would be measured by the stylometric similarity of the character's speech segments. We performed a cluster analysis on the 10 most frequent words (MFW), and the results in Figure 24 show that the software captured the distinctive features of the emails.

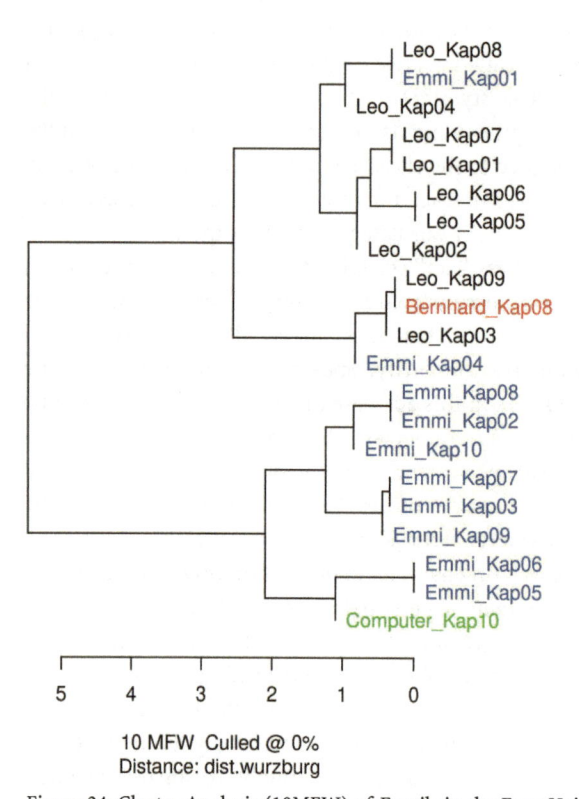

Figure 24: Cluster Analysis (10MFW) of Emails in the Four Voices of *Love Virtually*

The results of stylometric analysis show a clear separation between the emails written by Leo, which cluster at the top of the diagram, and those by Emmi, which appear at the bottom. In a way, the emails from Bernhard and the computer separate and frame them. The results change when the bar is raised to 1,000 words. By making the groupings more chapter-based and including more words in the corpus, the topics discussed by the two protagonists in their emails, among other aspects, are given greater weight.

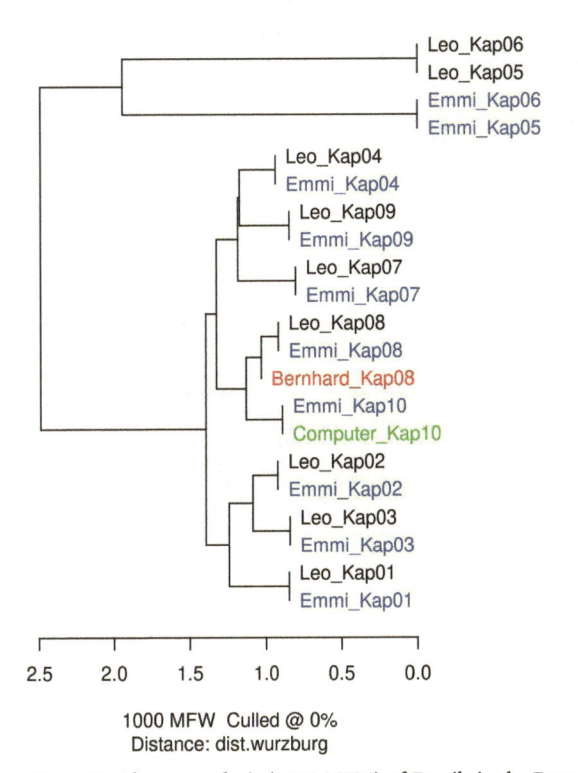

Figure 25: Cluster Analysis (1,000 MFW) of Emails in the Four Voices of *Love Virtually*

For this type of analysis, the concept of "style" is more problematic because many other aspects could influence results. Our operationalisation could partially respond to the issue of the difference between "figure style" and "act style" raised by Krautter (2020): the more MFW are included into the analysis, the more the content (that is, the context of speech or dialogue) becomes relevant. We therefore decided to take a closer look at the favourite words used by the four senders of the emails *in Love Virtually*, and the following list (Table 11) shows the twenty most common.

Emmi		Leo		Bern-hard		Computer	
Word	Frequency	Word	Frequency	Word	Frequency	Word	Frequency
sie	920	ich	826	ich	86	der	3
ich	857	sie	762	sie	84	adresse	2
nicht	380	und	338	und	39	e	2
und	343	nicht	294	die	38	achtung	1
leo	337	emmi	287	es	29	aufrufen	1
das	284	zu	243	habe	25	automa-tisch	1
mir	282	es	225	in	24	empfänger	1
es	279	das	218	mich	23	für	1
die	234	mir	213	mit	23	geänderte	1
ist	229	die	207	zu	23	gelöscht	1
mit	201	wir	199	das	21	gerne	1
so	201	mich	190	nicht	21	gewählten	1
der	192	ist	174	ihr	20	im	1
zu	191	der	167	wie	19	kann	1
wie	189	ein	158	ihnen	17	mail	1
ein	187	in	150	mir	17	mails	1
mich	185	ihnen	148	sich	17	mehr	1
ihnen	183	so	141	leike	16	neue	1
dass	170	wie	141	herr	15	nicht	1
sie	920	ich	826	ich	86	der	3

Table 11: The 20 MFWs among the Four Voices in *Love Virtually*

As is common, the MFW are function words such as articles and pronouns. Not coincidentally for an email novel like *Love Virtually*, "Emmi" and "Leo" are ranked at the fifth position among Leo's and Emmi's favourite words, indicating that the element of dialogue is a notable feature of the book.

When the emails *Love Virtually* are subjected to a sentiment analysis that differentiates the four voices, the results of operationalisation become even more interesting. Sentiment analysis (see Chapter 5 for details), which measures the emotionality of a text by drawing on a representative "vocabulary" for a given language, is particularly interesting in a romance novel. The positions within the Emmi, Leo, and Bernhard triad are, in fact, very different: Emmi and Bernhard are married, and Leo is the "third wheel" who undermines their relationship. These emotional flows are evident in Figure 26.

Unsurprisingly, the computer displays negative emotionality in all categories. Bernhard, surprisingly, prevails over Emmi and Leo in one positive emotion (happiness) and in all negative emotions (fear, disgust, sadness, and anger). His

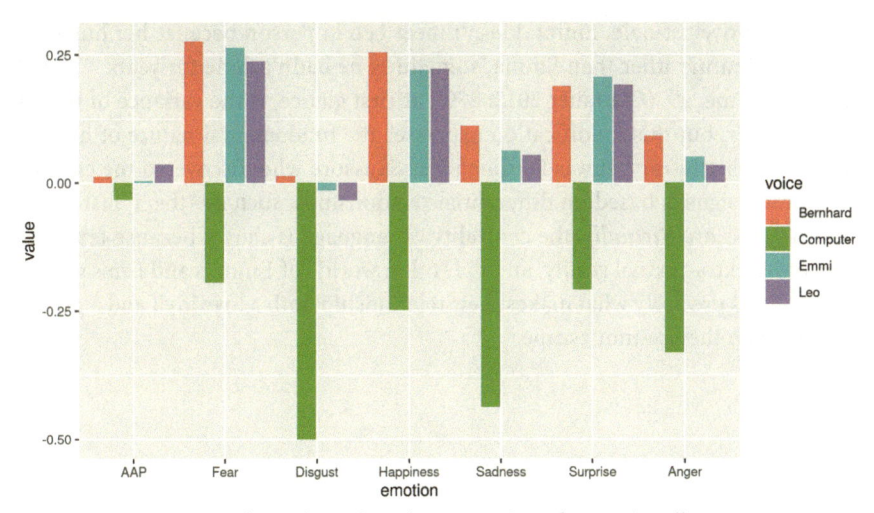

Figure 26: Sentiment Analysis of Emails in the Four Voices of *Love Virtually*

state of mind is in line with the plot of the novel, in which Bernhard's deepest affections are threatened. Leo and Emmi prevail in the lexicon of "surprise," perhaps because they were unprepared for the passion that overwhelmed their lives. When fictional characters express emotion, the reader's perception comes not only at the level of the vocabulary but also in the question of which characters experience particular emotions and why (Kim & Klinger 2018).

The above-described operationalisations offer intriguing insights into the nature of fictional characters, making it possible to distinguish them through stylometric and sentiment analysis. Readers generally consider literary characters to be similar to people in everyday life, with unique wills and personalities. Literary theory proposes more nuanced views, including "structuralist and semiotic approaches [that] highlight the difference between characters and human beings, focusing on the construction of characters and the role of the (linguistic, visual, auditive or audio-visual) text. [Structuralist and semiotic approaches] frequently regard characters as sets of signifiers and textual structures" (Eder *et al.* 2010: 5). The elements that define literary characters can be automatically identified, counted, and entered into a statistical calculation—that is, they can be operationalised (Silvi & Ciotti 2021: 189).

Along these lines, the distant reading proposed in this chapter makes it possible to see fictional characters as an effect of the text. They are, so to say, built by the words that denote them in a literary text, a linguistic operation that applies even more to Emmi and Leo, who exist for each other only in the emails they write.

In the novel's finale, Emmi doesn't meet Leo in person because her husband calls her Emmi rather than Emma, something he hadn't done for years. "The 'i' instead of the 'a'" (Glattauer 2012: 279), at first glance, is the variance of only a single letter, but this modification expresses the fundamental nature of human language as arbitrary. It was Ferdinand de Saussure who discovered the essence of human signs is based on differential relationships, such as "the 'i' instead of the 'a'". In *Love Virtually*, the centrality of language is shown because text prevails over extra-textual reality, and the "other world" of Emmi's and Leo's virtual existence is precisely what makes their relationship both a love idyll and a prison from which they cannot escape.

7. The Rating Culture of Online Reviewers vs. the Ivory Tower of Professional Reviewers: Assessing Literary Value in the Digital Age

Johannes Franzen (Franzen 2021) has described the phenomenon of massive online reviewing in which thousands of users publish product reviews over a short period of time. Such reviews become a dangerous "review bomb" when a product or service receives a large number of negative reviews at once. One striking example is the bomb "launched" by thousands of gamers against the videogame *The Last of Us: Part II*. In this controversy, reconstructed by Franzen, professional and non-professional critics clashed over two different assessment criteria (Franzen 2021: 2). The difference was quantitative as well: 121 professional reviews were opposed by feedback from 152,219 non-professionals. Critics of the game expressed their mistrust of professional reviews and demanded to participate in the evaluation procedure.

Clashes between contrasting forms of criticism concern not only many aspects of our lives but even more refined cultural artefacts such as literary texts. Lay criticism, for example, as it is carried out on platforms such as Amazon or Goodreads, is one manifestation of a culture of participation. With a record eighty million reviews, Goodreads represents a counterweight to the professional criticism that appears in journals and newspapers. Other venues for amateur literary criticism include book review blogs, websites, online forums, booktuber channels, and #instabook posts.

That the highly subjective and aesthetic experience of literary reading can be expressed in numbers is a recent phenomenon. In *The Metric Society* (2019), Stefan Mau discussed the massive power of "quantitative mentality" in every dimension of social life (Nassehi 2019; Stalder 2016; Reckwitz 2017). This mentality aims to organize social life according to principles of efficiency and predictability. Mau wrote that "quantification entails an act of translation" by reducing "a complex and confusing world to the standardized language of numbers" (Mau 2019: 13). We are in a new phase of this process because of the huge expansion of technologies for collecting, storing, and measuring data in a digitalized society. Big Data include not only shopping lists or professional-performance ratings, but emotional states, our taste in restaurants and hotels, health parameters (diet, sleeping, lifestyle), and behaviour quantified through self-tracking tools on smartphones. As Mau points out, humanity now produces more data in two days than in its entire history up to 2003 (2019: 22).

Data have enormous power: they "tell us how to look at things, thereby systematically excluding other perspectives" (Mau 2019: 15), and they always represent a particular form of value assignment. Quantification likewise touches diverse psychological mechanisms. As Mau (26) asserts, "We are natural comparatists" because we want to know whether we are superior or inferior to others. Data facilitate comparison because they create a common denominator across a range of dimensions. The result is "comparability," as Mau (31) states it, "by applying a common standard to disparate entities." This nearly infinite comparability, enhanced by our digital lives, produces a mechanism of "compare and despair." A widely publicized 2017 study by the Royal Society for Public Health, for instance, reported that constant comparisons can have a negative impact on the mental health of youth (Royal Society for Public Health 2017). In fact, quantification produces a correlation between estimated value and esteem—that is, the social recognition linked to that value. The notions of "prestige" and "value" occur several times in Mau's reflections (2019: 29; 50, and *passim*). These notions are important in relation not only to psychic states but to art and science as well. In the latter, the number of citations of a scholar's output—the so-called *h*-index or impact factor—is a crucial parameter in the performance evaluations of scientists or in recently introduced university rankings. The rating culture can also result in a *Tyranny of Metrics* (Muller 2018) when the "metric fixation" of our society is used in dysfunctional and oppressive ways.

Rating culture is exploited by social media like Instagram and Facebook as well (Frier 2020). Instagram gives its users three simple measures to show how they are performing: counts of "followers," likes on posts, and "engagement" (clicks on links, comments, and other user behaviours). These feedback scores make the Instagram experience competitive, emotional, and addictive. Facebook automatically catalogues its users' every small action. Knowledge about what people want is crucial to understanding Facebook's success, its pervasiveness, and its appeal for advertisers—but it involves pitfalls as well. The life of social media is a competition for attention that has created an "attention economy" (see Wu 2016; Tolentino 2019).

7.1. The Big Data of Online Reviewing

Strongly connected to the quantitative mentality is the new phenomenon of massive Internet reviewing. In the literary system, then, we can well claim that "Today, everyone is a critic" (Mahdawi 2016). In Franzen's view, the tendency of non-professional reviewers in the digital age is to distrust professional reviews and to demand to be involved in evaluation procedures. Franzen (2021), himself a professional literary critic, notes amateurish criticism of texts on Amazon or Goodreads. As an Amazon-owned, book-based social web site, Goodreads boasts some ninety million members as well as tens of millions of reviews and books catalogued; it employs review and rating systems similar to those on the Amazon website. Goodreads has become the most popular platform for readers to connect with one another through multiple opportunities to measure reading performance and text quality: they can list the books they have read, participate in reading challenges (that is, the number of books a user intends to read over the course of a year), offer ratings, and post reviews. On Goodreads, as well as on platforms such as Lovelybooks and Wattpad, books can be rated with stars, and the number of reviews and friend connections of a reviewer can be quantified. In our digital society, evaluation of cultural products has become synonymous with crowd evaluation.

On websites or in newspapers and magazines, rating culture produces a diverse range of big data. Quantitative or numerical ratings, for example, may appear on the websites of book retailers, and newspapers may use a "star system." For example, on "La Lettura," the cultural page of *Corriere della Sera*, which is among the most important newspapers in Italy, professional reviewers rate three parameters of a text from 1 to 5 stars: the "story," the "style," and the "cover."

In this context, two different evaluation systems exist. Online comments don't express evaluations based on assessed criteria, but they are mostly expressions of consumer satisfaction or dissatisfaction. In relation to these comments, Gerhard Lauer speaks about a "deconstruction of the hierarchies by pop-culture" (Lauer 2020: 157; Franzen 2022b: 123).

"Digital plenitude" has brought an end to the elite cultures typical of Modernism (Bolter 2019). Digital plenitude is a universe of digital products (websites, blogs, books, tv series) and practices on the Internet (by sharing and critiquing these products) so immense, varied, and dynamic that is not comprehensible as a whole. This digital universe is able to contain within itself the contradictory forces of high and popular culture, old and new media, conservative and radical social views which are practiced by different online communities. There is no longer an elite culture because there is no longer a single quality standard that is valid for all these communities. The distinction between high culture and popular culture has vanished; this can be seen, for example, in the current prominence of the graphic novel genre that was historically part of popular culture or in the disappearance of concepts such as entertainment literature (*Unterhaltungsliteratur* in German) or art films.

Consumers become "prosumers" in their digital lives and defend their right to express judgements. In literary debates—for example around Peter Handke's

Nobel prize or the publication of the novel *Marianengraben* by Jasmine Schreiber—social media played a significant role and competed with traditional criticism in newspapers and journals. Social-media users today refuse to accept the authority of traditional "gatekeepers" (Pianzola 2021: Chapter 5) who, in their eyes, follow outdated criteria, opening a debate between professional and lay readers regarding "Who has the power to establish what is tasteful and what is not?" (Franzen 2021: 14).

For Moritz Baßler (2019), this controversy brings back the old distinctions between low- and high-brow culture and between symbolic and economic capital, the latter of which indirectly reference the works of Pierre Bourdieu, the first to illustrate the forces and institutions of the "literary field." Bourdieu is surely the twentieth-century thinker who most compellingly described the logic of the "literary field," by which he meant "an independent social universe with its own laws of functioning, its specific relations of force, its dominants and its dominated" (Bourdieu 1993: 163). Far from being characterized by unselfishness and contemplation, the literary or artistic field is a "field of struggles" (Bourdieu 1993: 30). The main value generated by "innumerable struggles between agents" (authors, actors, writers, critics, directors, publishers, dealers etc.) (Bourdieu 1993: 79) is the artistic value or prestige of a literary text.

In pre-Internet times, the agents that determined symbolic capital in the literary field controlled both the social value of a literary text or an author and the categorization of what could be considered literature and what could not. The idea of literature that dominated until the digital age was born in the second half of the nineteenth century, when differentiations among commercial literature, popular literature, and high-brow artistic literature were already being made (Bourdieu 1993: 192ff; Neuhaus 2017). Modernist and avant-garde literature, dominated by the idea of renovation and of rupture with the past, adopted similar concepts. Modernist literature, in reaching for the status of art, held that literary writing should be difficult, complex—that is, different from everyday language. The literary writer, usually poor in economic terms, acquired a high symbolic power (Bourdieu 1993: 15) and a privileged position with reference to the reader. The might of the writer derived from indifference to the values of society, including current aesthetic values and public expectations (Bourdieu 1993: 200). Paradoxically, when a larger audience became accustomed to the new literature, economic success set in. In the view of Moretti (Moretti 2013: 31), modernism was "a sort of anti-market" that rejected the standardization of taste imposed by the genres of popular fiction that were typical at the end of the nineteenth century. The idea of "literariness" that emerged in the nineteenth century has largely dominated the concept of literature in the twentieth (Salgaro 2018). Literary theoreticians such as Viktor Shklovsky (1917) and Jan Mukarovský (1932), as agents of the literary field, have corroborated this notion of a complex and elitist literature.

Pierre Bourdieu also recognized the shift in the nineteenth century from the pre-mass-media age to mass media and the consequent movement from a concept of literature produced against market imperatives to the imposition of the sales model:

> [E]veryone is fixated on ratings. Wherever you look, people are thinking in terms of market success. Only 30 years ago, and since the middle of the 19th century [...] writers [were] acknowledged by other writers or even artists [were] acknowledged by other artists—immediate market success was suspect. It was taken as a sign of compromise with the times, with money. Today, on the contrary, the market is accepted increasingly as [a] legitimate means of legitimation. (Bourdieu 2001: 251)

With the development of the market, mediators—who include editors, critics, reviewers, publishers, libraries, and writers in the literary system—have taken on an increasingly crucial role in the careers of writers. They affect the economic success of a book or an author as well as the evaluation of the work and the establishment of an author's reputation. They are "gatekeepers" because they decide whether to admit individuals or works into a cultural field. Gatekeepers in the arts can exercise their function at different stages: publishers can prevent texts from being published, and critics can foster or impede a text's success (Janssen 2001).

Reviewing is a social praxis that brings social recognition to literary works that meet certain standards. The selection and valuation of literary texts is generally presented as personal, in which the intrinsic and "aesthetic" properties of the texts under consideration are scrutinized. Van Rees (1983) has noted how literary texts, if they are to be considered high-quality literature, must pass through the filters of three distinct types of critics: reviewers, essayists, and academic critics. Daily reviewers are the first gatekeepers to evaluate a literary text after publication, but essayists and academic critics have the power to legitimate the quality of a text and to introduce it into the "canon", that is, texts considered representative of a specific nation, culture, or epoch (Van Rees 1983: 403). In this process of canon formation (Rippl & Winko 2013), many factors and institutions may join forces: reviewers, publishers, readers, sales figures, film adaptations, literary prizes, and publication in a particular series or edition. While more normative canons were the standard in the past (Bloom 1995: 10), more descriptive approaches are now predominant (Rippl & Winko 2013: 66–76). Revisionist debates about the function and nature of canons during recent decades have encouraged rethinking of traditional concepts of literary prestige from a political point of view. As a result, more non-Western and non-European writers, more women, and more writers of popular fiction have been institutionalized within literary history (Löffler 2017: 13; Rippl & Winko 2013: 82). A canon therefore arises from an interplay of individual acts that are not necessarily aimed at canonizing a text. In the thinking of Simone Winko, these acts involuntarily form an "invisible hand" (Rippl & Winko 2013: 73).

In the twenty-first century, the Internet has revolutionized the "literary field"—that is, the reception and production of literary texts. The main institutions of the literary field have been dismantled and replaced over recent decades with new agents and institutions, to adopt Bourdieu's terms. The "Order of the (paper) book" (Weel 2011) shifted to an era of digital reading and writing. Today, books can be read on paper as well as in digital formats on computers, on eBook readers, and on smartphones. The circulation of the texts, which has been guaranteed for the last five centuries by publishing houses, is now provided by self-publishing, and the prestige acquired through reviews by literary critics in newspapers and journals can be obtained through discussions in blogs and online reading communities such as Goodreads. As we will see in the following chapter, the image of the writer as a quixotic bohemian has been replaced by that of a networked, self-promoting author on social media. Simultaneously, literary reviews and canonization have achieved a different status in the digitized world.

Thierry Chervel has provided a longitudinal study of literary reviews in the most important German journals and newspapers: *Frankfurter Allgemeine Zeitung*, *Frankfurter Rundschau*, *Neue Zürcher Zeitung*, *Süddeutsche Zeitung*, *Die Tageszeitung*, and *Die Zeit*. His main result is that, in recent decades, the number of reviews in these major newspapers has fallen sharply even as review sections have disappeared, including the feuilleton supplements of the *Neue Zürcher Zeitung* and *Die Zeit*. Because *Die Zeit* is doing brilliantly in economic terms, the shrinking of its review and criticism section is an editorial decision and not an expression of distress (Chervel 2021: 297–98).

Chervel studied the phenomenon of the "Popes of Literature" (*Literaturpäpste* in German) who, in German public life, are influential critics who determine the success or failure of a literary publication. During the twentieth century, these critics occupied the spotlight—Marcel Reich-Ranicki's television program, *Das Literarische Quartett*, for example, is a more intellectual version of Oprah Winfrey. At the beginning of the twenty-first century, three *Literaturpäpste* were still alive: Reich-Ranicki, Fritz J. Raddatz, and Joachim Kaiser.

In his historical reconstruction, Chervel convincingly showed that such agents of the literary field no longer exist and have not been replaced because newspapers and magazines have lost their power to determine the success of literary texts (Franzen 2022a). In the past, at least for newspaper readers, the critic had the last word. For these agents, reviewing was an "incontestable judgement" (Murray 2018: 115). The book critic's opinion regarding the quality of a text was unequivocal, and a title was reviewed only once by any given critic. The Internet has democratized reviewing praxes by creating space for a multitude of voices. Both phenomena—the shrinkage of review sections and the death of the "Popes of Literature"—are consequences of social reading and online reviewing. Chervel concluded with these words:

> However, nothing would be more wrong than to take a condescending view of the genre of user criticism. Often enough, user reviews measure up to critical standards—and they are written from a completely different point of view, not by journalists who, *nolens volens*, are also part of the literary establishment in which each element is considerate of the others, but from the perspective of a reader who has paid for his book and for whom it is actually relevant. The classic media will only survive if they see that their former gatekeeping function has become relative and recognize this as progress (Chervel 2021: 301).

Literary studies adopt a variety of positions regarding these new phenomena. Most literary scholars still ignore or even demonize them. In fact, online reviewing not only presents new forms of reviewing, it challenges the prestige of conventional criticism and the traditional distinctions between professional and non-professional criticism (*Laienkritik* in German). Professional reviewers such as journalists or literary scholars very often publish their evaluations online. Digital social reading (Rebora *et al.* 2019b) shows that the concept of reader should be revised and substituted with that of "wreader," a reader who is also an online writer. For Simone Murray (2018: 11), "The existence of book bloggers further problematizes book reviewers' liminal status between the amateur and professional domains." In her view:

> Social media has certainly rendered reviewing more democratically accessible and interactive than the traditional print reviewing paradigm. Yet, contrary to allegations, these coalescing digital cultural tastemakers are not reducible simply to the logic of quantification -whereby Internet traffic equates to cultural worth. We are witnessing the literary critical equivalent not of an absolute monarchy nor a proletarian revolt, but something poised ambiguously in between. (Murray 2018: 113; see also 119).

In Italy we have a related binary reviewing system. The Italian publisher Sandro Ferri released a memoir, *L'Editore Presuntuoso*, in which he stated the opinion that reviews and awards are among the least important reasons for which readers chose a book; they prefer to trust the judgements of their peers

> We can [take this position] with some certainty because it is readers themselves who do not seek the help of newspapers or of prizes to decide what they will read. Various surveys have indicated that reviews and awards are among the least important reasons for which readers chose a book… Nowadays, the public hardly reads—or reads only distractedly—newspaper literary inserts. They do not trust the judgments expressed there. As a publisher I can attest that even great reviews full of praise result in the sale of no more than a few dozen additional copies. This is a sign that few readers have been influenced by reviews, assuming they have even read them. (Ferri 2022)

The users of Twitter and Instagram have expressed a preference for the kind of literature that can be produced on social media. That preference resulted in the success of instapoets and, on Twitter, of the related phenomenon called "Twitterature." These genres were born within social media and did not exist before. Another consequence of the power of social media is that texts representing these new Internet-conceived genres are now published by traditional publishing houses, sometimes with great success. Another effect of these communities is that these new literary genres are now studied by literary scholars. Even if we cannot show that these works will stand "the test of time," scholarly publications and interest by literary scholars are clear signs of canonization (see Rippl & Winko 2013).

The presence of writers on social media is an international phenomenon that encompasses such diverse authors as Rupi Kaur, Sarah Berger, Stefanie Sargnagel, Marco Missiroli, Roberto Saviano, Margaret Atwood, Florian Meimberg, and many others. Recently, social-media-based literature has also been recognized by awards. In Germany, Stefanie Sargnagel, an author born in social media, is now published by the renowned Rowohlt-Verlag; in 2016, she received the Audience Award as part of the Ingeborg Bachmann Prize. Similarly, Florian Meimberg, a representative of German Twitterature, published his Tweets with S. Fischer Verlag, a major German publishing house, and received the 2010 Grimme Online Award.

In addition, online reviewing has changed the way literary texts are rewarded. For Philipp Ingold, "the only decisive factor is the number of spontaneous votes or the majority of thumbs up, which are extrapolated as "likes'," even for such an important award as the Ingeborg Bachmann prize (Ingold 2014).

> In Klagenfurt, as elsewhere, the lay public, which is predominant today in the cultural and entertainment industry, is satisfied (if not to say, shown respect) by the awarding of a so-called audience prize, which is exclusively determined by the criterion of majority approval. A discussion (or just an exchange of opinions) about the texts to be judged does not take place. The only decisive factor is the number of spontaneous votes or the majority of thumbs up, which are extrapolated as "likes." (Ingold 2014)

By analysing the justifications for awards, Ingold (2014) observed that they rarely went beyond declarations of subjective pleasure, which "makes desolately clear the extent to which professional criticism, which in Klagenfurt is always represented by well-known reviewers, has entered into a pact with the power of the non-professional public."

The evaluation of formal and experimental components of literary texts is neglected in favour of more emotional feedback (Martens *et al.* 2021). For these new evaluators, in Ingold's view, the understanding of literature is dictated solely by personal pleasure or displeasure. This, in principle, implies "realistic" texts, and the non-professional audience has succeeded in imposing this kind of "realism"—a concept of literature that remains fundamentally oriented toward reality, has "everyday life" as its constant point of reference, and is familiar, easily understandable, and "relatable." For Ingold, this state of affairs can easily be deduced from the Klagenfurt jury votes and prize speeches. This peculiar, realistic writing style, and thus, the focus on non-literary interests, has been permanently consolidated over the years and has now achieved clear dominance. As a result, the quality parameters of juries have changed: good is what goes down well, is easily understood, and can be conveniently shared online. He calls the decline of the professional critic "Instantcriticism"—perhaps a counterpart to "instapoets"—a phenomenon that induces, for him, a "McDonaldization" of the cultural scene.

Baßler (2021) expressed a similar view in observing the emergence of a so-called "Midcult"—a genre based on realistic literature. These texts are not challenging on a formal level and are not popular literature. Readers bring into them the good feeling of "having heard the heart of culture beating," as Umberto Eco put it. Writers like Daniel Kehlmann, Bernhard Schlink, Martin Suter, and Juli Zeh, as well as Elena Ferrante, Ian McEwan, Karl Ove Knausgård, and Haruki Murakami, are representatives of Midcult (Baßler 2019). Takis Würger's novel *Stella,* which deals with Germany's Nazi past, triggered a controversy regarding its literary quality. As Baßler reflected,

> I can say that there have never been such divergent ideas about what actually constitutes good literature as there are at the moment. Spectacle or not, heavy characters, legibility, pop? We simply no longer have a consensual standard of evaluation for it, and this also shakes the gatekeeper function that publishers, critics, and professors have had for so long. One can complain about this from a cultural point of view, but it is possibly just the logical effect of democratization, general education and access to the leading medium Web 2.0. (Baßler 2019)

Baßler considered changes in taste a consequence of "access to the web," which is the basis of social reading. Non-professional critics like Rupi Kaur's four million Instagram followers accuse professional critics of aloofness, elitism, incompetence, and arrogance (Baßler 2021). Professional literary critics have shifted parameters as well; what is now expected from literature is not aesthetic ambiguity but ethical and didactic insight. Nevertheless, Baßler doesn't perceive these phenomena as a decline of literature but as a challenge for the reading professionals in the book trade, critics, and universities, who must instead become better at justifying their aesthetic standards, adapting them to the current media and the social conditions of reading.

Because millions of online reviews cannot be captured with the typical tools of "close reading," this chapter proposes a proper methodological framework to account for changes in current literary criticism. Given that quantitative analysis is very uncommon among literary scholars (Salgaro 2018a), the field could easily ignore the big data produced by contemporary, real-world readers, but that would mean that literary theory had neglected an obviously significant phenomenon.

On the methodological level, then, literary theory should be able to analyse quantitative data and to integrate numbers into theoretical models. Secondly, literary theory could contribute to our society of metrics by itself producing quantitative data. This transformation of abstract concepts of theory into numbers is called operationalisation, and it has already been successfully applied in literary theory.

Operationalisation means (Chapter 2), in the vocabulary of the social sciences, the transformation of a concept into empirically observable properties. In operationalisation, data production and analysis feed each other and form a circular process (Salgaro 2018a: 55). As a consequence of this method, not only can the feedback of online reviewers be integrated into existing theories of literary evaluation, but the evaluations of professional and non-professional readers can be compared by quantifying and contrasting their subjective comments. In so doing, innovative form of online reviewing will be better recognized and anchored in the more traditional forms of literary criticism that appear in journals, magazines, and newspapers. To understand the "quantitative mentality" and the "rating culture" behind the big data of literature, literary theory itself must adopt data-driven methods.

7.2.   Publishing in the Digital Sphere

Means and methods of communication in publishing and bookselling have been revolutionized over recent decades. The communication among authors, writers, and readers was sporadic in the past. Publishing houses were the gatekeepers of the literary system, and writers could reach an audience only through them. Readers went to bookstores to buy books and were influenced in their choices by intermediary agents such as advertisements, literary reviews in journals, and bookstore staff. There was no direct communication among publishers, writers, and (non-professional) readers; the only feedback writers and publishers had was sales figures.

Communication within the "ecosystem of publishing" has been entirely revolutionized by the Internet and by social media, and important interactions among publishing houses, authors, and readers now take place there. Many writers interact with their readers through their social-media accounts, and publishing houses all have accounts of their own on Twitter, Instagram, and

Facebook (Murray 2018: 105 ff). Publishers can read and collect reader feedback in Amazon reviews and on social-reading platforms. They can assess readers' "sentiment" and base commercial decisions upon them. Consider such completely new phenomena as the BookTok subcommunity and hashtag #Booktok (more than 75 billion views worldwide; see Stamin 2022) and the widely used #instabook hashtag on Instagram (nearly fourteen million posts). These communication channels didn't exist until a few years ago, and direct-to-consumer communication has become the challenge for today's publishers. Simone Murray has also recognized "disintermediation" as the main characteristic of publishing in the digital sphere; it denotes the capacity of authors to publish and sell their texts "without the gatekeeper approval of mainstream media arbiters (agents, publishers, marketers, publicists, and retailers" (Murray 2018: 29). Consequently, publishing houses increasingly rely on the online reviews of non-professional readers for publicity more than on the great magazine or newspaper literary critics (see Chervel 2021). Smaller publishing houses use pitch parties on social media to find new authors. Following McGrath (2020) "Pitch Parties attempt to circumvent the systems of patronage on which the publishing industry relies" and provide an open alternative to a closed industry.

Literary texts are read today in many different formats and not only on paper —as printed books, as e-books, and on smartphones or other readers. The iPad and most e-readers allow readers to change and resize fonts, record and retrieve notes, and highlight passages. Other tools enable readers to know the number of others who have highlighted the same passage. According to Hayles, "In this sense, e-readers reinstitute communal reading" (Hayles 2020: 78) and, by entering into a collaboration with human readers, can sense and respond to their demands.

Another crucial phenomenon of the last decade is self-publishing which, according to publishers' statistics, constitutes 10% of publications in the current book market. Self-publishing is important not only because it is unprecedented, however, but also because it shows that the gatekeeper function of publishing houses is changing and demonstrates the increasing importance of social reading in pushing a literary text to success. E. L. James' *Fifty Shades of Grey* is only one of many examples. This erotic novel was analysed by the reputed sociologist Eva Illouz who tried to understand its huge appeal. Despite the text's formal limitations, Illouz considered it representative of the aspirations and self-understanding of contemporary women (Illouz 2014), further evidence that such tendencies as self-publishing, lay criticism, and new forms of literary evaluation and literary prestige cannot be neglected nor can their impact on the "literary field" be ignored.

This increased significance of social reading becomes clearer when analysing the recent evolution of China's publishing market (Anderson 2022). One of the most striking phenomena among many Asian reading cultures is that close to 40% of top-selling fiction originated as online literature. Generally produced as serials on major platforms, online literature is probably best known in the West through Wattpad's model of user-generated content (Pianzola 2021). Online reviewing and audience feedback have become determining factors in the success of texts because well-followed online digital series create publicity for a text until it appears as a physical book. In many cases, of course, the appeal of transforming a well-followed digital series into a published book is the text's built-in audience.

In the new literary system, producers and consumers are interchangeable: they became "prosumers" who produce "user-generated content." The principle of aesthetic genuineness applies in exchanges between producers and consumers and is a comparison mechanism that takes the form of affirmation or conformity ("Yes, that corresponds to me") or negation or delimitation ("No, that does not correspond to me"). The big names of literary criticism try to defend their positions: In an interview, Sigrid Löffler (2020) denounced the deprofessionalisation of online literary criticism disguised as democratization:

> The professional critic has got unwanted competition today, namely this electronic chatter at the regulars' table. Today, every consumer, every book buyer can automatically consider himself a critic. On the Internet, these amateurs then dominate for the most part; most are amateurs, bloggers, hobby critics. And they tweet to themselves with subjective judgments of taste. Arbitrary fits of enthusiasm that are usually not justified. Under the guise of an alleged democratization of criticism, literary criticism is in fact being literary criticism is actually being deprofessionalised. (Löffler 2020)

Löffler considered professional literary criticism to be an educational discipline whose aim was not to give recommendations on book purchases but to judge the literary quality of a book and possibly also to integrate it into the literary canon. Academic criticism has paid little attention to the frames of reference of lay literary criticism or to the ability of peer-to-peer recommendation systems to increase the "prestige" of a text in the literary system in innovative ways. In the digital age, two parallel ways of gatekeeping seem to exist: sometimes authors' online success induces traditional publishing houses to publish them. Consequently, online reviewers become the new gatekeepers because they not only express emotional judgements but are increasingly recruited by the literary system itself.

The phenomenon of social reading and online reviewing challenges traditional notions of both reviewing and literary prestige. Followers, likes, shares, and comments, all of which can be expressed numerically, represent the degree of social prestige of each #instapoet. For these writers, authority is conferred by likes (Penke 2022). The value of "likes," however, concerns not solely the social standing of a writer but income above all. Paradoxically, by increasing the number of followers, #instapoets can stimulate the interest of traditional "actors" in the literary field (e.g., literary agents; see Sovich 2017). The logic of likes is competitive: "the more, the better" (Passmann 2018: 15). To reference Bourdieu, symbolic and economic capital go hand in hand in such cases.

In the view of Simone Murray, Bourdieu's conceptual models require sensitive reframing if they are to engage with the current digital literary sphere. In the pre-Internet era, agents in the literary field held a monopoly on the award of the symbolic capital expressed by literary prizes, critical endorsement, and access to publication (Murray 2018: 18). Nowadays, the literary sphere is no longer characterized by cultural kingmakers but by mass democratic digital accessibility. The selection of cultural goods is no longer filtered by human gatekeepers but by algorithms. Amazon and Google use automated selection filters between authors and readers. These algorithms tend to be "black boxes" which, in Murray's view, "thus render ... the cultural encoded social and cultural priorities harder to identify and interrogate" (Murray 2018: 57).

While, for Bourdieu, a small number of individuals in the literary field masked their individual investments behind institutional values, "once cultural gate-keeping shifts to computer programs, sociological critiques of individual or small-group agency become far harder to sustain" (Murray 2018: 57). Algorithms additionally permit readers to "review the reviewer," and reviews with the highest reader preferences are sorted higher in the listings (Murray 2018: 135). If, in the past, agents in the literary sphere were individuals with specific interests and powers, discussion of and feedback on literary texts are now dominated by anonymous forces driven by multiple and highly complex quantitative elements. The fact is that the millions of reviewers on social media are, for these algorithms, more determinative than is the unique voice of the reviewer in the cultural page of a newspaper or magazine. The feedback instapoets receive therefore appears online, in social networks, and not in specialized academic journals or in printed newspapers.

Empirical studies on book purchases have similarly shown that, in today's publishing climate, the author functions as a brand name and must establish "brand loyalty" with readers (Kamphuis 1991). The rejection of the expertise of the traditional gatekeepers of "the literary system" denotes, in Bourdieu's vocabulary, a rejection of the symbolic capital of the literary field. The number of followers of the instapoets correlates with popularity and presumably with "economic capital." These writers seem to give up the laurels of the poet's symbolic capital deliberately in favour of commercial success and popularity. Their followers' likes seem preferable to reviews in important newspapers.

The traditional idea of the isolated poet, who stands in opposition to the social system, has been outclassed by the possibilities offered by social networks. Now authors are engaged in one-to-many relationships with readers, intervening in cultural debates and selectively updating their fans on the progress of their writing projects. "Interactivity" is one of the main features of literary communication in the digital sphere where authors have the possibility to interact with their readers through websites, blogs, vlogs, or Twitter and Facebook accounts and to maintain intimate connection with them (Murray 2018: 29).

7.3. Methodological Questions in the Analysis of Reviewing in the Digital Age

What can literary theory do in this neoteric context? Recent studies (Löffler 2020) mainly evoke institutions under threat and assume the vantage point of such traditional gatekeepers as professional literary critics. Some literary critics may prefer to retire to their ivory towers which, from the perspective of social media, is a stance that seems more and more obsolete. For Philip Ingold, literature that claims to be art—not on best or bestseller lists—can survive "only in the ivory tower ... finally becoming elitist and self-worthy again" (Ingold 2014). Ingold believes that popular fiction certified by ratings may be and remain what it has become—a part of entertainment literature and infotainment.

Ingold's critical position implies both ignoring the production of literature on social media that has created such important phenomena as instapoets and Twitterature and overlooking the millions of young readers who are a potential audience for high-brow (canonical) literature. Thomas Anz (2010) consequently recognized the positive evolution of online criticism and its ability to bring many new critics and new target groups to literary criticism.

First, it is important to understand that common ground exists between the lay reviewer and the professional: the reviewing activity itself, which implies the evaluation of the literary value of a text. Well before the institution of social reading and online book retailers, two German scholars, Renate von Heydebrand and Simone Winko, were studying the evaluation of literature. They developed a model that considered both the social and the individual aspects of reviewing by abandoning the notion of literary quality as an intrinsic characteristic of the text. Following their thinking, a literary text is not intrinsically valuable; rather, it only acquires an attributive value in relation to specific standards (Hedebrand & Winko 2008: 226). In appealing to the standards of cultivated readers, a "good" book should be "complex" or "rhetorically elaborated" to meet their expectations (values), while a "good" book can be a "suspenseful" love story or detective novel for less sophisticated readers. Interestingly, cultivated readers seem to share the criteria of literary value with modernist writers.

As Heydebrand and Winko have pointed out, "Literary evaluation is by no means limited to professional judgment on literary texts" (2008: 225). That is, different forms of professional reviewing—by journalists, literary critics, or literary scholars—also exist (Rippl & Winko 2013: 146–153). The actors in the "literary system" can express evaluations in a variety of ways, including through explicit verbal utterances and through non-linguistic acts of selection (e.g., buying one book instead of another). The indirect expression of preferences is multifaceted; it might occur in an author's choice of literary allusions, a reader's choice of one novel over another, an anthologist's inclusion or exclusion of a writer, a critic's comparison of several contemporary books, a professor's selection of works for a course syllabus, a student's choice of courses, or a journalist's survey of an author. Non-linguistic acts expressing intrinsic literary value can be expressed through numbers as well (a book's sales figures, for example).

The evaluative process might be elicited by aesthetic, educational, or economic factors because the assessment of literary quality is regulated by norms that are influenced by both the economic and the cultural spheres. While the former aims to maximise profits according to the law of supply and demand, the latter regulates "the possible gains in terms of knowledge, action orientation, gratification, prestige" (Heydebrand & Winko 2008: 230). Standards of value are governed by four dimensions: formal values, content values, relational values, and reception values. While the first three take place on a social level and refer to the text, the fourth takes place on an individual level.

The sub-dimension of individual value encompasses the quality of literary texts with regard to personal needs, and it includes the following psychological assets:
- Cognitive value (reflection, memorability)
- Practical value (making sense, significance)
- Hedonistic value (pleasure, entertainment)

Importantly, these values are valid for both professional and non-professional readers. What changes are the standards of values they use, which are often a consequence of their differing expertise. Individual values are not the only crucial aspect of the evaluation of books. Social value considers literary texts in terms of
- economic value (literary works as objects of the economic system)
- social prestige (symbolic capital within particular texts)

On the "economic value" sub-scale, a literary text is evaluated as a product. As with social prestige, the value of a text is determined by its capital—in this case, symbolic capital—and denotes the gain in prestige or social status that the handling of literature might bring to the actors (readers, editors, publishers, etc.).

Readers may also derive prestige from possessing books that reflect their intellectual and social status (Kamphuis 1991: 475). In a society in which literature is highly esteemed, the act of owning a book and the skill to talk about it competently might confer prestige on the owner (Heydebrand & Winko 1996: 131). This model confirms existing research on the attribution of literary value and, in Verboord's view, four indicators determine "institutional literary prestige": entries in literary encyclopaedias, literary prizes, the attention of literary critics, and the status of a publishing house (Verboord 2003: 277). Literary prestige can also be expressed by the numbers of reviews in elite periodicals (Underwood 2019: 68–111).

The Heydebrand/Winko models encompass professional and non-professional readers as well as linguistic and non-linguistic acts of evaluation and can capture all the new tendencies of online reviewing (Rippl & Winko 2013: 147–48). This is precisely the praxis that has grown exponentially in recent years and created a challenge for criticism. As one consequence, online reviewing has become a smaller branch within the larger research field of digital social reading. Because many projects and research groups are focused on these phenomena, an accurate "snap-shot" of this young and vital field is difficult. Current research has taken a variety of approaches to the big data of modern literary reviewing as professional and non-professional reviewers practice it, which can be summarized as follows:

1. Analysis of literary reviews based on quantitative evaluations, such as the stars on Amazon or Goodreads;
2. Investigation of qualitative (non-numerical) literary reviews on websites and social media;
3. Analysis and comparison of professional and non-professional (online) criticism.

Valid applications already exist for each of these research paths. Quantitative evaluations of literary reviews can compare numerical data, expressed with stars, on Amazon or in print publications. These numbers can be correlated with other numbers—for example, sales figures—which are often published in newspapers or on websites. A good example of this research line is a study in which Goodreads book metrics were compared to a range of book-based impact indicators for 15,928 academic books across broad fields (Kousha *et al.* 2017). Other studies using quantitative measures have created a corpus in which 15,454 unique book titles from the BKCI-Web of Science were matched with Tweets retrieved from Altmetrics.com to observe the use of Twitter by commercial publishers (Wang & Zuccala 2021). Other research (Maity *et al.* 2018) has shown how much user behaviour on Goodreads is indicative of sales on retail book platforms such as Amazon.

Investigation of qualitative literary reviews on websites and social media brings the concept of operationalisation into play, which is already common in the Digital Humanities. Operationalisation can be implemented, for example, by observing the occurrence of certain adjectives in online reviews. Using LIWC software, a 2019 study linguistically analysed 474,803 unique reviews posted on Goodreads between 2014 and 2016 (Hajibayova 2019). The high rate of function words coupled with positive emotion words suggests that reviewers tend to convey their opinions with the aim of influencing the reading choices of other individuals. These observations were confirmed by reviews of graphic novels (Hajibayova & McCorkhill 2021). Other studies have confirmed the emotionality of reviews by highlighting the fact that 70% of emotion words appear in the first sentence of a book review and noting that reviewers mostly discuss the book's content rather than its formal characteristics (K. Wang *et al.* 2019).

In another study, the book reviews of twenty-five 2009 bestsellers listed on Amazon were analysed to understand which factors induced people to buy a book. Margrit Schreier's premise is that the internet has changed the literary field with regard to the reputation of the book. While critics in the past have acted as experts guiding the public and participating in creating the literary status and reputation of a book (Schreier 2010: 309), Twitter, Facebook, and other social-reading mechanisms, conversely, have increasingly taken over as critics, informing their peers' reading choices. Schreier coded Amazon reviews to understand reviewers' reasons for liking or recommending a book and showed that the main reason given was "involvement," which had the highest frequency in the sample. A closer inspection showed that readers' involvement concerned, in hierarchical order, plot and characters. "Aesthetic involvement" which, for literary scholars is the main factor in appreciating a text, ranked only seventh on this list (Schreier 2010: 312).

For authors, these results raise concerns about the evaluation parameters, prestige, and value of reviews on such platforms as Amazon, Goodreads, and others. Quantitative methods can be used to study reader response in social-reading platforms and understand how fiction is read nowadays, gaining unprecedented access to readers' interactions with texts and with other readers in an "ecologically valid" (that is, natural) environment. Other studies have investigated various aspects of Goodreads reviews, such as their characteristics compared to Amazon reviews (e. g. Dimitrov *et al.* 2015) and gender differences across reviewers and authors (Thelwall and Kousha 2017). Similar studies have been carried out for platforms such as Wattpad.com (Pianzola 2021; Pianzola *et al.* 2020) or LovelyBooks.de, the largest German-language book community (340,000 members and 1.2 million reviews).

These studies show, among others, that a novel that becomes a show will receive about four times as many ratings on Goodreads.com as a novel that has never been adapted to TV or film (Porter 2021).

Most of these studies have focused on social-reading reviews alone (Rebora *et al.* 2021), sometimes giving the impression that book reviewing was born with the internet. But rating culture actually has a history (Spoerhase 2018). Only a few studies have tried to bridge the gap between professional and non-professional criticism, a comparison that could shed light on current evaluation practices in literary reading by showing continuities and ruptures between traditional and online criticism.

Finally, an example of analysis and comparison of professional and non-professional criticism is the work of Harada and Yamashita (2010), who investigated the characteristics of online book reviews in comparison to those published in print newspapers. Their results showed that the difference between the two evaluative practices was their point of focalization. While reviews in print newspapers focused on "writing style," online reviews emphasized "plot," and "setting." In addition, online reviews included more subjective and negative evaluations.

Another succinct example of comparisons of online, non-professional reviewing with professional criticism was proposed by Stefan Neuhaus (2017). After reconstructing the birth of literary reviews, Neuhaus analysed lay reviews on Amazon. Because they appeared on a commercial website, these comments became part of advertising and public relations. He analysed two online reviews, one of Franz Kafka's *Process* and one of John Grisham's *Sycamore Row*, to show their emphatic tone, the low quality of writing, and the lack of argumentation. The most amusing one included this line: "I would love to build a time machine, go back in time, and murder Franz Kafka before he ever had the opportunity to write a book."

An alternative approach was proposed by Peter Boot, who studied Dutch blogs to understand which persons or institutions were considered authoritative by online reviewers (Boot 2013). Frequently mentioned authorities were authors, companies and institutions, online critics, and prizes, a noteworthy result because it suggests that the influence of critics is still powerful.

Another project, "Evaluation of Literature by Professional and Layperson Critics," led by Gunther Martens at the Ghent University, is studying the differences between professional critics and lay readers by contrasting their criteria for distinguishing "good" from "bad." To do this, the project is using corpus and sentiment analyses to explore the visibility and popularity of literary awards such as the Ingeborg Bachmann prize on social media (Martens *et al.* 2021).

In line with the above-mentioned approaches, a study by Salgaro and Rebora (2018) used LIWC software to compare book reviews published on social networks with those that appear in paper magazines and literary journals. As a means to bridge the gap between professional and non-professional criticism, they focused explicitly on the precise vocabulary used in online and print reviews to express "critical distance" in literary reading. As expected, the analysis showed that "affect words" dominated on social networks in comparison to print magazines (>44%) and literary journals (>95%). This emotional or "affective" approach did not impede "cognitive processes," showing that no interference exists between cognitive and emotive/biological/perceptual processes in book reviewing.

7.4. Operationalising Literary Value

Professional criticism is changing because of online reviewing. In the current context, a multiplicity of criteria exist for evaluating literature, though common ground can be found between professional and lay reviewers. Literary reviews online or in traditional papers or journals are, first, acts of evaluation. Every evaluation determines the value of a certain object in relation to specific criteria, including norms, interests, desires, conventions, and motivations. For Friedericke Worthmann, literary evaluation is guided not only by social and aesthetic norms but by readers' and critics' needs. Needs and norms guide cognition and the experience of reading and justify statements of judgment. A needs-oriented evaluation of literature takes place when a reader perceives that a text has created a pleasant and enjoyable state (Worthmann 2016: 12), and the choice of text implies an act of preference based on standards that satisfy readers' needs and motivate the evaluation process. Worthmann thus merges normative criteria and psychological needs in the act of literary evaluation. During their literary socialization, readers acquire knowledge of what literature is and how it must or must not be valued (Worthmann 2016: 21), but, of course, aesthetic judgements have a strong subjective and idiosyncratic nature.

Research has shown that critics cannot identify either objective textual properties in an unequivocal way or what properties in a text imply an automatic value judgement. Van Rees (1983: 406) commented that, "in epistemological and methodological respects no form of literary criticism can be regarded as better founded than other." A critic is idiosyncratically attached to a peculiar concept of literature and evaluates texts with reference to the norms of that concept. Nevertheless an intersubjective consensus of critics can be reached by "orchestration"—that is, an attunement of their judgements to each other (Janssen 1997). As a result, for Worthmann, subjective factors will always affect literary evaluation:

> In any case, the individual will develop, among other things, subjective literary evaluation knowledge in the course of his socialization: subjective literary *values* (opinions about which characteristics of literature are desirable, e.g., the opinion "originality is good"); subjective literary *needs* (desired states of subjective well-being, for the realization of which literature is suitable, e.g., after emotional involvement, tension, relaxation); subjective literary *attitudes* (opinions and expectations about typical qualities

of the elements of text classes such as the attitude "poems are boring"). (Worthmann 2016: 21)

Every act of reading is linked to an emotional experience which, in turn, is influenced by the personality and the needs of the reader, and a text will be evaluated based on these subjective conditions. Feelings that arise because of an assessment of a text are experienced as positive or negative for the reader's subjective well-being, and evaluations are based on whether the reader achieves desired states of that well-being. Textual comprehension and the feelings that occur in reading are, as it were, two sides of the same coin in the reception process. For Worthmann, the aim is to develop a model that accounts for the multitude of psychological processes that are at work in the evaluation of literature. Importantly for us, these models can be applied to professional and non-professional reviewers who share the "reviewing activity." Following Worthmann's hypothesis, professional evaluations of books would seem to be no less subjective and emotional than those of lay reviewers.

Although Worthmann's model offers a deep description of the cognitive and emotional concepts involved in literary evaluation, it isn't able to tell what is going on in actual reviews, nor does it allow literary critics and online reviewers to be compared or distinguished. For that to take place, the abstract, non-countable concept of literary evaluation must be operationalised by building a questionnaire that assesses literary evaluation and submits it to flesh-and-blood readers.

In fact, the Heydebrand/Winko model has already been operationalised in the form of a questionnaire I developed with Arthur Jacobs and Jana Lüdtke, two neuropsychologists at the Free University of Berlin. The questionnaire has been tested and validated in other studies (see Chapter 2). In addition, we used this questionnaire to operationalise the distinction between reviews of professional and non-professional reviewers. To our knowledge this was the first attempt to compare these two categories, which were born with the internet and the practices of rating culture. In consequence, this survey was intended to be an exploratory study that lay the methodological foundations for future research. We chose items for the questionnaire according to the definition that von Heydebrand and Winko gave for each of the five subscales and adapted them to our aims (Table 12).

Items	Values	Nr. in the questionnaire
1.I think the text introduces a new perspective. 2.The text makes me look at things differently. 3.The subject of the text concerns questions which I often thought. 4.The text makes me stop and think.	Cognitive value	4 5 6 7

(Continued)

Items	Values	Nr. in the questionnaire
1.I felt that some aspects of the text were important for my everyday life.	Practical value	8
2.This text continued to influence my mood after I finished reading it.		9
3.After reading, it was easy to concentrate again on other things.		10
4.After reading this text, I felt refreshed, renewed, and revitalized		11
1.While reading the text I noticed the style.	Hedonistic value	12
2.The text is fascinating.		13
1.The Italian publisher has not yet set the price of the literary text of which you have read some extracts. How much would you be willing to pay for the paper version of the text? 10–13–16–19–22 euro	Economic value	14
1.Do you think that this text won a literary prize?	Social prestige	15
2.Do you think that the literary critics rated this text as an important text?		16
3.Do you think that this text should be taught in school?		17
4.Do you find this text trivial?		18

Table 12: The Operationalisation of the Heydebrand/Winko Model into a Questionnaire

We submitted this questionnaire on the literary value to seventy-seven Italian subjects and, based upon their replies to the question "Are you professionally involved in literature (professor, librarian, editor, writer, journalist)?" divided them into two groups: amateur, online reviewers and professional print reviewers. Forty-two of the subjects were classified as professionals, and thirty-six were amateurs.

To better differentiate the two groups, we added questions like "Have you written book reviews in trade journals in the last ten years?" (Question = Q1) or "Have you written online book reviews (on amazon.co.uk; internetbookshops, social-reading platforms: Goodreads etc.) in the last 10 years" (Q3)? We also asked our subjects their age, gender, reading habits, and professions. To test their different concepts of literary value, we asked subjects to read the following eleven Tweets from Florian Meimberg's *Tiny Tales* (see Chapter 5):

Was it really me?" asked God, while his head was still throbbing from the hangover. "Of course," sneered the devil. "It lasted six days."

The world population was stunned. The rumours were true: a second civilisation had been discovered. On the surface of the Earth.

That 37 planets were exactly aligned only happened once every 146 million years. God wielded his billiard cue.

The discovery was truly shocking to scientists: in ancient times there had been a primitive computer network: "Internet."

The president walked through the hangar, scanning the containers with the captured aliens. His chief of staff whispered, "They are called men."

His arrival on the unknown planet was a shock. The alien race proved to be hostile and aggressive. It hated men.

Brian threw himself into the festive crowd. It was the one day of the year he dared to be amongst people. Halloween.

"Sorry. I have a boyfriend," Eva lied. She had disliked the guy from the start. "Too bad," Adam muttered and disappeared back into the woods.

The line was blue. Pregnant. He returned to the bedroom, slipped into bed, snuggled into her warm body. "You are going to be an uncle."

"No, my darling." The old man smiled at his nephew. "The scar on my arm is from World War II. I have this from the Third."

Alex looked around. His parents' house had hardly changed at all. He placed the parcel in a drawer. Then he dialled the FBI number. (Meimberg 2011)

These texts were chosen for their brevity and because they had never been translated into Italian, thus avoiding familiarity effects. After reading these texts, the subjects completed the questionnaire based on the Heydebrand/Winko model described earlier (Q4–18), wrote a short review of the Meimberg text of a maximum of ten sentences, and answered the following questions:

How would you rate the review you just wrote? (Q19)
How do you rate reviews on amazon? (Q20)
How many hours does it take to write a good review of a novel? (Q21)

These three questions assessed subjects' metacognitive abilities in reviewing. Research has shown that these abilities are better on paper than on screen (Ackerman & Goldsmith 2011). For our purposes, we wanted to assess whether amateur and professional reviewers had different concepts of the activity of reviewing.

The outcome of the survey presented several interesting results. The pool of participants was well balanced in terms of gender (forty-four women, thirty-two men, one nonbinary) and professional employment: among the participants were professors; editors and journalists in the category of professional reviewers; and employees, students, judges, lawyers and entrepreneurs in the category of amateur reviewers. Given the pool of participants, their education level was not surprising: in no fewer than thirty-one cases, subjects claimed to hold a PhD and, in twenty-one cases, a master's degree. It follows that their reading habits were well above the national average: on average, they claimed to read between thirteen and twenty-four books per year. According to data from the Italian National Institute of Statistics (2018), 47.6% of Italian adults read fewer than three books per year in 2017; strong readers were those who read one book per month.

The "professional reviewer," of course, does not actually exist, strictly speaking. In fact, the review has an ambiguous, even subordinate position among academic publications. University professors often write the reviews in newspapers and journals, which, however, are not held in high scientific or academic regard. Given that nobody lives from reviews, there are no professional reviewers on the job market. Professional reviewers, then, are those who, by virtue of their profession (as writers, literary figures, or journalists) have or would have the tools to write and who have already done so.

Nevertheless, our results (see Figure 27) showed that the categories of professional and amateur reviewers were justified in statistical terms. To the question "Have you written book reviews in trade journals in the last 10 years? (Q2)" (possible answers: 1 to 5, corresponding to "no reviews," "one review," "two to five reviews," "six to ten reviews," "more than ten reviews"), professional reviewers answered with a mean of 3.14 (corresponding to a value between "two to five reviews" and "five to ten reviews"), while the amateur reviewers yielded a mean of 1.41 (corresponding to a value between "no reviews" and "one review"). This result was confirmed by a t-test (M = mean; SD = standard deviation; p = p value). In Q2, the forty-two professionals ($M = 3.14$, $SD = 1.49$) compared to the thirty-six amateurs ($M = 1.44$, $SD = 1.18$) had written significantly more reviews in journals and newspapers ($t(74) = 5.3$, $p = 1.14E-06$).

A similar result occurred for answers to the question: "Have you written online book reviews (on amazon.co.uk; internetbookshops, social-reading platforms: Goodreads etc.) in the last ten years?" (Q3) (possible answers: 1 to 5, to be interpreted as above). In this case, the result for professional reviewers was 1.39 in contrast to 2.36 for amateur and potential online reviewers. These statistics confirmed that, on average, professional reviewers had written more reviews in papers and journals in the previous ten years while amateur reviewers wrote more online reviews. In Q3, the forty-one professionals ($M = 1.39$, $SD = 1.03$) compared to the thirty-six amateurs ($M = 2.36$, $SD = 1.58$) had written significantly more online reviews ($t(73) = 2.9$, $p = 0.004$).

Another behavioural aspect distinguished amateur from professional reviewers: 86% of professional reviewers wrote the requested review of Meimberg's text in contrast to 66.6% of amateur reviewers. Writing reviews therefore came easily to professional reviewers, which was not the case for amateurs.

Although amateur and professional reviewers could clearly be distinguished in our analysis, their evaluation of Meimberg's text, assessed through the questionnaire based on the Heydebrand/Winko model (Table 12), didn't significantly differ as Figure 27 shows.

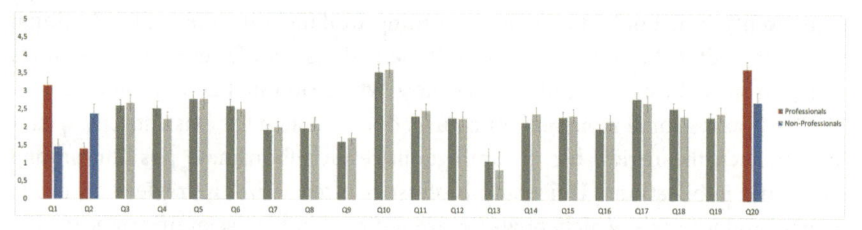

Figure 27: Results of the Survey (on Reading Habits, Reviewing, and Literary Prestige) of Amateur vs. Professional Reviewers

Figure 27 shows the data analysed through a t-test, assuming equal variances. In grey are the data that didn't yield a statistically significant result; the coloured bars (red professional/blue amateur) indicate statistically significant ones. (The *** in the graph indicates a p-value of < 0.001 with a 95% confidence interval; the * in the graph indicates a p-value of < 0.05 with a 95% confidence interval.) For some of the questions, professionals and amateurs did not provide a response, leading to a discrepancy in the degrees of freedom observed.

Because we were able to confirm the distinction between the two groups statistically, (Q1–3) something in the text we chose must have led to these un-differentiated results (Q4–18). With regard to the distinction between professional and amateur reviewers: in the data of Q1, the forty-one professionals ($M = 0.61$, $SD = 0.49$) compared to the thirty-six amateurs ($M = 0.17$, $SD = 0.37$ demonstrated a significantly better level of education (answering the question: What degree do you have?; $t(73) = 4.1$, $p = 9.06E-05$). As many as twenty-five individuals classified as professionals declared that they held the PhD.

A closer look at the evaluations of the literary value of Meimberg's Tweets yielded results well below the mean of 3. The highest result came from Q18: "Do you find this text trivial?," respectively 2.8 from professionals and 2.69 from amateur reviewers. The reviews also showed that readers failed to consider these short texts as a whole to which they could attribute an overall meaning.

The short reviews we asked subjects to write could fall, at least for the amateur reviewers, into the five categories for online reviewing proposed in a witty article by Marco Archetti:

– First category: the Iconoclasts. (e.g., *Anna Karenina*, "A novel with excellent possibilities, in my opinion inadequately exploited").
– Second category: the Oppositionals. Those who write, "it may be so, but," and who, with contempt for authority, affirm the ineluctability of their own opinion... their first interest is not to destroy, but to affirm themselves through their own judgement...
– Third category: the Naïfs. They trumpet an innocent opinion and leave us bewildered (e.g., *The Decameron* "is not very good, but somehow it interests me and I did not mind reading it.")
– Fourth category: the Melodramatics. If they don't like a book, they are sad...

- Fifth category: the Dispossessed. (e. g., "*Crime and Punishment*, a little story, nothing much"). (Archetti 2017)

As Archetti thought about the comments he read, what continued to amaze him was not so much "the individual judgement as the general method, i. e., the blithe zeroing out of perspective. The bystander, promoted to reviewer, descends upon the subject and judges it. He does so in no uncertain terms, based upon what [the text] appears to him to be and divorced from any context.... He has only one outcome in mind: perceiving himself to be on the same level as the material he is judging" (Archetti 2017).

Concerning our fifty-nine reviewers (out of seventy-seven who concluded the first part of the survey), we observed that, in general, they disliked the Meimberg text. In one representative example, a subject wrote, "The text plays on trivial clichés borrowed from the world of the post-human, the dystopian, and the post-apocalyptic."

In their reviews, readers, both amateurs and professionals alike, tried to attribute meaning to all eleven of Meimberg's Tweets as a whole, as if they were a single text, and criticised their fragmentary nature and disconnected sentences. They tried in vain to find a genre for them: "Classifying the story into a genre is difficult. [It could be] fantasy, science fiction, detective story, spy story, generational tale." Most readers focused on the Biblical references in three Tweets. In professional reviews, in contrast, the classic vocabulary of criticism was employed, with terms such as postmodern, plot, deconstruction, dystopia, or stylistic signature, as well as no shortage of references to other authors.

The tools and style of amateur reviewers seemed poorer, and they often concluded their commentaries by recommending or discouraging the purchase of the book. One reviewer in particular deserved credit for recognizing the link to Twitter: "Short sentences, written according to the strict canons of Twitter. The sentences seem unfinished, but perhaps because they are extrapolated. A few (not all) successful puns.... I would not recommend buying the volume. However, if you have already bought it: happy reading."

Many comments fell into the category of "oppositional," as classified by Archetti, such as these two: "Pretentious text. Better to spend one's time on more constructive reading" and "But what is this text? It sounds like it was written by David Lynch."

These attitudes may be part of the "illusion of competence" studied by Dunning and Kruger (1999). According to their well-known experiments, when people are incompetent, they not only arrive at erroneous conclusions but are deprived of the ability to recognise their own mistakes. In the comments by amateur reviewers, they overestimated their own ability to judge a literary text both with respect to professionalism and level of education (note the different levels of education compared to professionals) and with respect to their own metacognitive abilities (Q21) in completing the task that was asked of them.

The three bars on the far left (Q19–21) of Figure 27 show the results of the metacognitive abilities of the subjects with regard to reviewing. Metacognition is the way professionals vs. amateur reviewers intend reviewing activity, how they see themselves as reviewers, and it is an indicator of the awareness that the two groups have with respect to sharing their opinions regarding the texts they read.

Here again, it came as no surprise that professionals (Q21) were more aware that a good book review required an average of some four hours of work, while amateurs thought less than three would be sufficient (in answer to the question "How many hours does it take to write a good review of a novel?"). In Q21, thirty-six professionals who decided to write a review ($M = 3.60$, $SD = 1.32$) compared to the twenty-five amateurs who did not ($M = 2.62$, $SD = 1.40$), and the results were significantly larger ($t(57) = 2.7$, $p = 0.008$).

To analyse reviews, we submitted them to a sentiment analysis. As Figure 28 shows, no large differences emerged between amateur and professional reviews; indeed, paradoxically, professionals had slightly higher values on body, emotion, and social, while non-professionals were higher on cognitive processes, confirming a similar result discussed in a previous study (Salgaro & Rebora 2018).

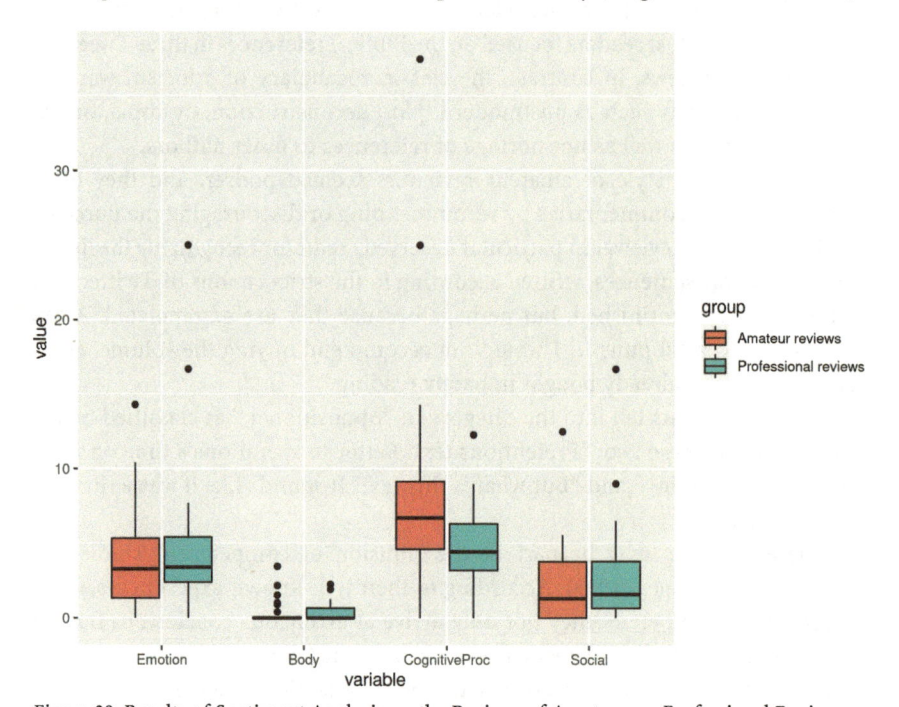

Figure 28: Results of Sentiment Analysis on the Reviews of Amateur vs. Professional Reviewers

One of the main findings concerned the length of the reviews, which was highly dependent upon differences between professional and amateur reviewers. While professional reviewers wrote reviews of an average of 109 words, amateurs on average used somewhat over half that number (62). The brevity of Meimberg's texts obviously had an impact on their vocabulary. Though we asked subjects to write reviews of at least ten sentences, only a fraction complied with this instruction. The results, consequently, were closer to the kinds of commentaries that appear on social-reading sites than to actual reviews.

Despite its limitations, our questionnaire is an instrument of a renewed methodological framework that can provide a snapshot of the ways in which reviewing is carried out in today's media landscape. In this multifaceted environment, traditional and newer media, paper and digital, alternate without being mutually exclusive; both a passion for reading and the desire to express opinions on books have found new forms of expression. Traditional books have been joined by audio books, and new genres such as Twitterature, literary weblogs (Fassio 2022), and instapoets have emerged within social media. The operationalisation of literary theory may help #instapoetry find its way to a new, more productive form of #instacriticism.

8. Measuring Readers' Reactions to Morally Bad Fictional Characters: Perpetrator Studies and the Shift of Empathy from Prosocial to Negative

The concept and the scientific study of empathy have boomed so dramatically in the last twenty years that the fences of academia can no longer contain them. The notion of being able to put oneself in other people's shoes (or in other people's clothes, as Italian has it) has entered everyday conversation and become a coveted quality, a so-called soft skill, that is both demanded and exhibited in the private and professional spheres. The transfer of this concept from the scientific field into general conversations was energized by the astonishingly large number of books on the subject that have been published in a wide range of fields: philosophy, aesthetics, evolutionary psychology, and the educational sciences; ethics and politics; linguistics, communication science, and media theory; cultural and gender studies; medicine and caregiving; law; neuroeconomics and neuromarketing; and theology. To mention only one example, the economist Jeremy Rifkin and the primatologist Frans de Waal almost simultaneously published large studies entitled, respectively, *The Empathic Civilization* (Rifkin 2009) and *The Age of Empathy* (de Waal 2010). Their approaches to empathy cover a great deal of territory: According to Rifkin, Darwin's evolutionary theory must be reconsidered because *Homo empathicus,* rather than *Homo homini lupus*, is the key to improving the fitness of humankind. In de Waal's opinion, *Homo* is *empathicus* because the empathic monkey still resides in each individual.

The concept of empathy has spread so widely and become so familiar that we do not question its exact definition. Simultaneously, the many discussions inside and outside academia hide the lack of a clear concept of empathy (Pinotti & Salgaro 2019). A 2016 article identified up to forty-three distinct definitions of empathy (Cuff *et al.* 2016), suggesting that one obstacle to the study of empathy is the absence of consensus regarding its meaning (Coplan 2011b). Researchers, meanwhile, are playfully asking "Will the real empathy please stand up?" (Coplan 2011a).

One reason for this vagueness is that the history of the concept of empathy is as complex as is the phenomenon it describes (Pinotti 2011). Andrea Pinotti recognized four main phases in the history of this concept, the first two of which are strongly linked to German culture. The term *Einfühlung* (translated from German into "empathy") made his first appearances in late eighteenth century and gained force between the late nineteenth and early twentieth centuries. The third phase began with the English translation of *Einfühlung* into *empathy* by Titchener in 1909 during the Anglo-Saxon dominance of psychological research. The neurosciences triggered the fourth phase of empathy studies, which started in the 1980s as the result of the discovery of mirror neurons by a team of neurologists at the University of Parma around Giacomo Rizzolatti. This brief historical excursus shows that, during the last century, concepts of empathy have crossed disciplines and cultural and linguistic contexts, contributing not only to their popularity but to the term's conceptual vagueness.

8.1.   Literary Empathy and Prosociality

A further striking feature of the fourth and current phase of empathy is the concept's ideological use. Such important philosophers as Martha Nussbaum (1997), have claimed that empathy triggers a human capacity for prosocial behaviour, thus creating a link between empathy and ethical behaviour. For Nussbaum, the reading of literature triggers an empathic involvement that is "an essential ingredient of an ethical stance that asks us to concern ourselves with the good of other people whose lives are distant from our own" (Nussbaum 1995: xvi).

More recently, the popular concept of empathy has spread into empirical research on literary reading, and experiments have shown that literary reading has a positive short- and long-term effect on our empathic abilities, a viewpoint that work by (Johnson 2013; 2012; Bunce & Stansfield 2014; Kidd & Castano 2013; Mar *et al.* 2011) seems to confirm. Our educational system is widely based on the assumption that literary reading improves students as people and citizens, and literature and the arts are thus seen as enhancing moral and prosocial attitudes (Koopman & Hakemulder 2015). In empathy studies, empathy not only describes a psychological phenomenon but becomes intertangled with the ideological perspectives of authors and researchers.

Such an ideological perspective on literary empathy has resulted in methodological shortcomings in studies such as those mentioned above. The stimuli used in experiments were not texts that could be considered representative of the history of literature. The fictional characters of these stories—an orphan girl in Botswana, for example, in Bunce and Stansfield (2014)—are so sui generis that they preclude a generalization of the results. In other cases, the stimuli "were designed to induce compassionate feelings for the characters and model prosocial behaviour" (Johnson 2012: 151). This description of the stimulus text in a recently published paper provides one example:

The intervention text in this study consisted of three selected passages from Richard Wagamese's novel, *Indian Horse* (2012). The novel presents a fictionalized, but realistic, portrayal of how the Residential Schools System has impacted and continues to impact the lives of Canadian Indigenous people. The first passage [...] powerfully describes the protagonist's and fellow Residential School children's feeling of being robbed of their freedom and their feeling of suffocation from having their identity and culture taken away from them. In the second passage [...] the protagonist recalls the tragic story of two sisters, the younger of whom died after being repeatedly placed in solitary confinement by the nuns running the school, after which the older sister committed suicide at her sister's funeral. The third passage [...] portrays the painful memory of the protagonist's extended sexual abuse by one of the Catholic Fathers running the school, who was also the protagonist's ice hockey coach. (Sopčák *et al.* 2022)

This kind of literary texts present a black-and-white morality in which the protagonist is depicted as both unambiguously positive and as holding victim status because she was abused. Even if the quoted text is contemporary, the unequivocal morality of this kind of fictional character is more in line with fables than it is with contemporary texts.

Beginning with Modernism, and even earlier, literature began to focus on morally ambiguous and even evil characters that audiences seem to appreciate: Faust, Raskolnikov, Madame Bovary, Iago, and Humbert Humbert are among the most notorious characters in world literature. While the experiments we have described assess empathy with morally good fictional characters, the history of literature offers numerous examples of amoral attitudes in novels, the theatre, and other forms of art (Ercolino & Fusillo 2022). By reconstructing the evolution of the concept of empathy, Ercolino (2018) theorized a sort of negative empathy in a fictional context. His thesis was that even negative empathy holds a cathartic function for the reader:

As far as literature is concerned, negative empathy, a form of high-level empathy, can be defined as a potentially regressive aesthetic experience, consisting in a cathartic identification with negative characters, which can be either open to agency—indifferently leading either to pro- or antisocial behaviour—or limited to the inner life of the empathizing subject. (Ercolino 2018: 252)

This empathic link between audience and morally negative or hybrid heroes dominates the reception of TV series (Salgaro & Tourhout 2018). In the last decade, the links among literature, empathy, and prosocial behaviour have been overemphasized and have occluded significant aspects of the aesthetic experience of literary texts. Another problem is a unilateral view of empathy which becomes an equivalent of "compassion" (Johnson 2012: 151). In fact, one reason for the predominantly positive connotation of empathy in studies of literary reception is that empathy has been narrowly defined as "sympathy and concern for unfortunate others" (Bal & Veltkamp 2013: 2).

The distinction between empathy and sympathy, which is the psychological term for compassion, is crucial in the study of immoral characters because, as research has shown, only sympathy involves a moral judgement. Recent studies have demonstrated that sympathy seems to involve an emotional understanding implying a moral evaluation, whereas empathy, "feeling with" another, is more neutral and could exist without identification (Jolliffe & Farrington 2006). Furthermore, even the most well-known questionnaire on empathy, Davis's "Interpersonal Reactivity Index" (1980), may "equate sympathy with empathy" (Jolliffe & Farrington 2006: 591).

Another shortcoming in studies on literary empathy is that, rather than underscore the peculiarities of *literary* empathy, psychological research tends to consider *literary* empathy and what we might call "everyday" empathy to be equivalent (Mar & Oatley 2008). Keith Oatley, who laid the groundwork in psychology for research of this kind, seems to adopt such a misinterpretation when he claims that "fiction is a set of simulations of social worlds that we can compare, as it were stereoscopically, with aspects of our everyday world" (Oatley 2016: 618).

In contrast to this equivalence of fiction and reality, Suzanne Keen has emphasized that the fictional quality of the imaginary world elicited by literary texts has no consequence on everyday life. Fictionality does have an impact on empathic feelings because "the perception of fictionality releases novel-readers from the normal state of alert suspicion of others' motives that often acts as a barrier to empathy" (Keen 2007: 169). Precisely because fiction and reality are not the same thing, readers experience them differently. Fictional framing, for example, leads to a "suspension of moral judgement" or "suspension of values" (Vaage 2013: 226–27).

8.2. The Shift toward Empathy with Morally Negative Characters and Perpetrators

The research described in the previous chapter was state-of-the-art until not long ago. In very recent years, a clear counter-trend has emerged to this understanding of the concept of empathy, a shift that has been due in part to the emergence of a new type of fictional hero in the contemporary imagination. Narratological analysis has emphasized that since 9/11, a shift has led to the development of a contemporary heroic model, the *hybrid hero*, a character that challenges both audience and creators on empathic, moral, and narrative levels (Salgaro & Tourhout 2018). In TV series like *Breaking Bad*, *Dexter*, or *House of Cards*, the hybrid hero is neither wholly a hero nor wholly a villain. The prevalent

trait of this typology of hero, then, is moral ambiguity. Contemporary heroes do not necessarily seek the moral approval of audiences but are looking for ways to arouse audiences and to gain their complicity, suggesting "the need of a turn in the concept of fictional empathy" (Salgaro & Tourhout 2018) that could revise at least three aspects of the concept of fictional empathy:
1. The distinction between empathy and sympathy or compassion;
2. The disentanglement of empathy from morality;
3. The link between negative empathy and aesthetic enjoyment.

The rise of the hybrid hero in contemporary media induced a shift in aesthetic criticism and in the study of empathic reactions to fictional characters. In recent years, research in media psychology has focused on more challenging moral contexts, including morally ambiguous characters. Experiments in this field have revealed that morally questionable protagonists were perceived to be more realistic and to elicit more enjoyment in readers. Creating a good, a bad, and a morally ambiguous version of an invented story, Krakowiak and Oliver (2012) showed that a good protagonist was better liked than were the morally ambiguous and the bad character and that narratives featuring good characters were more affectively enjoyed. Though morally ambiguous characters were liked less than good characters, they were nevertheless equally enjoyed.

This experiment shows that the notion of aesthetic enjoyment is multidimensional and cannot be compressed into the black-and-white schema of much empathy research. Konijn and Hoorn (2005: 110), for example, have noted that "characters deemed fascinating combine good and bad features, which for the observer, may evoke desirable inner conflicts, such as agreeable sensations of suspense." Other research in media psychology seems to support this view by showing that a moral violation in fiction elicits mixed responses in enjoyment and emotion (McGraw & Warren 2010).

The concept of empathy seems to have changed in recent years in fields other than media psychology. Contemporary researchers have tried to decouple empathy from morality (Prinz 2011; Bloom 2016) by showing the lack of evidence for a strong correlation between empathy and prosocial motivation. Other research goes further in overturning the link between empathy and morality. In their paper *The Dark Side of Empathy: Mimesis, Deception, and the Magic of Alterity*, Bubandt and Willerslev (2016) reported two cases of field research related to the social phenomena of hunting and political violence, in both of which the empathic faculty was used for deceptive and ultimately violent purposes. The two ethnologists labelled such behaviour "tactical empathy" in which the empathetic incorporation of others' perspectives is motivated by seduction, deception, or manipulation with an ultimate violent intent. Like Prinz and Bloom, these researchers broke with the implicit moral economy of the concept of empathy and criticised dominant academic trends in the study of empathy that "see it not only as a human capacity, but also as a human virtue" (Bubandt & Willerslev 2015: 11).

In literary studies as well, more and more criticism has been raised against a singular understanding of empathy. Suzanne Keen (2007: 99) first observed that "the faith in the relationship between reading narratives and moral or social benefits is so strong that it remains a bedrock assumption of many scholars, philosophers, critics, and cultural commentators," suggesting that empathy is more easily engaged in the domain of fiction because there are fewer costs and risks associated with it.

Inspired by Keen, Fritz Breithaupt proposed, in his 2016 *Empathy for Empathy's Sake: Aesthetic and Everyday Aesthetic Sadism,* that the dark sides of empathy could be approached by examining morally bad acts to experience empathy. For Breithaupt (2016: 155), the aesthetic experience provided a risk-free involvement that made it possible "to enjoy empathy devoid of any obligation." Thus "the involvement of spectators in tragedies would be an ideal form of this empathy for empathy's sake" (2016: 156) because audiences are not truly interested in the fate of the hero rather in the overwhelming emotions and deep reflections it elicits. Breithaupt considered empathy to be self-centred and observed that the aesthetic dimension triggered empathic feelings for selfish reasons. Only an understanding of empathy as "empathy for empathy's sake" can explain the reactions of audiences to the hybrid hero in TV series or theatre (Breithaupt 2019).

This turn toward morally negative characters is visible in Holocaust Studies as well, which has witnessed a shift to the figure of the Perpetrator. This new focus, at the centre of so-called "Perpetrator Studies," comes after years in which attention was paid mostly to the representation of victims of the Holocaust, who were rightly given precedence. More than a few literary texts have been written from a fictional perpetrator's perspective, however, including *La Mort est Mon Métier* (1952) by Robert Merle, *La Danse de Gengis Cohn* (1967) by Romain Gary, and *Der Nazi und der Friseur* (1977) by Edgar Hilsenrath. More recent novels such as *Er Ist Wieder Da* (2012) by Timur Vermes and *Der Kommandant: Monolog* (2012) by Jürg Amann further constitute this highly problematic genre.

The "Perpetrator Genre" is thorny for several reasons. Fictionalization is generally considered inadequate when dealing with the Shoah, especially if a Nazi perspective is involved, because it pushes historical fact into an "unreal" dimension. In addition, the subject is "taboo, which places the imagination of the consciousness of the perpetrator outside acceptable discourse on the Holocaust" (McGlothlin 2010: 213). The representation of the perpetrators of a genocide puts both authors and readers on challenging ethical ground where aesthetic criteria seem to fail. Very often these fictional texts seem manipulative, inducing empathy and sympathy for the vicious protagonists and exculpating them.

8.3   The Operationalisation of Empathy in the Case of Morally Negative Characters

In studying reception to literary texts, the notion that "bad is stronger than good"—a phrase used in the psychology of emotions—has been operationalised, and empirical evidence has been found for its existence in research conducted at the Max Planck Institute for Empirical Aesthetics in Frankfurt in collaboration with Winfried Menninghaus and Valentin Wagner (Salgaro *et al.* 2021). In this experiment, the stimulus material was created by manipulating the initial paragraphs of the José Saramago's 1997 novel, *Blindness,* to change the moral nature of the protagonist. The experimental modification was limited to the addition of a few words that referred abstractly to good, bad, and evil actions that the characters had carried out many years prior. Compared to the length of the original excerpt (2,380 words), the word count for the three insertions was marginal (57, 62, and 64 words for the good, bad, and evil versions, respectively).

In the "good" variant, one character was a doctor who had worked in a hospital in Africa and had saved many patients; in the "bad" variant, he had previously served in an Egyptian secret service prison and was involved in torture. In a third "evil" variant, the character was identified as a Nazi officer who had killed prisoners in a concentration camp during World War II. The passage describes a man who becomes blind while waiting at a red light in his car and focusses on how he navigates the world around him given his sudden loss of sight. To offer a glimpse into this highly engaging text, this passage comes from the beginning of the novel used in the experiment:

> The green light came on at last, the cars moved off briskly, but then it became clear that not all of them were equally quick off the mark. The car at the head of the middle lane has stopped, there must be some mechanical fault, a loose accelerator pedal, a gear lever that has stuck, problem with the suspension, jammed brakes, breakdown in the electric circuit, unless he has simply run out of gas, it would not be the first time such a thing has happened. The next group of pedestrians to gather at the crossing see the driver of the stationary car wave his arms behind the windshield, while the cars behind him frantically sound their horns. Some drivers have already got out of their cars, prepared to push the stranded vehicle to a spot where it will not hold up the traffic, they beat furiously on the closed windows, the man inside turns his head in their direction, first to one side then the other, he is clearly shouting something, to judge by the movements of his mouth he appears to be repeating some words, not one word but three, as turns out to be the case when someone finally manages to open the door, I am blind. (Saramago 1997)

In the original text, the main character is a man whose name the reader will not discover; in the experimental conditions, the following sentences were changed:

1. He has observed these uncontrolled responses among the patients in the African hospital (good)/inmates in the high security prison in Egypt (bad)/ prisoners in the concentration camp where he once worked (evil);
2. That happened often in the hospital (good)/prison (bad)/concentration camp (evil), that valuables suddenly disappeared;
3. Spontaneously, he attributed the blindness to the medicines (good)/drugs (bad)/gas (evil) he was shown in the clinic in Africa (good)/in the concentration camp (evil)/during the interrogations in Egypt (bad);
4. It was in this dream that he saw the faces of the people whom he had saved (good)/tortured (bad)/killed (evil). (Salgaro *et al.* 2021)

The texts presented were in German, and the 196 participants who completed the online experiments were also German. We excluded from this pool of participants (a) participants who showed an unrealistically high reading speed; (b) participants who made mistakes in responding to the control questions; (c) participants who reported that they had read the novel or seen the film, and (d) participants who reported a language other than German as their native language. The final sample thus consisted of 141 participants. The mean age of the final sample was 39.9 years (SD = 17.8, min = 18, max = 79), with 100 women (71%) and 41 men (29%). Besides collecting data on gender and age, a German version of the author recognition test (Stanovich & West 1989) was employed to evaluate the participants' exposure to literature. After reading one version of Saramago's manipulated text, subjects were asked to complete questionnaires regarding their reactions. Table 13 shows the results of their answers to such questions as "How beautiful/entertaining/boring (Knoop *et al.* 2016) did you find the text?"—in other words, their aesthetic evaluations

Variable	contrast	η_G^2/est.	MSE/SE	df	F/t	p	
suspenseful		.038	2.59	(2,138)	2.71	.070	†
	bad—evil	0.68	0.33	138	2.07	.040	*
	bad—good	0.65	0.34	138	1.93	.055	†
	evil—good	-0.03	0.34	138	-0.09	.928	
captivating		.044	2.72	(2,138)	3.18	.045	*
	bad—evil	0.66	0.34	138	1.96	.052	†
	bad—good	0.80	0.34	138	2.34	.021	*
	evil—good	0.15	0.34	138	0.42	.672	
carrying_away		.003	2.77	(2,138)	0.22	.799	
	bad—evil	0.08	0.34	138	0.25	.805	
	bad—good	0.23	0.35	138	0.67	.507	
	evil—good	0.15	0.35	138	0.42	.675	
interesting		.012	2.22	(2,138)	0.84	.434	
	bad—evil	0.20	0.30	138	0.66	.513	

(Continued)

Variable	contrast	η_G^2/est.	MSE/SE	df	F/t	p	
	bad—good	0.40	0.31	138	1.30	.197	
	evil—good	0.20	0.31	138	0.65	.516	
boring		.012	2.48	(2,138)	0.83	.438	
	bad—evil	-0.02	0.32	138	-0.06	.957	
	bad—good	0.36	0.33	138	1.10	.273	
	evil—good	0.38	0.33	138	1.15	.253	
entertaining		.136	2.45	(2,138)	10.82	<.001	***
	bad—evil	1.29	0.32	138	4.07	<.001	***
	bad—good	1.28	0.33	138	3.94	<.001	***
	evil—good	-0.01	0.33	138	-0.04	.968	
surprising		.003	2.52	(2,138)	0.22	.805	
	bad—evil	0.20	0.32	138	0.63	.529	
	bad—good	0.16	0.33	138	0.47	.636	
	evil—good	-0.05	0.33	138	-0.14	.887	
well_made		.018	2.20	(2,138)	1.28	.282	
	bad—evil	0.06	0.30	138	0.20	.846	
	bad—good	0.46	0.31	138	1.48	.141	
	evil—good	0.40	0.31	138	1.29	.201	
aesthetically_valuable		.002	2.96	(2,138)	0.11	.897	
	bad—evil	0.06	0.35	138	0.17	.865	
	bad—good	0.17	0.36	138	0.46	.644	
	evil—good	0.11	0.36	138	0.30	.768	
beautiful		.009	2.60	(2,138)	0.62	.537	
	bad—evil	0.36	0.33	138	1.11	.271	
	bad—good	0.23	0.34	138	0.67	.501	
	evil—good	-0.14	0.34	138	-0.41	.686	
morally_valuable		.012	2.87	(2,138)	0.85	.429	
	bad—evil	0.03	0.34	138	0.08	.940	
	bad—good	0.41	0.35	138	1.18	.241	
	evil—good	0.39	0.35	138	1.10	.274	

Table 13: Version Contrasts of Text-Focused Ratings (Salgaro *et al.* 2021) Note. † p < .10, * p < .05, ** p < .01, *** p < .001.

After the reading task, empathy, perspective taking, and sympathy were assessed with items adopted from Busselle and Bilandzic's (2009) questionnaire, which they called the "Narrative Engagement Scale," including twelve items from the German version of the transportation scale (Green & Brock 2000; Appel & Richter 2010). The term "transportation" indicates a specific kind of narrative engagement: the extent to which a reader became immersed in or "transported" by a narrative (Busselle & Bilandzic 2009).

Subjects rated the items on seven-point scales ranging from 1 = *does not at all apply* to 7 = *strongly applies*. As an example, subjects replied to the following questions intended to assess "transportation" and "suspense": "After finishing the narrative, I found it easy to put it out of my mind"; "I wanted to learn how the narrative ended"; "I was impatient to see how the story would end"; "The narrative affected me emotionally."

Figure 29 shows the numerical data of responses to all the dimensions we tested.

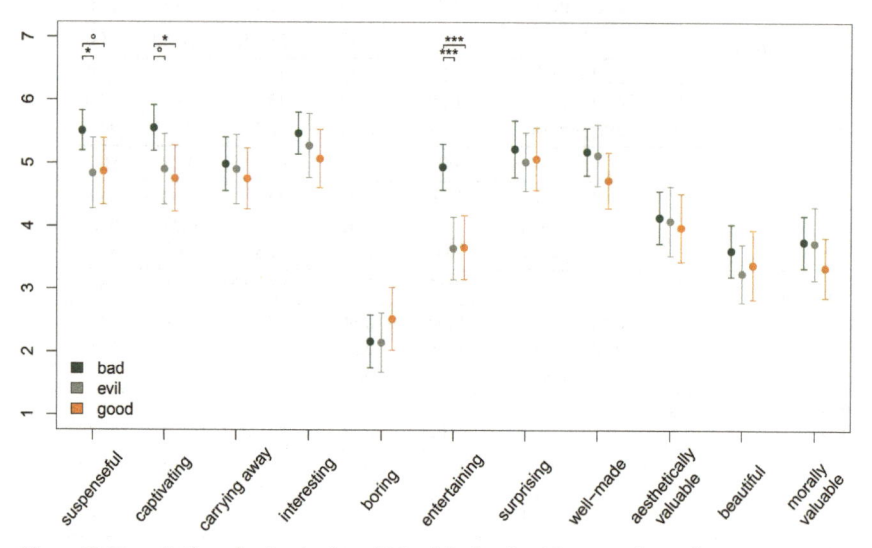

Figure 29: Mean Ratings for Aesthetic and Moral Evaluation Measures. (Error bars represent the 95 % CI. Significant differences between conditions are designated by p < .1, * p < .05, ** p < .01, *** p < .001.)

Statistical analysis showed that the three groups differed significantly:

(1) The BadCharacter version was rated as significantly more "captivating" and "entertaining" than the GoodCharacter version: $t = 2.34$, $p = .021$ and $t = 3.94$, $p < .001$. Ratings for "suspenseful" were also higher for the BadCharacter version, but this effect was only marginally significant.

(2) The BadCharacter version was also rated as significantly more "suspenseful" and "entertaining" than the EvilCharacter version: $t = 2.07$, $p = .040$ and $t = 4.07$, $p < .001$, respectively. Ratings for "captivating" showed a trend in the same direction, but the effect was only marginally significant.

(3) The ratings for the GoodCharacter and the EvilCharacter versions did not differ significantly on any of the eleven dimensions of aesthetic evaluation (all $ps > 0.2$). (Salgaro *et al.* 2021)

These results suggest that sympathy for an evil character was significantly lower than sympathy for either the good character or the bad character (which did not differ significantly from each other). The ANOVA for the mean sympathy score yielded a significant version-effect, $F(2, 138) = 3.47$, $MSE = 2.09$, $p = .034$, $\eta G2 = .048$, but no significant effects for empathy or perspective-taking were noted. The results for empathy showed no significant version-effect at all, lending at least partial support to the distinction between empathy and sympathy discussed previously (that is, that sympathy is more likely to involve dimensions of moral judgment than does empathy). These results are shown in Figure 30:

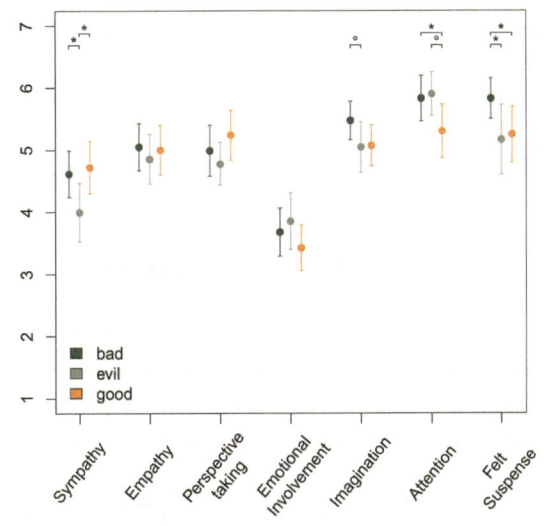

Figure 30: Mean Scores for Person State Measures. (Error bars represent the 95 % CI. Significant differences among the conditions are designated by p < .1, * p < .05, ** p < .01, *** p < .001. See Salgaro *et al.* 2021)

Most notably, even though the differences were small, the "bad character" version was rated as more "suspenseful," "captivating," and "entertaining" compared to both the good and the evil character version. Another outcome of the experiment is that because empathy did not differ in any of the three conditions, we concluded it was not crucial for the appreciation of characters. Taken together, these results problematize the link between empathy and "morally good" fictional characters.

The Frankfurt study showed that the shift toward "morally negative" and "morally ambiguous" fictional characters postulated in media psychology and literary theory is confirmed by readers' appreciation of morally bad characters. Nevertheless, gaps still exist in the research. For example, the experiment does not make clear whether there is a difference between the moral nature of the protagonists and readers' perception of the nature of the protagonists.

Another question is linked to cultural constraints in the moral evaluation of fictional characters. The subjects in the experiment were German, and one of the manipulations introduced a character with a Nazi past, which is highly relevant to Germany's history. The second issue touched upon the intercultural validity of the study's results. In the original experiment, German readers encountered a story about a former Nazi in the evil version of the narrative, but it is unclear whether the topic would be treated in the same way by readers from another cultural context—Italians, for example, for whom Fascism existed in their historic reality but who underwent a different process of education and coming to terms with the legacies of World War II.

To replicate our 2021 study (Salgaro *et al.* 2021) and, at the same time, to address questions of causality and intercultural validity, we carried out a similar between-subjects experiment. Italian-speaking participants read the same adapted excerpts—featuring a good, bad, or evil main character—from the Italian translation of *Blindness*.

We used a slightly different experimental design in this second experiment. Rather than asking the subjects if they find the text "morally valuable" to measure moral evaluation—as we had done previously (Salgaro *et al.* 2021)—we assessed participants' judgement of the character's morality through their responses to a more focused prompt: "In my eyes, the protagonist is a good person." As in the Frankfurt experiment, subjects were asked to reply on a seven-point scale.

Because the goal was to replicate our earlier findings, we tested *sympathy* alone in the second phase. Sympathy for the main character was measured through such prompts as, "I was sorry for what happened to the protagonist"; and "While I was reading, I was worried about Marco," items taken from the "sympathy" dimension of Busselle and Bilandzic's Narrative Engagement Scale (2009).

To assess the intercultural validity of the results of the original study, we introduced a measurement of Character Realism. In fact, we specifically wanted to test whether the evil Nazi character had a different impact on German readers in contrast to Italians. Research has shown that "perceived realism," meaning the closeness between fictional characters and readers, plays a role in responses to literary characters (Krakowiak & Oliver 2012). The more a character is perceived as close, the less she or he is considered fictional. Because evil fictional characters don't suffer real-life consequences, readers allow them a much higher degree of moral disengagement. Salgaro *et al.* (2021) believed that German readers in the original experiment submitted the protagonists of the excerpt, and the former Nazi in particular, to a so-called "reality check" that prevented them from enjoying the fictional nature of the stories. In consequence, they couldn't experience the "moral disengagement" or "suspension of moral judgement" that are typical of reading fiction.

Character Realism was measured using a combination of three items (based on Potter 1986; Shapiro & Chock 2003; Krakowiak & Oliver 2012), including (1) "The protagonist reminds me of someone I know"; and (2) "The protagonist acts like someone I know."

Two hundred and sixteen students at the University of Verona participated voluntarily in an online experiment conducted in March 2021 (for details, see De Jonge *et al.* n.d.). The students were presented with the experiment through their electronic-learning environment, "Moodle." From the pool, participants were deleted if they either were familiar with the narrative or incorrectly answered two or more of the four attention questions—leaving a sample of 202 participants (77.2% bachelor's students; 88.6% women). Seventy-three subjects participated in the "good" character condition, seventy in the "bad" condition, and fifty-nine in the "evil" condition.

Here, we mention only results that contributed to the discussion regarding the reception of negative heroes in literary reading. To test our hypotheses on the impact of the protagonist's morality, we conducted a MANOVA with character morality as a fixed factor; aesthetic evaluation, sympathy, transportation, and character realism as dependent variables; and moral judgement as a covariate. MANOVA was used to test all variables at once and thus control for non-normality and reduce type-1 errors.

	Character Morality	Moral Judgement	Sympathy	Aesthetic Evaluation	Transportation	Character Realism
Mean (SD)	Good	5.58 (1.26)	5.65 (1.34)	4.33 (1.05)	4.20 (.81)	2.32 (1.58)
	Bad	4.27 (1.55)	5.52 (1.45)	4.44 (.91)	4.26 (.73)	2.34 (1.61)
	Evil	4.19 (1.43)	5.20 (1.40)	4.52 (.93)	4.29 (.72)	2.13 (1.58)

Table 14: Descriptive Statistics

As Table 14 shows, character morality had only a marginally significant effect on aesthetic evaluation. The "good" character was evaluated as the least aesthetically pleasing ($M = 4.33$, $SD = 1.05$) and the "evil" character as most aesthetically pleasing ($M = 4.52$, $SD = .93$); the "bad" character was evaluated somewhere in between ($M = 4.44$, $SD = .91$). Compared to the Frankfurt study, the Verona study explored protagonists' morality more broadly, assessing the impact of moral judgements on ratings. In effect, moral judgement significantly predicts aesthetic evaluation—especially the aesthetic evaluations "beautiful," "suspenseful," "interesting," and "entertaining." We performed a mediation analysis using the PROCESS macro, Model 4, to explore the indirect relationships among character morality, moral judgement, and aesthetic evaluation to emphasize that moral judgement of a character is crucial to enjoyment of a fictional narrative. Figure 31 shows that an increased positive moral judgement was linked to an increased positive aesthetic evaluation.

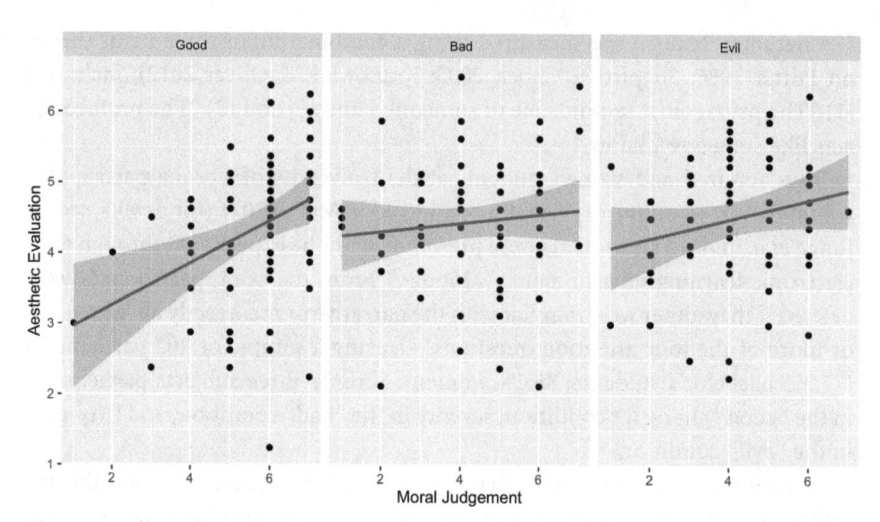

Figure 31: Effect of Moral Judgement on Aesthetic Evaluation, Sorted by Character Morality

Moreover, moral judgement had a significant effect on sympathy and a slightly significant effect on "transportation." Descriptive statistics in Table 14 show that the "good" character was evaluated as more of a good person ($M = 5.58$, $SD = 1.26$) than were the "bad" or "evil" character. As a result, we decided to use mediation analysis through the PROCESS macro, Model 4, to show that a character who is perceived as a morally better person elicits more sympathy than does a character who is perceived as less morally good. Figure 32 shows that if *perceived* morality (positive moral judgement) increases, sympathy increases.

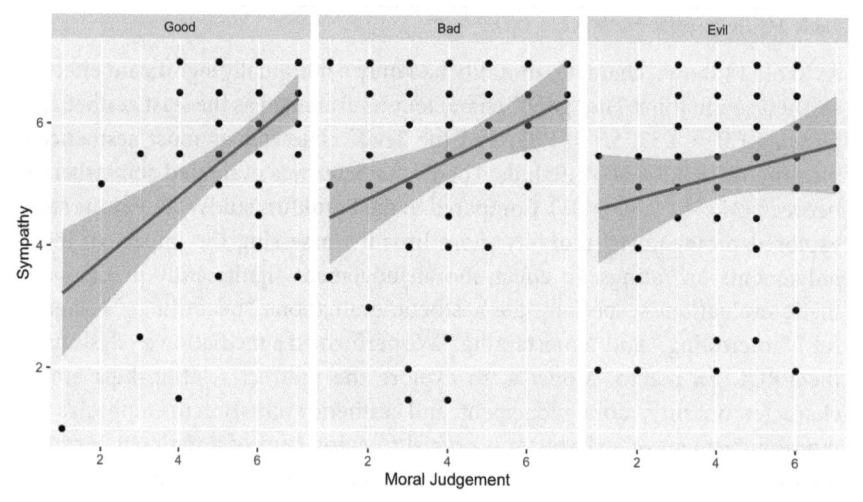

Figure 32: Effect of Moral Judgement on Sympathy, Sorted by Character Morality

Taken as a whole, these results confirm that "bad is preferred over good". The most interesting results of the Verona study underscore the finding that the crucial element was not the moral nature of the fictional character per se, but rather the reader's evaluation of the morality of that character. Thus, we might argue that the causal element in readers' aesthetic evaluations of and involvement in narratives with a "good," "bad," or "evil" character was indeed readers' *perception* of the character's moral nature.

With regard to intercultural validity, we found no effects among Italian readers of character morality or moral judgement on our measure of Character Realism. Italian readers may have performed a "reality check" on the former Nazi character but didn't feel the historic proximity German readers may have experienced (Salgaro *et al.* 2021). Scores of overall character realism were low. More interestingly, the "evil" character was perceived as less realistic than either the "good" or the "bad" character, perhaps explaining why Italian readers aesthetic evaluation of the narrative was high. Italian readers could experience moral disengagement while German readers could not. These results need further investigation, perhaps in other cultural contexts.

The Frankfurt and Verona experiments confirmed readers' preferences for morally negative fictional characters over positive ones, leaving open questions regarding, first, an explanation for the cause of this preference. Does fictional framing really allow readers to experience moral disengagement? Second, what are the limits of acceptance for morally negative behaviour? In the Verona experiment, subjects aesthetically appreciated the Nazi-version of the story, but would they have done so if the Nazi character were the protagonist of the story and actively involved in the Shoah? From the text used in the Verona and Frankfurt experiments, we only ascertain the past of the evil character and not the present. To answer these questions, we carried out a third experiment, once again at the University of Verona, using a novel with a Nazi protagonist as stimulus material (Jonathan Littell's 2006 *Les Bienveillantes*, translated by Charlotte Mandell as *The Kindly Ones* in 2009). This novel holds a privileged position in Perpetrator Studies because of both its literary qualities and its success. The protagonist's persona is complex: He is a Nazi officer, holds a law degree, has a deep knowledge of literature and philosophy, is homosexual, and has engaged in an incestuous relationship with his sister.

The novel has been criticized for its violence and its simulation of authenticity (Manoschek 2008) but most of all for inducing empathy and sympathy for the perpetrator (Richards 2009: 136; 142). Erin McGlothin distinguishes five types of identification in interactions between the protagonist and the novel's readers: the weakest form was "existential identification," or "the reader's basic recognition of the perpetrator as a human agent" (McGlothlin 2016: 260), and the strongest was "ideological identification," which was "the strength of the reader's alignment with the perpetrator's moral and ethical worldview and his justification for his own behaviour" (McGlothlin 2016: 264). Eva Mona Altmann (2021: 236–39) offered a more detailed analysis of the text by exactly describing the literary features that promoted or hindered empathy, sympathy, and antipathy. She also accused Littell of intending to elicit empathy or sympathy from the reader (2021: 334).

In the new experiment at the University of Verona, we tested two assumptions: Did fictionality foster moral disengagement? and, in turn, Did moral disengagement foster empathy for a perpetrator protagonist (a Nazi, in this case)?

We used passages from the two chapters of *The Kindly Ones* that Altmann (2021) had analysed: the first and another that recounted the Babi Yar episode in which masses of Jews in the Ukraine were executed during World War II. Participants read these excerpts and answered questions concerning their feelings toward and judgment of the protagonist and the events depicted in the narrative. In choosing these passages, we wanted to capture the complexity of the character of Maximilien Aue, the protagonist, as well as his constant and varied attempts to minimize his role in the horrors. The participants numbered 104, including B.A. and M.A. students of foreign languages and literature and staff at the University of Verona. They were divided into two groups: fifty-seven participants read the excerpts under the assumption that they had been taken from a novel, and forty-seven read the same text having been told it was an excerpt from an autobiography.

To measure actual moral disengagement, we followed the work of Krakowiak and Tsay (2011) and formulated nine items that fit both our text and Bandura's (2002) dimensions of moral disengagement: moral justification, euphemistic labelling, advantageous comparison, displacement of responsibility, diffusion of responsibility, disregard or distortion of consequences, dehumanization, and attribution of blame. Three items were added to measure overall moral disengagement (see Table 15; Cronbach's alpha: 0.816).

Item	Corrected item—Total correlation
Maximilien Aue is a person like any other. He behaved like everyone else.	0.535
Maximilien Aue is not to be blamed for his action during the war, because he was simply carrying out orders.	0.732
The Nazi regime is to be blamed for the killings Maximilien Aue committed, not Maximilien Aue himself.	0.621
Maximilien Aue is an intellectual with a passion for the absolute and for overcoming limits. What he did in war was a consequence of this creativity.	0.229
It is impossible to establish who is guilty in a genocide because so many people are involved.	0.185
Maximilien Aue never wanted to become a murderer, he was forced to do it.	0.535

(Continued)

Item	Corrected item— Total correlation
Maximilien Aue is right when he says that in most cases the man standing above the mass grave no more asked to be there than the one lying, dead or dying, at the bottom of the pit.	0.473
Because the Jews who were deported and arrested were dirty, without proper clothes and without documents, Maximillian Aue could consider them non-humans.	0.047
In the circumstances of war a man is forced to kill, so Maximilien Aue had no other choice.	0.720
Maximilien Aue was morally justified in all his actions during the war.	0.617
I consider Maximilien Aue's actions incorrect.	0.366
I believe that, in general, Maximilien Aue is a morally just person.	0.590

Table 15: Reliability Analysis of "Moral Disengagement" (De Jonge *et al.* 2022)

Empathy for Maximilien Aue was measured using the State Empathy Scale During Message Processing constructed by Shen (2010). The scale captures three dimensions of state empathy in four items each, affective empathy, cognitive empathy, and associative empathy (see Table 16; Cronbach's alpha: 0.903). Answers to all items were measured on a seven-point Likert scale: 1 = not at all, 7 = very much.

Item	Corrected item— Total correlation
Affective Empathy	
Maximilien Aue's emotions are genuine.	0.520
I experienced the same emotions as Maximilien Aue when reading this story.	0.696
I was in a similar emotional state as Maximilien Aue when reading this story.	0.696
I can feel Maximilien Aue's emotions.	0.605
Cognitive Empathy	
I can see Maximilien Aue's point of view.	0.622
I recognize Maximilien Aue's situation.	0.715
I can understand what Maximilien Aue was going through.	0.501
Maximilien Aue's reactions to the situation are understandable.	0.663
Associative Empathy	
When reading the story, I was fully absorbed.	0.377
I can relate to what Maximilien Aue was going through in the story.	0.682
I can identify with the situations described in Maximilien Aue's story.	0.670
I can identify with Maximilien Aue in the story.	0.736

Table 16: Reliability Analysis of "Empathy" (De Jonge *et al.* 2022)

Our results showed that the fictional variant of the story had an indirect effect on empathy through moral disengagement ($B = 0.190$; 95% CI [0.005, 0.415]). Fictionalization had a significant effect on moral disengagement because readers who read the text presented to them as an excerpt from a novel ($M = 3.76$, $SD = 0.86$) experienced significantly higher levels of moral disengagement than did readers who read the narrative presented to them as an autobiography ($M = 3.41$, $SD = 0.96$), $t(102) = 1.990$ $p = 0.049$. Moreover, higher levels of moral disengagement led to significantly higher levels of empathy for Maximilien Aue ($B = 0.535$, $t(101) = 4.708$, $p < 0.001$).

We can therefore conclude that fictionality does foster moral disengagement by allowing the reader to experience empathy for a perpetrator protagonist such as a Nazi.

The success of negative or hybrid heroes in films and TV series is perhaps the result of the fact that, in a fictional context, we look less for opportunities to confirm existing moral values and express prosocial thoughts and intentions and more for chances to experience the moral disengagement allowed by a dimension that exists apart from everyday life. Disengagement makes it possible to experience new selves in contrast with our everyday morality. Taken as a whole, the results of our experiments show that a significant part of modern of contemporary literature makes it possible to experience negative empathy which, according to Ercolino and Fusillo:

> is an aesthetic experience that consists of a cathartic empathising with characters [...] who are connoted in a way that is negative, seductive, and disturbing and who evoke a destabilising violence capable of triggering deep empathic anguish, insistently asking the reader to engage in moral reflection and pushing him or her to take an ethical stance. (Ercolino & Fusillo 2022)

This liminal experience renders literature a privileged and enriching dimension of existence for readers. From the point of view of literary theory, operationalisation is a way for us to value the richness and complexity of literary experience through various tools and methods.

Index

References

Ackerman, Rakefet, and Morris Goldsmith. 2011. 'Metacognitive Regulation of Text Learning: On Screen versus on Paper.' *Journal of Experimental Psychology: Applied* 17 (1): 18–32. https://doi.org/10.1037/a0022086.

Adorno, Theodor W. 2002. 'Late Style in Beethoven'. In *Essays on Music by Theodor W. Adorno*, edited by Richard Leppert, 564–68. Berkeley: University of California Press.

Ajouri, Philip, Katja Mellmann, and Christoph Rauen. 2013. *Empirie in der Literaturwissenschaft*. Münster: mentis Verlag.

Allesch, Johannes von. 1921. *Wege zur Kunstbetrachtung*. Dresden: Sybillen Verlag.

Altmann, Eva Mona. 2021. *Das Unsagbare verschweigen: Holocaust-Literatur aus Täterperspektive: eine interdisziplinäre Textanalyse*. Bielefeld: Transcript.

Alvarado, Rafael C. 2019. 'Digital Humanities and the Great Project: Why We Should Operationalize Everything—and Study Those Who Are Doing So Now'. In *Debates in the Digital Humanities 2019*, edited by Matthew K. Gold and Lauren F. Klein, 75–82. University of Minnesota Press. https://doi.org/10.5749/j.ctvg251hk.

Amann, Klaus, Karl Corino, and Walter Fanta. 2009. *Robert Musil: Klagenfurter Ausgabe: kommentierte Edition sämtlicher Werke, Briefe und nachgelassener Schriften, mit Transkriptionen und Faksimiles aller Handschriften*. Klagenfurt: Robert Musil-Institut, Alpen-Adria Universität Klagenfurt.

Anderson, Porter. 2022. 'The Lunar New Year: China's Book Market in 2021'. Publishing Perspectives. 1 February. https://publishingperspectives.com/2022/02/on-the-lunar-new-year-chinas-market-in-2021-covid19/.

Antonakaki, Despoina, Paraskevi Fragopoulou, and Sotiris Ioannidis. 2021. 'A Survey of Twitter Research: Data Model, Graph Structure, Sentiment Analysis and Attacks'. *Expert Systems with Applications* 164 (February): 114006. https://doi.org/10.1016/j.eswa.2020.114006.

Anz, Thomas. 2010. 'Kontinuitäten und Veränderungen der Literaturkritik in Zeiten des Internets: Fünf Thesen und einige Bedenken'. In *Digitale Literaturvermittlung: Praxis, Forschung, Archivierung*, edited by Renate Giacomuzzi, Stefan Neuhaus, and Christiane Zintzen, 48–63. Innsbruck: StudienVerlag.

Appel, Markus, and Tobias Richter. 2010. 'Transportation and Need for Affect in Narrative Persuasion: A Mediated Moderation Model'. *Media Psychology* 13 (2): 101–35. https://doi.org/10.1080/15213261003799847.

Archetti, Marco. 2017. 'Viaggio tra i commenti ai libri su Amazon, dove l'ignoranza dei passanti si fa giudice supremo'. *Il foglio*, 11 December. https://www.ilfoglio.it/cultura /2017/12/11/news/viaggio-tra-i-commenti-ai-libri-su-amazon-dove-lignoranza-dei-pa ssanti-si-fa-giudice-supremo-168164/.

Bal, P. Matthijs, and Martijn Veltkamp. 2013. 'How Does Fiction Reading Influence Empathy? An Experimental Investigation on the Role of Emotional Transportation'. Edited by Liane Young. *PLoS ONE* 8 (1): e55341. https://doi.org/10.1371/journal.pone.0055341.

Bally, Charles. 1970. *Traité de stylistique française*. Genève: Librarie de l'Université.

Bandura, Albert. 2002. 'Selective moral disengagement in the exercise of moral agency'. *Journal of Moral Education* 31(2). 101–119.

Baßler, Moritz. 2019. 'Der Konsens ist weg. In Leipzig treffen Leserschaft, KritikerInnen, Verlage und Buchhandel aufeinander. Zuletzt haben sie sich allerlei Kränkungen zugefügt'. *Tageszeitung*, 16.03. https://taz.de/Buchmesse-in-Leipzig/!5577851/.

–. 2021. '"Der Neue Midcult"'. *POP-ZEITSCHRIFT* 18: 132–149. https://pop-zeitschrift.de /2021/06/28/der-neue-midcultautorvon-moritz-bassler-autordatum28-6-2021-datum/.

Bell, Alice, Sam Browse, Alison Gibbons, and David Peplow, eds. 2021. *Style and Reader Response: Minds, Media, Methods*. Amsterdam: John Benjamins Publishing Company. https://doi.org/10.1075/lal.36.

Benn, Gottfried. 1989. 'Altern als Problem für Künstler'. In *Gottfried Benn. Sämtliche Werke*, edited by Gerhard Schuster and Holger Hof, 6:123–51. Stuttgart: Klett.

Bloom, Paul. 2016. *Against Empathy: The Case for Rational Compassion*. New York, NY: Ecco.

Blumenberg, Hans. 1997. 'Letzte Bücher'. *Marbacher Magazin* 2: 165–172.

Blumesberger, Susanne. 2006. 'Felix Salten und seine vielfältigen Beziehungen zu Wien'. In *Felix Salten. Der unbekannte Bekannte*, edited by Ernst Seibert and Susanne Blumesberger, 13–26. Wien: Praesens.

Bolter, J. David. 2019. *The Digital Plenitude: The Decline of Elite Culture and the Rise of Digital Media*. Cambridge, Massachusetts: The MIT Press.

Boot, Peter. 2013. 'The Desirability of a Corpus of Online Book Responses'. In *Proceedings of the Second Workshop on Computational Linguistics for Literature*, 32–40. https://aclan thology.org/W13-1405.

Bourdieu, Pierre. 2001. 'Television'. *European Review* 9 (3): 245–56. https://doi.org/10.10 17/S1062798701000230.

Bourdieu, Pierre, and Randal Johnson. 1993. *The Field of Cultural Production: Essays on Art and Literature*. New York: Columbia University Press.

Braidotti, Rosa. 2014. *Il postumano. La vita oltre l'individuo, oltre la specie, oltre la morte*. Roma: Derive Approdi.

Breithaupt, Fritz. 2016. 'Empathy for Empathy's Sake: Aesthetics and Everyday Empathic Sadism'. In *Empathy and Its Limits*, edited by Aleida Assmann and Ines Detmers, 151–65. London: Palgrave Macmillan UK. https://doi.org/10.1057/9781137552372_9.

–. 2019. *The Dark Sides of Empathy*. Translated by Andrew B. B. Hamilton. Ithaca [New York]: Cornell University Press.

Bridgman, Percy Williams. 1927. *The Logic of Modern Physics*. New York: Macmillan.

Broch, Herrmann. 1995. 'Mythos und Altersstil'. In *Schriften zur Literatur 2. Theorie*, edited by Paul Michael Lützeler, 212–34. Frankfurt am Main: Suhrkamp Verlag.

Bruneau, Charles. 1951. 'La stylistique'. *Romance Philology*, 1951, 5(1): 1–14.

Bryman, Alan. 2003. *Quantity and Quality in Social Research*. London: Routledge. https://doi.org/10.4324/9780203410028.

Bubandt, Nils, and Rane Willerslev. 2015. 'The Dark Side of Empathy: Mimesis, Deception, and the Magic of Alterity'. *Comparative Studies in Society and History* 57 (1): 5–34. https://doi.org/10.1017/S0010417514000589.

Bunce, Louise, and John Stansfield. 2014. 'The Relationship Between Empathy and Reading Fiction: Separate Roles for Cognitive and Affective Components'. *Journal of European Psychology Students* 5 (July): 9–18. https://doi.org/10.5334/jeps.ca.

Burke, Michael. 2018a. 'Rhetoric and Poetics: The Classical Heritage of Stylistics'. In *The Routledge Handbook of Stylistics*, edited by Michael Burke, 11–31. London; New York: Routledge.

–. ed. 2018b. *The Routledge Handbook of Stylistics*. London; New York: Routledge.

Burke, Michael, and Kristy Evers. 2018. 'Formalist Stylistics'. In *The Routledge Handbook of Stylistics*, edited by Michael Burke, 31–45. London; New York: Routledge.

Burke, Michael, and Michaela Mahlberg, eds. 2018. 'Corpus Stylistics'. In *The Routledge Handbook of Stylistics*, 378–93. London; New York: Routledge.

Burrows, John, and Hugh Craig. 2012. 'Authors and Characters'. *English Studies* 93 (3): 292–309. https://doi.org/10.1080/0013838X.2012.668786.

Burrows, John Frederick. 1987. *Computation into Criticism: A Study of Jane Austen's Novels and an Experiment in Method*. Oxford [Oxfordshire]: New York: Clarendon Press; Oxford University Press.

Busselle, Rick, and Helena Bilandzic. 2009. 'Measuring Narrative Engagement'. *Media Psychology* 12 (4): 321–47. https://doi.org/10.1080/15213260903287259.

Cafiero, Florian, and Jean-Baptiste Camps. 2022. *Affaires de style*. Paris: Le Robert.

Catano, James V. 1988. *Language, History, Style: Leo Spitzer and the Critical Tradition*. London: Routledge.

Chang, Hasok. 2021. 'Operationalism'. In *The Stanford Encyclopedia of Philosophy*, edited by Edward Zalta. https://plato.stanford.edu/archives/fall2021/entries/operationalism/.

Chervel, Thierry. 2021. 'Die Kritik und ihre Päpste: Rückblick auf ein Genre'. In *Rezensiv – Online-Rezensionen und Kulturelle Bildung*, edited by Guido Graf, Ralf Knackstedt, and Kristina Petzold, 297–302. Bielefeld: transcript Verlag. https://doi.org/10.1515/978383 9454435-019.

Cieliebak, Mark, Jan Milan Deriu, Dominic Egger, and Fatih Uzdilli. 2017. 'A Twitter Corpus and Benchmark Resources for German Sentiment Analysis'. In *Proceedings of the Fifth International Workshop on Natural Language. Processing for Social Media*, 45–51. Valencia, Spain: Association for Computational Linguistics. https://doi.org/10.186 53/v1/W17-1106.

Ciula, Arianna, and Øyvind Eide. 2016. 'Modelling in Digital Humanities: Signs in Context'. *Digital Scholarship in the Humanities*, September, i33–46. https://doi.org/10.1093/llc /fqw045.

Coplan, Amy. 2011a. 'Will the Real Empathy Please Stand up? A Case for a Narrow Conceptualization'. *The Southern Journal of Philosophy* 49 (1): 40–65. https://doi.org/10.1 111/j.2041-6962.2011.00056.x.

–. 2011b. 'Understanding Empathy: Its Features and Effects'. In *Empathy: Philosophical and Psychological Perspectives*, edited by Amy Coplan and Peter Goldie, Oxford: Oxford University Press. https://doi.org/10.1093/acprof:oso/9780199539956.003.0002.

Corbetta, Piergiorgio. 2014. *Metodologia e tecniche della ricerca sociale*. Bologna: Il Mulino.

Craig, Hugh, and Arthur F Kinney. 2009. *Shakespeare, Computers, and the Mystery of Authorship*. Cambridge: Cambridge University Press. http://dx.doi.org/10.1017/CBO97 80511605437.

Crane, Gregory. 2006. 'What Do You Do with a Million Books?' *D-Lib Magazine* 12 (3). https://doi.org/10.1045/march2006-crane.

Cuff, Benjamin M.P., Sarah J. Brown, Laura Taylor, and Douglas J. Howat. 2016. 'Empathy: A Review of the Concept'. *Emotion Review* 8 (2): 144–53. https://doi.org/10.1177/1754 073914558466.

Dalen-Oskam, Karina van. 2014. 'Epistolary Voices. The Case of Elisabeth Wolff and Agatha Deken'. *Literary and Linguistic Computing* 29 (3): 443–51. https://doi.org/10.1 093/llc/fqu023.

De Jonge, Julia, Serena Demichelis, Simone Rebora, and Massimo Salgaro. 2022. 'Operationalizing Perpetrator Studies. Focusing Readers' Reactions to The Kindly Ones by Jonathan Littell'. *Journal of Literary Semantics*, 1–15. https://doi.org/10.1515/jls-2022-2057.

De Jonge, Julia, Massimo Salgaro, Simone Rebora, Frank Hakemulder, and Elly A. Konijn. n.d. (in press). Literary Figures Who Are "Breaking Bad". Moral and Aesthetic Appreciation of Immoral Characters.

DeCarlo, Matthew. 2018. *Scientific Inquiry in Social Work*. Open Social Work Education: Minneapolis. https://open.umn.edu/opentextbooks/textbooks/591.

Delgado, Pablo, Cristina Vargas, Rakefet Ackerman, and Ladislao Salmerón. 2018. 'Don't Throw Away Your Printed Books: A Meta-Analysis on the Effects of Reading Media on Reading Comprehension'. *Educational Research Review* 25 (November): 23–38. https://doi.org/10.1016/j.edurev.2018.09.003.

Dimino, Mariaelisa, Simone Rebora, and Massimo Salgaro. 2021. 'Ein Schlachtfeld der Zuschreibung von Autorschaft. Musils propagandistische Beiträge in der Frontzeitung "Heimat" (1918)'. *Studia Theodisca* 28: 101–132. https://doi.org/10.54103/1593-2478/1 6674.

Dimitrov, Stefan, Faiyaz Zamal, Andrew Piper, and Derek Ruths. 2015. 'Goodreads Versus Amazon: The Effect of Decoupling Book Reviewing And Book Selling'. In *Proceedings of the Ninth International AAAI Conference on Web and Social Media in Oxford*, 602–5. AAAI Press.

Drees, Jan, and Sandra Annika Meyer. 2013. *Twitteratur. Digitale Kürzestschreibweisen*. Berlin: Frohmann.

Dupont, Bruno. 2014. 'Erzählen im Zeitalter des Internets'. *Germanica* 55: 189–207. https://doi.org/10.4000/germanica.2702.

Eco, Umberto. 1979. *Lector in fabula: la cooperazione interpretativa nei testi narrativi*. Milano: Bompiani.

Eddy, Beverley D. 2010. *Felix Salten: Man of Many Faces*. Riverside, California: Ariadne Press.

Eder, Jens, Fotis Jannidis, and Ralf Schneider, eds. 2010. *Characters in Fictional Worlds: Understanding Imaginary Beings in Literature, Film, and Other Media*. Berlin; New York: De Gruyter.

Eder, Maciej. 2015. 'Rolling Stylometry'. *Digital Scholarship in the Humanities*, 2015, 31(3): 457–469, https://doi.org/10.1093/llc/fqv010.

–. 2017. 'Visualization in Stylometry: Cluster Analysis Using Networks'. *Digital Scholarship in the Humanities* 32 (1): 50–64. https://doi.org/10.1093/llc/fqv061.

Eder, Maciej, Jan Rybicki, and Mike Kestemont. 2016. 'Stylometry with R: A Package for Computational Text Analysis'. *The R Journal* 8 (1): 107–21.

Ehrenfels, Christian von. 1890. 'Über Gestaltqualitäten'. *Vierteljahrsschrift für wissenschaftliche Philosophie* 14: 249–292.

Eichhorn, Peter. 1971. *Idee und Erfahrung im Spätwerk Goethes.* Freiburg: K. Alber.

Elkins, James. 2003. 'Style'. In *Oxford Art Online.* Oxford: Oxford University Press. https://doi.org/10.1093/gao/9781884446054.article.T082129.

Elliot, Mark, Fairweather, Ian, Wendy Kay Olsen, and Maria Pampaka. 2016. *A Dictionary of Social Research Methods.* Oxford: Oxford University Press. http://oxfordreference.com/view/10.1093/acref/9780191816826.001.0001/acref-9780191816826.

Engel, Manfred, and Bernd Auerochs, eds. 2010. *Kafka-Handbuch: Leben, Werk, Wirkung.* Stuttgart: Metzler.

Ercolino, Stefano. 2018. 'Negative Empathy: History, Theory, Criticism'. *Orbis Litterarum* 73 (3): 243–62. https://doi.org/10.1111/oli.12175.

Ercolino, Stefano, and Massimo Fusillo. 2022. *Empatia negativa. Il punto di vista del male.* Milano: Bompiani.

Evert, Stefan, Thomas Proisl, Fotis Jannidis, Isabella Reger, Steffen Pielström, Christof Schöch, and Thorsten Vitt. 2017. 'Understanding and Explaining Delta Measures for Authorship Attribution'. *Digital Scholarship in the Humanities* 32 (suppl_2): ii4–16. https://doi.org/10.1093/llc/fqx023.

Fanta, Walter. 2000. *Die Entstehungsgeschichte des 'Mann ohne Eigenschaften' von Robert Musil.* Wien: Böhlau.

Fassio, Marcella. 2022. 'Prädigitale Autorschaft und auktoriale Deutungshoheit in literarischen Weblogs'. *Sprache und Literatur* 51 (1): 36–51. https://doi.org/10.30965/25890859-05002013.

Ferri, Sandro. 2022. *L'editore presuntuoso.* Assolo. Roma: Edizioni E/o.

Fialho, Olivia, and Sonia Zyngier. 2018. 'Quantitative Methodological Approaches to Stylistics'. In *The Routledge Handbook of Stylistics*, edited by Michael Burke, 329–46. London; New York: Routledge.

Fish, Stanley Eugene. 1980. *Is There a Text in This Class?: The Authority of Interpretive Communities.* Cambridge: Harvard University Press.

–. 2000. *Is There a Text in This Class? The Authority of Interpretive Communities.* Cambridge: Harvard University Press.

Franzen, Johannes. 2021. 'Everyone's a critic: Rezensieren in Zeiten des ästhetischen Plebiszit'. In *Unterstellte Leseschaften: Tagung, Kulturwissenschaftliches Institut Essen, 29. bis 30. September 2020.* DuEPublico. https://doi.org/10.37189/duepublico/74186.

–. 2022a. 'Echtzeitfeuilleton? Kulturjournalismus nach der Digitalisierung'. In *Feeds, Tweets & Timelines – Schreibweisen der Gegenwart in Sozialen Medien*, 111–29. Bielefeld: transcript Verlag. https://www.degruyter.com/document/isbn/9783839463857/html?lang=de.

–. 2022b. 'Die Trennung von Publikum und Autor: Neue Näheverhältnisse in der literarischen Öffentlichkeit nach der Digitalisierung'. *Sprache und Literatur* 51 (1): 116–33. https://doi.org/10.30965/25890859-05002017.

Frenzel, Herbert A., and Elisabeth Frenzel. 1985. *Daten deutscher Dichtung: chronologischer Abriss der deutschen Literaturgeschichte.* München: Deutscher Taschenbuch-Verlag.

Freuler, Regula. 2011. 'Zwitschern mit Goethe. Viel Blabla und etwas Twitteratur'. *Neue Zürcher Zeitung*, 13 February 2011. http://www.nzz.ch/aktuell/feuilleton/uebersicht/zwi tschern-mit-goethe-1.9498080.

Frier, Sarah. 2020. *No Filter: The inside Story of Instagram.* New York: Simon & Schuster.

Ganascia, Jean-Gabriel. 2015. 'The Logic of the Big Data Turn in Digital Literary Studies'. *Frontiers in Digital Humanities* 2 (December). https://doi.org/10.3389/fdigh.2015.00007.

Gazzaley, Adam, and Larry D. Rosen. 2016. *The Distracted Mind: Ancient Brains in a High-Tech World.* Cambridge: MIT Press.

Gellai, Szilvia. 2015. 'Dramatische Vernetzung in Daniel Glattauers E-Mail-Romanen'. *Text&Kritik:* 151–163.

Gerlach, Jin, and Peter Buxmann. 2011. 'Investigating the Acceptance of Electronic Books: The Impact of Haptic Dissonance on Innovation Adoption'. Presented at the 19th European Conference on Information Systems, ECIS 2011, Helsinki, Finland, June 9–11.

Ginzburg, Carlo. 2013. 'Clues. Roots of an Evidential Paradigm'. In *Clues, Myths, and the Historical Method*, 96–126. Baltimore: Johns Hopkins University Press.

Gius, Evelyn. 2019. 'Computationelle Textanalysen als fünfdimensionales Problem: Ein Modell zur Beschreibung von Komplexität'. *Pamphlet #8*, 2019.

Gius, Evelyn, Anna Murawska, Oliver Schmidt, Carla Sökefeld, and Michael Vauth. 2020. 'Sentiment Sensitivity. Using Sentiment Analysis in Literary Studies to Analyze Genre and the Depiction of Illness'. Presented at the DH 2020. https://dh2020.adho.org/wp -content/uploads/2020/07/470_SentimentsensitivityUsingsentimentanalysisinliterarys tudiestoanalyzegenreandthedepictionofillness.html.

Glattauer, Daniel. 2009. *Alle sieben Wellen: Roman.* Wien: Deuticke.

–. 2012. *Love Virtually.* Translated by Jamie Bulloch. London: MacLehose Press.

Green, Melanie C., and Timothy C. Brock. 2000. 'The Role of Transportation in the Persuasiveness of Public Narratives.' *Journal of Personality and Social Psychology* 79 (5): 701–21. https://doi.org/10.1037/0022-3514.79.5.701.

Gregoriu, Christiana. 2018. 'The Linguistic Levels of Foregrounding in Stylistics'. In *The Routledge Handbook of Stylistics*, edited by Michael Burke, 87–101. London New York: Routledge.

Grimm, Jacob. 2010. *Rede über das Alter.* Göttingen: Steidl.

Hajibayova, Lala. 2019. 'Investigation of Goodreads' Reviews: Kakutanied, Deceived or Simply Honest?' *Journal of Documentation* 75 (3): 612–26. https://doi.org/10.1108/J D-07-2018-0104.

Hajibayova, Lala, and Mallory McCorkhill. 2021. 'Graphic Novels through the Lens of Goodreads Reviews: Artistic, Textual, or Blend of Both?' *Journal of Librarianship and Information Science*, July, 09610006211033898. https://doi.org/10.1177/0961000621103 3898.

Hall, Murray G. 2015. 'Josef und Josefine Mutzenbacher. Oder Recycling der Pornographie'. In *Erotisch-Pornografische Lesestoffe: Das Geschäft mit Erotik und Pornografie im Deutschen Sprachraum vom 18. Jahrhundert bis zur Gegenwart*, edited by Christine Haug, Johannes Frimmel, Anke Vogel, Teresa Lang, and Franz Adam, 159–81. Wiesbaden: Harrassowitz Verlag.

–. 2019. '"zu einem recht negativen Ergebnis für Sie". Vielleicht besser: Ein recht negatives Ergebnis. Die Erben Felix Saltens und der Rechtsstreit um Josefine Mutzenbacher (courtesy of the author)'. Presented at: Im Schatten von Bambi. Felix Salten zum 150. Geburtstag, 5.–6. September 2019, Wienbibliothek. https://www.wienbibliothek.a t/veranstaltungen-ausstellungen/veranstaltungskalender/im-schatten-bambi-felix-salt en-150-geburtstag.

Hansen-Löve, Aage Ansgar, Brigitte Obermayr, and Georg Witte, eds. 2013. *Form und Wirkung: phänomenologische und empirische Kunstwissenschaft in der Sowjetunion der 1920er Jahre; [Beiträge der Konferenz 'Die vergessene Akademie. Interdisziplinäre Kunstwissenschaft, phänomenologische und psychologische Ästhetik in Russland 1920–1930' vom 4. – 6. Dezember 2009 an der Freien Universität Berlin].* München: Fink.

Harada, Takashi, and Sawako Yamashita. 2010. 'The Analysis of Differences between Online Book Reviews and Those in Newspapers'. *Joho Chishiki Gakkaishi* 20 (2): 65–72. https://doi.org/10.2964/jsik.20_65.

Harding, Jennifer Riddle. 2018. 'Reader Response Criticism and Stylistics'. In *The Routledge Handbook of Stylistics*, edited by Michael Burke, 68–85. Routledge Handbooks in English Language Studies. London, New York: Routledge.

Hayer, Björn. 2015. 'Der E-Mail-Roman in der Schule: didaktische Überlegungen zur Medialiät in Daniel Glattauers Roman "Gut gegen Nordwind"'. *Literatur in Wissenschaft und Unterricht* 48: 121–130.

Hayles, N. Katherine. 2020. *Postprint: Books and Becoming Computational.* New York: Columbia University Press.

Herrmann, Berenike, and Gerhard Lauer. 2017. 'KOLIMO. A Corpus of Literary Modernism for Comparative Analysis'. https://kolimo.uni-goettingen.de/about.

Herrmann, J. Berenike. 2018. 'In a Test Bed with Kafka. Introducing a Mixed-Method Approach to Digital Stylistics'. *Digital Humanities Quarterly* 011 (4). http://www.digi talhumanities.org/dhq/vol/11/4/000341/000341.html.

Herrmann, J. Berenike, Christof Schöch, and Karina van Dalen-Oskam. 2015. 'Revisiting Style, a Key Concept in Literary Studies'. *Journal of Literary Theory* 9 (1): 25–52.

Herrmann, Jasmin, Moritz Ingwersen, Björn Sonnenberg-Schrank, and Olga Tarapata, eds. 2020. *Revisiting Style in Literary and Cultural Studies: Interdisciplinary Articulations.* New York: Peter Lang.

Holmes, David. 1998. 'The Evolution of Stylometry in Humanities Scholarship'. *Literary and Linguistic Computing* 13 (3): 111–17. https://doi.org/10.1093/llc/13.3.111.

Hoover, David. 2013. 'Almost All the Way Through — All at Once'. In *DH2013 Conference Abstracts*, 223–26. http://dh2013.unl.edu/abstracts/ab-124.html.

–. 2014. 'Modes of Composition in Henry James: Dictation, Style, and What Maisie Knew'. *The Henry James Review* 35 (3): 257–77. https://doi.org/10.1353/hjr.2014.0024.

–. 2017. 'The Microanalysis of Style Variation'. *Digital Scholarship in the Humanities* 32 (suppl_2): ii17–30. https://doi.org/10.1093/llc/fqx022.

Horstmann, Jan, and Rabea Kleymann. 2019. 'Alte Fragen, neue Methoden – Philologische und digitale Verfahren im Dialog. Ein Beitrag zum Forschungsdiskurs um Entsagung und Ironie bei Goethe'. *Zeitschrift für digitale Geisteswissenschaften.* https://doi.org /10.17175/2019_007.

Illouz, Eva. 2007. *Cold Intimacies: The Making of Emotional Capitalism.* Cambridge, UK; Malden, MA: Polity Press.

Ingold, Philipp. 2014. 'Laienherrschaft – in Klagenfurt und anderswo', *Volltext* 3. https://www.lyriktext.de/ingold-essays/laienherrschaft-n-in-klagenfurt-und-anderswo.

ISTAT. 2018. 'La produzione e la lettura di libri in Italia'. https://www.istat.it/it/archivio/225610.

Jacobs, Arthur M. 2019. 'Sentiment Analysis for Words and Fiction Characters From the Perspective of Computational (Neuro-)Poetics'. *Frontiers in Robotics and AI* 6 (July). https://doi.org/10.3389/frobt.2019.00053.

Jannidis, Fotis and Lauer, Gerhard. 2014. 'Jannidis, Fotis/Gerhard Lauer, Burrows's Delta and Its Use in German Literary History'. In *Distant Readings. Topologies of German Culture in the Long Nineteenth Century*, edited by Erlin Matt and Tatlock Lynne, 29–54. Rochester NY: Camden House.

Janssen, Susanne 2001. 'The Empirical Study of Careers in Literature and the Arts'. In *The Psychology and Sociology of Literature: In Honor of Elrud Ibsch*, edited by Elrud Ibsch, Dick H. Schram, and Gerard Steen, 323–57. Amsterdam; Philadelphia: Benjamins.

–. 1997. 'Reviewing as Social Practice: Institutional Constraints on Critics' Attention for Contemporary Fiction'. *Poetics* 24 (5): 275–97. https://doi.org/10.1016/S0304-422X(96)00010-1.

Jeffries, Lesley, and Dan McIntyre. 2010. *Stylistics.* Cambridge Textbooks in Linguistics. New York: Cambridge University Press.

Jockers, Matthew. 2014. 'A Novel Method for Detecting Plot'. http://www.matthewjockers.net/2014/06/05/a-novel-method-for-detecting-plot/.

–. 2013. *Macroanalysis: Digital Methods and Literary History.* Topics in the Digital Humanities. Urbana: University of Illinois Press.

Johnson, Dan R. 2012. 'Transportation into a Story Increases Empathy, Prosocial Behavior, and Perceptual Bias toward Fearful Expressions'. *Personality and Individual Differences* 52 (2): 150–55. https://doi.org/10.1016/j.paid.2011.10.005.

–. 2013. 'Transportation into Literary Fiction Reduces Prejudice against and Increases Empathy for Arab-Muslims'. *Scientific Study of Literature* 3 (1): 77–92. https://doi.org/10.1075/ssol.3.1.08joh.

Jolliffe, Darrick, and David P. Farrington. 2006. 'Development and Validation of the Basic Empathy Scale'. *Journal of Adolescence* 29 (4): 589–611. https://doi.org/10.1016/j.adolescence.2005.08.010.

Kafka, Franz. 1988. *The Complete Stories.* Translated by Nahum N. Glatzer. New York: Schocken Books.

Kahle, P., S. Colutto, G. Hackl, and G. Mühlberger. 2017. 'Transkribus – A Service Platform for Transcription, Recognition and Retrieval of Historical Documents'. In *2017 14th IAPR International Conference on Document Analysis and Recognition (ICDAR)*, 04:19–24. https://doi.org/10.1109/ICDAR.2017.307.

Kamphuis, Jan. 1991. 'Satisfaction with Books: Some Empirical Findings'. *Poetics* 20 (5–6): 471–85. https://doi.org/10.1016/0304-422X(91)90021-G.

Kastenbaum, R. 1985. 'Program of the Thirty-Eighth Annual Scientific Meeting of the Gerontological Society of America'. *Gerontologist* 25 (3): 252.

Kayser, Wolfgang. 1948. *Das sprachliche Kunstwerk. Eine Einführung in die Literaturwissenschaft.* Bern: Francke.

Keen, Suzanne. 2007. *Empathy and the Novel.* Oxford: Oxford University Press.

Kelih, Emmerich. 2008. *Geschichte der Anwendung quantitativer Verfahren in der russischen Sprach- und Literaturwissenschaft*. Hamburg: Kovač.

Kermode, Frank. 2000. *The Sense of an Ending: Studies in the Theory of Fiction: With a New Epilogue*. New York: Oxford University Press.

Kestemont, Mike. 2014. 'Function Words in Authorship Attribution. From Black Magic to Theory?' In *Proceedings of the 3rd Workshop on Computational Linguistics for Literature (CLFL)*, 59–66. Gothenburg, Sweden: Association for Computational Linguistics. https://doi.org/10.3115/v1/W14-0908.

Ketelsen, Uwe-Karsten. 2009. '"Ich weiß nicht, ob Sie der sind, als der Sie schreiben": eine Liebe in Zeiten der digitalisierten Kommunikation; Daniel Glattauer "Gut gegen Nordwind" (2006)'. In *Literarische Koordinaten der Zeiterfahrung*, edited by Joanna Ławnikowska-Koper, 132–42. Wrocław: Oficyna Wydawnicza ATUT.

Key, Ellen. 1919. *The Century of the Child*. New York; London: The Knickerbocker Press.

Kharde, Vishal. A., and Sheetal. Sonawane. 2016. 'Sentiment Analysis of Twitter Data: A Survey of Techniques'. *International Journal of Computer Applications*, no. 139(11): 5–15. https://doi.org/10.48550/ARXIV.1601.06971.

Kidd, David Comer, and Emanuele Castano. 2013. 'Reading Literary Fiction Improves Theory of Mind'. *Science* 342 (6156): 377–80. https://doi.org/10.1126/science.1239918.

Kim, Evgeny, and Roman Klinger. 2018. 'A Survey on Sentiment and Emotion Analysis for Computational Literary Studies'. *ArXiv:1808.03137 [Cs]*, August. http://arxiv.org/abs/1808.03137.

Kleinwort, Malte. 2013. *Der späte Kafka. Spätstil als Stilsuspension*. Paderborn: Fink.

Knoop, Christine A., Valentin Wagner, Thomas Jacobsen, and Winfried Menninghaus. 2016. 'Mapping the Aesthetic Space of Literature "from Below"'. *Poetics* 56 (June): 35–49. https://doi.org/10.1016/j.poetic.2016.02.001.

Konijn, Elly A., and Johan F. Hoorn. 2005. 'Some Like It Bad: Testing a Model for Perceiving and Experiencing Fictional Characters'. *Media Psychology* 7 (2): 107–44. https://doi.org/10.1207/S1532785XMEP0702_1.

Koopman, Eva Maria (Emy), and Frank Hakemulder. 2015. 'Effects of Literature on Empathy and Self-Reflection: A Theoretical-Empirical Framework'. *Journal of Literary Theory* 9 (1): 79–111. https://doi.org/10.1515/jlt-2015-0005.

Kousha, Kayvan, Mike Thelwall, and Mahshid Abdoli. 2017. 'Goodreads Reviews to Assess the Wider Impacts of Books'. *Journal of the Association for Information Science and Technology* 68 (8): 2004–16. https://doi.org/10.1002/asi.23805.

Krakowiak, K. Maja, and Mary Beth Oliver. 2012. 'When Good Characters Do Bad Things: Examining the Effect of Moral Ambiguity on Enjoyment'. *Journal of Communication* 62 (1): 117–35. https://doi.org/10.1111/j.1460-2466.2011.01618.x.

Krakowiak, K. M. and Tsay, M. 2011. 'The role of moral disengagement in the enjoyment of real and fictional characters'. *International Journal of Arts and Technology*, 4(1), 90–101. https://doi.org/10.1504/IJART.2011.037772.

Krautter, Benjamin. 2020. 'Figurenstil im deutschsprachigen Drama (1740–1930): Eine stilometrische Annäherung'. In *Reflektierte algorithmische Textanalyse*, edited by Nils Reiter, Axel Pichler, and Jonas Kuhn, 299–326. Berlin: De Gruyter. https://doi.org/10.1515/9783110693973-013.

Kreuzmair, Elias. 2017. '"The Dissociation Technique" – "Twitteratur" und das Motiv der Schreibszene in Texten von Renate Bergmann, Florian Meimberg und Jennifer Egan'.

Textpraxis. Digitales Journal für Philologie. www.uni-muenster.de/Textpraxis/elias-kre uzmair-twitteratur.

Kreuzmair, Elias, and Magdalena Pflock. 2020. 'Mehr als Twitteratur. Eine kurze Twitter-Literaturgeschichte, 24. 09. 2020'. *54books*.

Kruger, Justin, and David Dunning. 1999. 'Unskilled and Unaware of It: How Difficulties in Recognizing One's Own Incompetence Lead to Inflated Self-Assessments.' *Journal of Personality and Social Psychology* 77 (6): 1121–34. https://doi.org/10.1037/0022-3514.7 7.6.1121.

Kusche, Sabrina. 2012. 'Der E-Mail-Roman. Zur Medialisierung des Erzählens in der zeitgenössischen deutsch- und englischsprachigen Literatur'. Doctoral Thesis in German at Stockholm University, Stockholm. http://geb.uni-giessen.de/geb/volltexte/201 2/8903/pdf/KuscheSabrina_2012_05_25.pdf.

Lauer, Gerhard. 2015. 'Introduction: Empirical Methods in Literary Studies'. *Journal of Literary Theory* 9 (1): 1–3. https://doi.org/10.1515/jlt-2015-0001.

–. 2020. *Lesen im digitalen Zeitalter.* Geisteswissenschaften im digitalen Zeitalter, Band 1. Darmstadt: Wbg Academic.

Leech, Geoffrey N. 2007. 'New Resources, or Just Better Old Ones? The Holy Grail of Representativeness'. In *Corpus Linguistics and the Web*, edited by Marianne Hundt, Nadja Nesselhauf, and Carolin Biewer, 133–49. Amsterdam: Brill. https://doi.org/10.1 163/9789401203791.

Leech, Geoffrey N., and Mick Short. 2007. *Style in Fiction: A Linguistic Introduction to English Fictional Prose.* New York: Pearson Longman.

Leeder, Karen. 2015. 'Figuring Lateness in Modern German Culture'. *New German Critique* 42 (2 125): 1–29. https://doi.org/10.1215/0094033X-2889224.

Liebrand, Claudia, and Stefan Börnchen. 2019. 'Pikara-Roman, Meta-Pornografie und Institutionenkritik. Zur sexuellen Ethnografie der "Josefine Mutzenbacher"'. *Hofmannsthal-Jahrbuch. Zur Europäischen Moderne* 27: 275–97.

Liu, Bing. 2015. *Sentiment Analysis: Mining Opinions, Sentiments, and Emotions.* Cambridge: Cambridge University Press. https://doi.org/10.1017/CBO9781139084789.

Lodge, David. 1966. *Language of Fiction: Essays in Criticism and Verbal Analysis of the English Novel.* New York: Columbia University Press.

Löffler, Philipp, ed. 2017. *Reading the Canon: Literary History in the 21st Century.* Heidelberg: Universitätsverlag Winter.

Löffler, Sigrid. 2020. 'Machen Blogger die Literaturkritik kaputt?' *Deutschlandfunk Kultur.* https://www.deutschlandfunkkultur.de/sigrid-loeffler-ueber-amateure-vs-profis-ma chen-blogger-die-100.html.

Maar, Michael. 2021. *Die Schlange im Wolfspelz: das Geheimnis grosser Literatur.* Hamburg: Rowohlt.

Mahdawi, Arwa. 2016. 'Are You Ready for a Future Where We're All Reviewed like Uber Drivers?' *The Guardian*, 15.03. https://www.theguardian.com/technology/commentisf ree/2016/mar/15/rating-culture-score-personal-privacy-uber-sharing-economy.

Maity, Suman Kalyan, Ayush Kumar, Ankan Mullick, Vishnu Choudhary, and Animesh Mukherjee. 2018. 'Understanding Book Popularity on Goodreads'. *Proceedings of the 2018 ACM Conference on Supporting Groupwork – GROUP '18*, 117–21. https://doi.org /10.1145/3148330.3154512.

Mangen, Anne, and Don Kuiken. 2014. 'Lost in an IPad: Narrative Engagement on Paper and Tablet'. *Scientific Study of Literature* 4 (2): 150–77. https://doi.org/10.1075/sso l.4.2.02man.

Manoschek, Walter. 2008. '"Wir werden es nie erfahren"'. *Die Presse*, 17 March. https://www.diepresse.com/370435/bdquowir-werden-es-nie-erfahrenldquo.

Mar, Raymond A., and Keith Oatley. 2008. 'The Function of Fiction Is the Abstraction and Simulation of Social Experience'. *Perspectives on Psychological Science* 3 (3): 173–92. https://doi.org/10.1111/j.1745-6924.2008.00073.x.

Mar, Raymond A., Keith Oatley, Maja Djikic, and Justin Mullin. 2011. 'Emotion and Narrative Fiction: Interactive Influences before, during, and after Reading'. *Cognition & Emotion* 25 (5): 818–33. https://doi.org/10.1080/02699931.2010.515151.

Marks, Peter. 2017. *Imagining Surveillance: Eutopian and Dystopian Literature and Film.* Edinburgh: Edinburgh University Press.

Martens, Gunther, Lore de Greve, and Pranaydeep Singh. 2021. 'Literary Criticism 2.0: A Digital Analysis of the Professional and Community-Driven Evaluative Talk of Literature Surrounding the Ingeborg Bachmann Prize'. In *DH Benelux 2021*,. https://2021. dhbenelux.org/home/abstracts/.

Mau, Steffen. 2019. *The Metric Society: On the Quantification of the Social.* Cambridge; Medford: Polity Press.

McCarty, Willard. 2004. 'Modeling: A Study in Words and Meanings'. In *A Companion to Digital Humanities.* Malden: Blackwell Publishing: 254–70.

McGlothlin, Erin. 2010. 'Heorizing the Perpetrator in Bernhard Schlink's The Reader and Martin Amis's Time's Arrow'. In *After Representation? The Holocaust, Literature, and Culture*, edited by R. Clifton Spargo, Robert M. Ehrenreich, and United States Holocaust Memorial Museum, 210–30. New Brunswick, N.J: Rutgers University Press.

–. 2016. 'Empathetic Identification and the Mind of the Holocaust Perpetrator in Fiction: A Proposed Taxonomy of Response'. *Narrative* 24 (3): 251–76. https://doi.org/10.1353/nar.2016.0016.

McGrath, Laura B. 2020. 'America's Next Top Novel'. *Post45*. 8 April. https://post45.org/2020/04/americas-next-top-novel/.

McGraw, A. Peter, and Caleb Warren. 2010. 'Benign Violations: Making Immoral Behavior Funny'. *Psychological Science* 21 (8): 1141–49. https://doi.org/10.1177/09567976103760 73.

McMullan, Gordon. 2016. 'The "Strangeness" of George Oppen'. In *Late Style and Its Discontents: Essays in Art, Literature, and Music*, edited by Gordon McMullan and Sam Smiles, 31–48. Oxford University Press. https://doi.org/10.1093/acprof:oso/978019870 4621.001.0001.

McMullan, Gordon, and Sam Smiles, eds. 2016. *Late Style and Its Discontents: Essays in Art, Literature, and Music.* Oxford: Oxford University Press. https://doi.org/10.1093/acprof:oso/9780198704621.001.0001.

Meimberg, Florian. 2011. *Auf die Länge kommt es an: Tiny Tales; sehr kurze Geschichten.* Frankfurt am Main: Fischer Taschenbuch Verlag.

–. 2022. 'Webpage'. https://florian-meimberg.com/pages/about.

Meyer, Anne-Rose. 2014. 'Innovationen aus dem Netz? Kürzestgeschichten 'to go''. In *Die deutschsprachige Kurzgeschichte*, 166–69. Berlin: Erich Schmidt Verlag.

Meyer, Sandra Annika. 2019. 'Von Strom, Zeit und Raum. Digitale Kürze als literarisches Experimentierfeld'. In *Internet – Literatur – Twitteratur: Erzählen und Lesen im Medienzeitalter: Perspektiven für Forschung und Unterricht*, edited by Anne-Rose Meyer, 235–54. Berlin; Bern; Bruxelles; New York; Oxford; Warszawa; Wien: Peter Lang. https://doi.org/10.3726/b15191.

Monti, Claudia. 1995. 'Mancanza-pienezza. L'inversione percettiva di Musil'. *Cultura Tedesca* 3: 71–84.

–. 2000. 'L'altro lato dell'amore, Considerazioni su Die Amsel e Der Mann ohne Eigenschaften'. In *Robert Musils "Die Amsel". Kritische Lektüren. Materialien aus dem Nachass*, edited by Walter Busch and Ingo Breuer, 225–53. Innsbruck; Wien; Bozen: Sturzflüge/Edition Studienverlag.

Montini, Donatella. 2020. *La stilistica inglese contemporanea: teorie e metodi*. Roma: Carocci editore.

Moretti, Franco. 2013a. *Distant Reading*. London; New York: Verso.

–. 2013b. '"Operationalizing": Or, the Function of Measurement in Modern Literary Theory'. *Pamphlet of the Stanford Literary Lab*, 1–15.

–. 2022. *Falso movimento: la svolta quantitativa nello studio della letteratura*. Extrema ratio. Milano: Nottetempo.

Mosteller, Frederick, and David L. Wallace. 2007. *Inference and Disputed Authorship: The Federalist*. Stanford: Center for the Study of Language and Information.

Muller, Jerry Z. 2018. *The Tyranny of Metrics*. Princeton: Princeton University Press.

Müller-Seidel, Walter. 1993. 'Spätwerk und Alterskunst. Zum Ort Fontanes an der Schwelle zur Moderne.' In: '*Was hat nicht alles Platz in eines Menschen Herzen …*'. *Theodor Fontane und seine Zeit*, edited by Evangelische Akademie Baden, 120–51. Karlsruhe: Evangelischer Presseverband.

Murray, Simone. 2018. *The Digital Literary Sphere: Reading, Writing, and Selling Books in the Internet Era*. Baltimore: Johns Hopkins University Press.

Musil, Robert. 1987. *Posthumous Papers of a Living Author*. Hygiene, Colo: Eridanos Press.

Nassehi, Armin. 2019. *Muster: Theorie der digitalen Gesellschaft*. München: C.H. Beck.

Neuhaus, Stefan. 2017. 'Vom Anfang und Ende der Literaturkritik. Das literarische Feld zwischen Autonomie und Kommerz'. In *Die Rezension: aktuelle Tendenzen der Literaturkritik*, edited by Andrea Bartl, Markus Behmer, Martin Hielscher, Internationale Buchwissenschaftliche Gesellschaft, and Otto-Friedrich-Universität Bamberg. Würzburg: Königshausen & Neumann. https://literaturkritik.de/id/20276.

Nicoli, Roberto. 2013. '"Auf die Länge kommt es an": Florian Meimbergs "Tiny Tales" als Neuinterpretation der Kürzestgeschichte im Zeitalter von Twitter'. *Confronto Letterario* 60, 217–239.

–. 2016. 'Incompiutezza compiuta. Sulla Twitteratura di Florian Meimberg'. In *Open Literature. La cultura digitale negli studi letterari*, edited by Virginia Pignagnoli and Silvia Ulrich, 101–18. Torino: Dipartimento di Lingue e Letterature Straniere e Culture Moderne, Università di Torino. https://iris.unito.it/retrieve/handle/2318/1622379/6187 99/Trinchero_Articolo_Ricognizioni_2016.pdf.

Nussbaum, Martha C. 1997. *Cultivating Humanity: A Classical Defense of Reform in Liberal Education*. Harvard University Press.

–. 1995. *Poetic Justice: The Literary Imagination and Public Life*. Beacon Press.

Oatley, Keith. 2016. 'Fiction: Simulation of Social Worlds'. *Trends in Cognitive Sciences* 20 (8): 618–28. https://doi.org/10.1016/j.tics.2016.06.002.

Paccagnella, Ivano, and Elisa Gregori, eds. 2010. *Leo Spitzer. Lo stile e il metodo.* Padova: Esedra Editrice.

Passmann, Johannes. 2018. *Die soziale Logik des Likes: eine Twitter-Ethnografie.* Frankfurt: Campus Verlag.

Patton, Michael Quinn. 1990. *Qualitative Evaluation and Research Methods.* SAGE Publications.

Penke, Niels. 2022. 'Akzeleration und Experiment über Variation und Wiederholung in der Instapoetry'. In *Feeds, Tweets & Timelines – Schreibweisen der Gegenwart in sozialen Medien,* 77–93. Bielefeld: transcript Verlag. https://www.degruyter.com/document/isbn /9783839463857/html?lang=de.

Pennebaker, James W., and C.K. Chung. 2014. 'Counting Little Words in Big Data. The Psychology of Individuals, Communities, Culture, and History'. In *Social Cognition and Communication,* edited by Joseph P. Forgas, Orsolya Vincze, and János László, 25–42. Sydney Symposium of Social Psychology Series. New York: Psychology Press, Taylor & Francis Group.

Pförtner, Carmen. 2011. 'Florian Meimberg serviert Poesie als Espresso. Bielefelder schreibt knackig- kurze Twitter-Tiny Tales', *Neue Westfälische Zeitung,* 29 October.

Pianzola, Federico. 2021. *Digital Social Reading.* MIT Press. https://doi.org/10.1162/ba67f 642.a0d97dee.

Pianzola, Federico, Simone Rebora, and Gerhard Lauer. 2020. 'Wattpad as a Resource for Literary Studies. Quantitative and Qualitative Examples of the Importance of Digital Social Reading and Readers' Comments in the Margins'. Edited by David Orrego-Carmona. *PLOS ONE* 15 (1): e0226708. https://doi.org/10.1371/journal.pone.0226708.

Pichler, Axel, and Nils Reiter. 2020. 'Reflektierte Textanalyse'. In *Reflektierte algorithmische Textanalyse: interdisziplinäre(s) Arbeiten in der Creta-Werkstatt,* edited by Nils Reiter, Axel Pichler, and Jonas Kuhn, 43–59. Boston: De Gruyter.

–. 2021. 'Zur Operationalisierung literaturwissenschaftlicher Begriffe in der algorithmischen Textanalyse. Eine Annäherung über Norbert Altenhofers hermeneutische Modellinterpretation von Kleists Das Erdbeben in Chili'. *Journal of Literary Theory* 15 (1–2): 1–29. https://doi.org/10.1515/jlt-2021-2008.

Pinotti, Andrea. 2011. *Empatia: storia di un'idea da Platone al postumano.* Biblioteca di cultura moderna. Roma: Laterza.

Pinotti, Andrea, and Massimo Salgaro. 2019. 'Empathy or Empathies? Uncertainties in the Interdisciplinary Discussion'. *Gestalt Theory* 41 (2): 141–58. https://doi.org/10.2478/gth -2019-0015.

Pirro, Maurizio, and Luca Zenobi, eds. 2011. *Jugend: rappresentazioni della giovinezza nella letteratura tedesca.* Il quadrifoglio tedesco. Milano: Mimesis.

Plotnikov, Nikolaj. 2014. *Kunst als Sprache – Sprachen der Kunst. Russische Ästhetik und Kunsttheorie der 1920er Jahre in der europäischen Diskussion.* Hamburg: Meiner.

Porter, Alexander Manshel, Laura B. McGrath, J. D. 2021. 'The Rise of Must-Read TV'. The Atlantic. 16 July. https://www.theatlantic.com/culture/archive/2021/07/tv-adaptations-fiction/619442/.

Potter, W. James. 1986. 'Perceived Reality and the Cultivation Hypothesis'. *Journal of Broadcasting & Electronic Media* 30: 159–74. https://doi.org/10.1080/088381586093866 17.

Prensky, Marc. 2001. 'Digital Natives, Digital Immigrants Part 1'. *On the Horizon* 9 (5): 1–6. https://doi.org/10.1108/10748120110424816.

Prinz, Jesse J. 2011. 'Is Empathy Necessary for Morality?' In *Empathy: Philosophical and Psychological Perspectives*, edited by Amy Coplan and Peter Goldie, 211–29. Oxford: Oxford University Press. https://doi.org/10.1093/acprof:oso/9780199539956.003.0014.

Rebora, Simone. 2020a. 'Critica letteraria e metodi computazionali. Il caso della sentiment analysis'. In *Letteratura e altri saperi: influssi, scambi, contaminazioni*, edited by Anna Maria Babbi and Alberto Comparini, 209–30. Roma: Carocci editore.

–. 2020b. 'La stilometria per gli studi letterari: Un'introduzione'. *Symbolon*, 2020, 14 (11): 19–34.

Rebora, Simone, Peter Boot, Federico Pianzola, Brigitte Gasser, J. Berenike Herrmann, Maria Kraxenberger, Moniek M. Kuijpers, et al. 2021. 'Digital Humanities and Digital Social Reading'. *Digital Scholarship in the Humanities* 36 (Supplement_2): ii230–50. https://doi.org/10.1093/llc/fqab020.

Rebora, Simone, J. Berenike Herrmann, Gerhard Lauer, and Massimo Salgaro. 2018. 'Robert Musil, a War Journal, and Stylometry: Tackling the Issue of Short Texts in Authorship Attribution'. *Digital Scholarship in the Humanities*, October. https://doi.org/10.1093/llc/fqy055.

Rebora, Simone, and Massimo Salgaro. 2018. 'Is "Late Style" Measurable? A Stylometric Analysis of Johann Wolfgang Goethe's, Robert Musil's, and Franz Kafka's Late Works'. *Elephant & Castle* 18: 3–39.

–. 2022. 'Is Felix Salten the Author of the Mutzenbacher Novel (1906)? Yes and No'. *Language and Literature: International Journal of Stylistics* 31 (2): 243–64. https://doi.org/10.1177/09639470221090384.

Reckwitz, Andreas. 2017. *Die Gesellschaft der Singularitäten: zum Strukturwandel der Moderne*. Berlin: Suhrkamp.

Reeve, Jonathan. 2018. 'Does "Late Style" Exist? New Stylometric Approaches to Variation in Single-Author Corpora'. *DH2018 Book of Abstracts*, 2018, ADHO edition.

Reiter, Nils, Axel Pichler, and Jonas Kuhn, eds. 2020. *Reflektierte algorithmische Textanalyse: interdisziplinäre(s) Arbeiten in der Creta-Werkstatt*. Boston: De Gruyter.

Richards, Earl Jeffrey. 2009. 'Fiktionen des Bösen und "das Gewissen" der Nazis: "Les Bienveillantes" von Jonathan Littell'. In *Observatoire de l'extreme contemporain. Studien zur französischsprachigen Gegenwartsliteratur*, 129–47. Tübingen: Gunther Narr.

Richter, Sandra. 2020. 'Reading with the Workflow. Arbeitsprozesse in den Computational Literary Studies – Beiträge zur Empirisierung literaturwissenschaftlicher Verfahren'. In *Reflektierte Algorithmische Textanalyse: Interdisziplinäre(s) Arbeiten in Der Creta-Werkstatt*, 143–69. Boston: De Gruyter.

Riffaterre, Michael. 1959. 'Criteria for Style Analysis'. *WORD* 15 (1): 154–74. https://doi.org/10.1080/00437956.1959.11659690.

–. 1971. *Essais de stylistique structurale*. Paris: Flammarion.

Rifkin, Jeremy. 2009. *The Empathic Civilization: The Race to Global Consciousness in a World in Crisis*. New York: TarcherPerigee.

Rippl, Gabriele, and Simone Winko, eds. 2013. *Handbuch Kanon und Wertung*. Stuttgart: J.B. Metzler. https://doi.org/10.1007/978-3-476-05306-0.

Ronzon, Francesco. 2008. *Sul campo: breve guida pratica alla ricerca etnografica*. Milano: Meltemi Editore.

Rougemont, Denis de. 1983. *Love in the Western World*. Princeton: Princeton University Press.

Royal society for public health. 2017. '#StatusofMind'. https://www.rsph.org.uk/our-work/campaigns/status-of-mind.html.

Rushkoff, Douglas. 2013. *Present Shock: When Everything Happens Now*. New York, NY: Current.

Ruthner, Clemens. 2011. 'The Back Side of Fin-de-Siècle Vienna: The Infamously Infantile Sexuality of Josefine Mutzenbacher'. In *Contested passions: sexuality, eroticism, and gender in modern Austrian literature and culture*, edited by Modern Austrian Literature and Culture Association, Ruthner Conference Clemens, and Raleigh Whitinger, 91–105. New York: Peter Lang.

Ruthner, Clemens, Matthias Schmidt, and Carolin Schmieding, eds. 2019. *Die Mutzenbacher: Lektüren und Kontexte eines Skandalromans*. Wien: Sonderzahl.

Rybicki, Jan. 2017. 'Reading Novels with Statistics: What Numbers of Words Tell Us about Authorship, Genre, or Chronology'. In *Models and Reality: Festschrift For James Robert Thompson*, edited by John A. Dobelman, 207–24. Chicago: T&NO Company.

Rybicki, Jan, Katarzyna Biernacka-Licznar, and Monika Wozniak. 2018. 'Polysystem Theory and Macroanalysis. A Case Study of Sienkiewicz in Italian'. *DH2018 Book of Abstracts*, 2018, ADHO edition.

Sahle, Patrick, and Ulrike Henny. 2015. 'Klios Algorithmen: Automatisierte Auswertung von Wikipedia-Inhalten Als Faktenbasis Und Diskursraum'. In *Wikipedia und Geschichtswissenschaft*, edited by Thomas Wozniak, Jürgen Nemitz, and Uwe Rohwedder. Berlin, München, Boston: De Gruyter, 113–148. https://doi.org/10.1515/9783110376357-010.

Said, Edward W. 2006. *On "Late Style": Music and Literature Against the Grain*. New York: Pantheon.

Salgaro, Massimo. 2008. 'Kafka è Kafkiano?' *Cultura Tedesca* 35: 211–226.

–. 2015. 'How Literary Can Literariness Be?: Methodological Problems in the Study of Foregrounding'. *Scientific Study of Literature* 5 (2): 229–49. https://doi.org/10.1075/ssol.5.2.06sal.

–. 2018a. 'The Digital Humanities as a Toolkit for Literary Theory: Three Case Studies of the Operationalization of the Concepts of "Late Style," "Authorship Attribution," and "Literary Movement."' *Iperstoria* 12: 50–60.

–. 2018b. 'Historical Introduction to the Special Issue on Literariness'. *Scientific Study of Literature* 8 (1): 6–18. https://doi.org/10.1075/ssol.00005.sal.

–. 2019. 'Albert Ritter, der ghostwriter in der Redaktion der Tiroler Soldatenzeitung – ein biographisches Profil'. In *Robert Musil als Redakteur der Tiroler Soldaten Zeitung.*, edited by Mariaelisa Dimino, Elmar Locher, and Massimo Salgaro, 107–19. Paderborn: Fink Verlag.

–. 2021a. '"Schreiben ist wie küssen, nur ohne Lippen". Die virtuelle Liebe in "Gut gegen Nordwind" (2006) von Daniel Glattauer'. *Studia Austriaca* 29: 159–84.

–. 2021b. 'The History of the Empirical Study of Literature from the Nineteenth to the Twenty-First Century'. In *Handbook of Empirical Literary Studies*, edited by Donald Kuiken and Arthur M. Jacobs, 515–42. Berlin: De Gruyter. https://doi.org/10.1515/978 3110645958-020.

–. 2022a. 'Il cervello antico dell'homo digitalis. Leggere e studiare nell'era del digitale'. *Babylonia Journal of Language Education* 2: 12–17.

–. 2022b. 'The Writer Who Refused to Sign His Work: The Case of B. Traven'. *Studi Germanici* 21: 79–99.

–. 2022c. 'How Soon Is Now?: Zeitmaschinen und Zeitreisen in den "Tiny Tales" von Florian Meimberg'. *Zeitschrift Für Germanistik* 32 (2): 395–412. https://doi.org/10.372 6/92171_395.

Salgaro, Massimo, and Simone Rebora. 2018. 'Measuring the "Critical Distance". A Corpus -Based Analysis of Italian Book Reviews'. In *AIUCD2018 – Book of Abstracts*, edited by Daria Spampinato, 161–63. https://doi.org/10.6092/unibo/amsacta/5997.

Salgaro, Massimo, Pasqualina Sorrentino, Gerhard Lauer, Theresa Sylvester, Jana Lüdtke, and Arthur M. Jacobs. 2020. 'Does Age Determine Whether We Read E-Books?' In *The Materiality of Reading*, edited by Theresa Shilhab and Sue Walker, 46–67. Aarhus: Aarhus University Press.

Salgaro, Massimo, Pasqualina Sorrentino, Jana Lüdtke, Arthur M. Jacobs, and Gerhard Lauer. 2018. 'How to Measure the Social Prestige of a Nobel Prize in Literature". *TXT* 138–148. Amsterdam University Press edition.

Salgaro, Massimo, and Benjamin Van Tourhout. 2018. 'Why Does Frank Underwood Look at Us? Contemporary Heroes Suggest the Need of a Turn in the Conceptualization of Fictional Empathy'. *Journal of Literary Theory* 12 (2): 345–68. https://doi.org/10.1515/jl t-2018-0019.

Salgaro, Massimo, Valentin Wagner, and Winfried Menninghaus. 2021. 'A Good, a Bad, and an Evil Character: Who Renders a Novel Most Enjoyable?'. *Poetics* 87 (August): 101550. https://doi.org/10.1016/j.poetic.2021.101550.

Salten, Felix. 1967. *The Memoirs of Josefine Mutzenbacher. Attributed to Felix Salten, Author of Bambi*. Translated by Rudolf Schleifer. North Hollywood: Brandon House.

–. 2020. *Bambi*. Translated by David Wyllie. https://www.gutenberg.org/ebooks/63849.

Salten, Felix, and Michael Farin. 1990. *Josefine Mutzenbacher oder Die Geschichte einer wienerischen Dirne von ihr selbst erzählt*. München: Schneekluth.

Sampaolo, Giovanni. 2009. 'Il Tardo Goethe'. In *L'età classico-romantica. La cultura letteraria in Germania tra Settecento e Ottocento*, edited by Michele Cometa, 87–99. Bari: Laterza.

Saramago, José. 1997. *Blindness*. London: Harvill Press.

Schmitt, Dietmar, and Claudia Öhlschläger. 1994. 'Weibsfauna. Zur Koinzidenz von Tiergeschichte und Pornographie am Beispiel von Bambi und Josefine Mutzenbacher'. *Hofmannsthal-Jahrbuch* 2: 237–86.

Schneider-Özbek, Katrin. 2011. 'Daniel Glattauers E-Mail-Roman "Gut gegen Nordwind": nur die Modernisierung eines alten Genres?' *Zeitenwende. Österreichische Literatur seit dem Millennium, 2000–2010*, edited by Michael Boehringer, Susanne Hochreiter, 352–370. Wien: Praesens.

Schöch, Christoph, Daniel Schlör, Albin Zehe, Henning Gebhard, Martin Becker, and Andreas Hotho. 2018. 'Burrows' Zeta: Exploring and Evaluating Variants and Parameters'. In *DH2018 Book of Abstracts*, 274–78. Mexico City: ADHO.

Schreier, Margrit. 2010. 'Is It Possible to Give a 6 out of 5 Stars?": Book Selection and Recommendation in the Internet Age'. *Primerjalna Književnost* 13(2): 195–207.

Seidler, Miriam. 2010. *Figurenmodelle des Alters in der deutschsprachigen Gegenwartsliteratur*. Tübingen: Narr.

Shapiro, Michael A., and T. Makana Chock. 2003. 'Psychological Processes in Perceiving Reality'. *Media Psychology* 5: 163–98. https://doi.org/10.1207/S1532785XMEP0502_3.

Silvi, Daniele, and Fabio Ciotti. 2021. *Lezioni di informatica umanistica*. Roma: Universitalia.

Sopčák, Paul, Don Kuiken, and Shawn Douglas. 2022. 'Existential Reflection and Morality'. *Frontiers in Communication*. https://doi.org/10.3389/fcomm.2022.991774.

Sotirova, Violeta, ed. 2016. *The Bloomsbury Companion to Stylistics*. London; New York: Bloomsbury Academic.

Sovich, Nina. 2017. 'My Love Is Like a Hashtag; Instagram Gives Rise to New Poets'. *Wall Street Journal*, September. https://www.wsj.com/articles/my-love-is-like-a-hashtag-instagram-gives-rise-to-new-poets-1504954801.

Spitzer, Leo. 1920. *Die Umschreibungen des Begriffes 'Hunger' im Italienischen: Stilistisch-onomasiologische Studie auf Grund von unveröffentlichtem Zensurmaterial*. https://doi.org/10.1515/9783112324967.

–. 1967. *Linguistics and Literary History: Essays in Stylistics*. Princeton University Press. https://doi.org/10.1515/9781400878109.

–. 1988. *Representative Essays*, edited by Alban K. Forcione, Herbert Lindenberger, and Madeline Sutherland. Stanford: Stanford University Press.

–. 2016. *Piccolo Puxi: saggio sulla lingua di una madre*, edited by Anna Maria Babbi. Translated by Massimo Salgaro. Milano: Il saggiatore.

Spoerhase, Carlos. 2018. 'Rankings: A Pre-History'. *New Left Review* 114(6): 99–112.

Stalder, Felix. 2016. *Kultur der Digitalität*. Berlin: Suhrkamp.

Stamin, Caterina. 2022. 'BookTok, il trend da 75 miliardi di visualizzazioni, al Festivaletteratura di Mantova: "Così i creator rilanciano i libri che amano"'. La Stampa. 11 September. https://www.lastampa.it/cultura/2022/09/11/news/booktok_il_trend_da_7 5_miliardi_di_visualizzazioni_al_festivaletteratura_di_mantova_cosi_i_creatorrilan ciano_i_libri_ch-8659629/.

Stanovich, Keith E., and Richard F. West. 1989. 'Exposure to Print and Orthographic Processing'. *Reading Research Quarterly* 24 (4): 402. https://doi.org/10.2307/747605.

Starobinski, Jean. 1970. 'Leo Spitzer et La Lecture Stylistique'. In *Ètudes Des Style*, by Leo Spitzer. Paris: Gallimard.

Stockwell, Peter, and Sara Whiteley. 2015. *The Cambridge Handbook of Stylistics*. Cambridge: Cambridge University Press.

Surma-aho, Antti, and Katja Hölttä-Otto. 2022. 'Conceptualization and Operationalization of Empathy in Design Research'. *Design Studies* 78 (January): 101075. https://doi.org/10.1016/j.destud.2021.101075.

Taberner, Stuart. 2013. *Aging and Old-Age Style in Günter Grass, Ruth Klüger, Christa Wolf, and Martin Walser: The Mannerism of a Late Period*. Studies in German Literature, Linguistics, and Culture. Rochester, New York: Camden House.

–. 2015. 'Aging, Late Style, and Untimeliness in Recent Literary Fiction by Martin Walser'. *New German Critique* 125: 97–113.

Tatar, Maria. 2003. *The Hard Facts of the Grimms' Fairy Tales*. Princeton Oxford: Princeton University Press.

Tausczik, Yla R., and James W. Pennebaker. 2010. 'The Psychological Meaning of Words: LIWC and Computerized Text Analysis Methods'. *Journal of Language and Social Psychology* 29 (1): 24–54. https://doi.org/10.1177/0261927X09351676.

Thelwall, Mike, and Kayvan Kousha. 2017. 'Goodreads: A Social Network Site for Book Readers'. *Journal of the Association for Information Science and Technology* 68 (4): 972–83. https://doi.org/10.1002/asi.23733.

Tolentino, Jia. 2019. *Trick Mirror: Reflections on Self-Delusion*. New York: Random House.

Trunz, Erich. 1990. *Ein Tag aus Goethes Leben*. München: Beck.

Underwood, Ted. 2019. *Distant Horizons: Digital Evidence and Literary Change*. Chicago: The University of Chicago Press.

Vaage, Margrethe Bruun. 2013. 'Fictional Reliefs and Reality Checks'. *Screen* 54 (2): 218–37. https://doi.org/10.1093/screen/hjt004.

Van Rees, C.J. 1983. 'How a Literacy Work Becomes a Masterpiece: On the Threefold Selection Practised by Literary Criticism'. *Poetics* 12 (4–5): 397–417. https://doi.org/10.1016/0304-422X(83)90015-3.

Verboord, Marc. 2003. 'Classification of Authors by Literary Prestige'. *Poetics* 31 (3–4): 259–81. https://doi.org/10.1016/S0304-422X(03)00037-8.

Verdaasdonk, Hugo, and Kees van Rees. 1992. 'The Narrow Margins of Innovation in Literary Research'. *Poetics* 21 (1–2): 141–52. https://doi.org/10.1016/0304-422X(92)90027-Z.

Waal, Frans de. 2010. *The Age of Empathy: Nature's Lessons for a Kinder Society*. Illustrated Edition. New York: Crown.

Wang, Kai, Xiaojuan Liu, and Yutong Han. 2019. 'Exploring Goodreads Reviews for Book Impact Assessment'. *Journal of Informetrics* 13 (3): 874–86. https://doi.org/10.1016/j.joi.2019.07.003.

Wang, Yajie, and Alesia Zuccala. 2021. 'Scholarly Book Publishers as Publicity Agents for SSH Titles on Twitter'. *Scientometrics* 126 (6): 4817–40. https://doi.org/10.1007/s11192-021-03947-6.

Wastl, Nora. 2010. 'Geschickte Liebe – Daniel Glattauers "Gut gegen Nordwind" oder die Geburt des E-Mail-Romans'. Masterarbeit, Graz.

Weel, Adriaan van der. 2011. *Changing Our Textual Minds: Towards a Digital Order of Knowledge*. Manchester; New York: Manchester University Press.

Weichinger, Robert. 1991. 'Schluß mit Genuß! Wer schrieb die Mutzenbacher? Wer kriegt die Tantiemen? Felix Saltens Erben wohl nicht'. *Die Presse* 2/3: 6.

Weitin, Thomas. 2021. *Digitale Literaturgeschichte: eine Versuchsreihe mit sieben Experimenten*. Digitale Literaturwissenschaft. Berlin [Heidelberg]: J.B. Metzler.

Weitin, Thomas, and Katharina Herget. 2017. 'Falkentopics: Über einige Probleme beim Topic Modeling literarischer Texte'. *Zeitschrift für Literaturwissenschaft und Linguistik* 47 (1): 29–48. https://doi.org/10.1007/s41244-017-0049-3.

White, Hayden V. 2000. *Metahistory: The Historical Imagination in Nineteenth-Century Europe.*. Baltimore: Johns Hopkins University Press.

Wilke, Beatrice. 2007. 'Computervermittelte Kommunikationsformen in literarischen Texten'. *Testi e linguaggi*, 1: 151–168.

Wolf, Markus, Andrea B. Horn, Matthias R. Mehl, Severin Haug, James W. Pennebaker, and Hans Kordy. 2008. 'Computergestützte quantitative Textanalyse: Äquivalenz und Robustheit der Deutschen Version des Linguistic Inquiry and Word Count'. *Diagnostica*. https://doi.org/10.1026/0012-1924.54.2.85.

Wolf, Maryanne, and Catherine J. Stoodley. 2018. *Reader, Come Home: The Reading Brain in a Digital World*. First edition. New York: Harper.

Worthmann, Friederike. 2016. 'Literarische Kanones als Lektüremacht. Systematische Überlegungen zum Verhältnis von Kanon(isierung) und Wert(ung)'. In *Kanon Macht Kultur Theoretische, historische und soziale Aspekte ästhetischer Kanonbildungen DFG-Symposion 1996*, edited by Renate von Heydebrand, 9–30. https://nbn-resolving.org/urn :nbn:de:101:1-2016100417103.

Wu, Tim. 2016. *The Attention Merchants: The Epic Scramble to Get inside Our Heads*. New York: Alfred A. Knopf.

Zanetti, Sandro. 2012. *Avantgardismus der Greise? Spätwerke und ihre Poetik*. Paderborn: Fink.

Zehe, Albin, Martin Becker, Fotis Jannidis, and Andreas Hotho. 2017. 'Towards Sentiment Analysis on German Literature'. In *KI 2017: Advances in Artificial Intelligence*, edited by Gabriele Kern-Isberner, Johannes Fürnkranz, and Matthias Thimm, 387–94. Cham: Springer International Publishing. https://doi.org/10.1007/978-3-319-67190-1_36.

Zimbler, Mattitiyahu, and Robert S. Feldman. 2011. 'Liar, Liar, Hard Drive on Fire: How Media Context Affects Lying Behavior: Media Context Affects Lying Behavior'. *Journal of Applied Social Psychology* 41 (10): 2492–2507. https://doi.org/10.1111/j.1559-1816.2 011.00827.x.

Zipes, Jack. 2006. *Fairy Tales and the Art of Subversion: The Classical Genre for Children and the Process of Civilization*. New York: Routledge.